D1093662

SCALE MODELS
IN PLASTIC

Frontispiece: Modelling in plastic can take a number of forms, involve a host of different materials, encompass a wide range of techniques and require a variety of skills. The degrees to which these different factors are employed will vary from modelmaker to modelmaker, but the underlying aim is common to all — the pursuit of realism. The plastic kit is one means by which this aim may be facilitated, and this model of a US M48A2 Patton tank (from the Monogram 1/32 scale kit) shows just how effectively it can be realised.
(Model: Sheperd Paine. Photo by courtesy of Monogram Models Inc)

SCALE MODELS
IN PLASTIC

by
ROGER CHESNEAU

with contributions from
Ray Rimell
Len Manwaring
Alan Edwards
Dave Patrick

Line drawings by Ted Wilson

CONWAY MARITIME PRESS
GREENWICH

First published in Great Britain 1979 by
Conway Maritime Press Ltd
2 Nelson Road, Greenwich, London SE10 9JB

ISBN 0 85177 139 4

Designed by Ray Fishwick

Typesetting by Jilarana Ltd
Southend-on-Sea

Printed in Great Britain by Page Bros (Norwich) Ltd

Foreword

Modelmaking is as old as the history of man itself, but modelling as a leisure time activity enjoyed by millions is a much more recent development and may be considered as being a product of twentieth-century prosperity and technology, since the introduction of new materials and new industrial techniques has meant that less time is now required, and less skill needed, to produce a reasonably realistic model. This situation has of course been realised by the appearance of the model kit.

The availability of models in kit form has meant that anyone possessing average skills, a reasonable amount of patience and an ability to follow instructions can produce a miniature representation of a prototype that is unmistakably such. Furthermore, the plastic kit is in essence a product of the toy industry and therefore marketed with children as the principal recipients, a consideration not divorced from the fact that such a kit usually has a low retail price and requires merely a tube of cement to effect a scaled-down imitation of the object it attempts to portray.

However, the hobby is enjoyed, albeit in a somewhat refined manner, by a considerable number of adults. That this relatively small but not insignificant section of the plastic kit buying public is recognised by the manufacturers is reflected in the fact that their products have become more sophisticated in design, more accurate in appearance, more esoteric in the choice of subject – and more expensive – as the number of adult modellers has grown. A model created merely by assembling a contemporary plastic kit is a much more impressive affair today than it was twenty or so years ago, although merely assembling a plastic kit is a procedure that is more and more being rejected.

A hobby can only be termed as such if the result of his efforts bring pleasure and satisfaction to the participant. With modelling, the creation of a familiar shape in three dimensions is often sufficient to satisfy him, but at the other extreme there are those whose sole objective is to recreate, in perfect miniature detail, every single feature of their chosen subject. Between thse two ideals – and ideals they are, since the sense of achievement in a hobby is, ultimately, a very personal thing – is a bewildering array of individual interests, of differing approaches to the techniques associated with plastic modelling, and of opinions as to what constitutes a good model. To assist the modeller, there are an equally perplexing number of aids in the form of reference literature, accessories, tools, paints and miscellaneous materials and equipment. Modelling societies abound; model exhibitions, competitions and expositions proliferate; month by month the range of kits and products available in the hobby shop grows. Plastic modelling is indeed big business.

The purpose of *Scale Models in Plastic* is to provide, in a single volume, an up-to-date guide to the basic techniques and approaches associated with the creation of plastic models and to illustrate the application of these approaches and techniques by examples of models built by enthusiasts from several different countries. It is not possible for the book to be totally comprehensive, nor indeed is it desirable, since part of the pleasure of modelling is derived from the modeller's own discovery of a method as to how a particular end might best be achieved or how a skill might best be developed. In addition, a number of personal philosophies are behind the way in which the book has been produced, and it is felt that the reader should be made aware of these. First, it is the *appearance* of the finished model that is considered all-important: all plastic models are composed of prepared parts, and whether these parts are produced by a kit manfacturer or whether they are hand made by the modelmaker himself is largely irrelevant in this context. There is a feeling amongst a small number of modelmakers that the methods used to create a plastic model are more important than the model itself. Whilst this may be true insofar as the development of the modeller's personal skills is concerned, it is of far less significance with regard to the appearance of the final result. In other words, a model built entirely of hand made components is not necessarily 'better' than one constructed of kit parts: how much work with materials such as plastic card is incorporated into it is largely a matter of degree and of personal requirements, not necessarily of merit. Secondly, it should be borne in mind that a model is much more carefully scrutinised than its full size prototype, and frequently from unnatural angles and in peculiar lighting conditions. Thirdly, it is probably true to say that there are three categories of modelmakers who work with plastics: there are the 'builders', whose interests lie in the constructional techniques associated with the production of a model; there are the 'painters', whose forte is the application of an eyecatching exterior finish to their models; and there are the 'collectors', who wish only to amass a large number of recognisable models in a short time. Modelmakers may come into one or more (possibly all three) of these categories, and the work of all is represented in the photographs contained in this book.

In order to include as much information as possible, the text has been organised into two main sections. The first outlines the approaches and techniques pertinent to all forms of plastic modelling, and includes a discussion of the processes involved in kit manufacture. This last topic has never really been considered in a modelling publication, but its significance is fundamental and it is hoped that the inclusion of a chapter about it will go some way to explain the many limitations of kit technology, limitations which most modellers are aware of but relatively few tend to appreciate fully. The second section concentrates on the five major interest areas of plastic models and concludes with a brief discussion on model storage and display.

ROGER CHESNEAU

Acknowledgements

A book such as this is of course to some extent a co-operative project, and a special word of thanks must go to the four contributors, Ray Rimell, Len Manwaring, Alan Edwards and Dave Patrick, whose expertise has been of immeasurable benefit to its contents. The assistance offered by Barry Wheeler and the staff of Airfix Products Ltd, Maurice Landi and Don Baker of Lesney Products & Co Ltd, Peter and Pamela Veal of Pamela Veal Ltd and Gordon Stevens of Rareplanes with respect to the various manufacturing processes involved in kit production was invaluable, and the help received from Imperial Chemical Industries (Plastics Division) Ltd, G H Bloore Ltd, May & Baker Ltd and M L Shelley and Partners Ltd must also be acknowledged. I am indebted to Bob Reder of Monogram Models Inc for permission to include some photographs of dioramas created by Sheperd Paine; to Lesney Products & Co Ltd for permission to photograph manufacturing equipment within the company's factory; and to Airfix Products Ltd for supplying many photographs and for permission to reproduce tooling diagrams. I am particularly grateful to Greg Bieszczad and Donn Buerger for co-ordinating the supply of many of the model photographs originating in the USA, to Susumu Yoshida for arranging the photography of models in Japan, and to Norman Sharpen for his helpful comments during the preparation of the text. Several other people were of considerable assistance, either in supplying photographs or in allowing their models to be photographed for the purposes of this book, and they are acknowledged individually in the captions. Uncredited models are from the author's collection; most of the uncredited photos were taken by my wife Joananne, to whom I owe my thanks. Finally, acknowledgement must be made of the multitude of anonymous modellers who, through contact either in casual conversation or via the modelling media, have made known their techniques and methods – this kind of information is picked up and stored for future reference almost unconsciously over the years by all connected with the hobby, and organisations such as the International Plastic Modellers Society are of immense benefit in this respect. The list is long and the names cannot always be recalled, but by making known their experiences these people have enabled many others, including the author, to derive increased pleasure from modelling in plastic. It is hoped that this book will serve the same ends.

ROGER CHESNEAU

Contents

Chapter 1

Plastic and plastic kits

There can be little denying that one of the most startling developments of the twentieth century has been the way in which synthetic materials have gradually replaced traditional, extractive substances in the manufacture of a wide range of merchandise and of these synthetic materials plastics form perhaps the most interesting and versatile group. Instead of adapting techniques of production to suit the vagaries of naturally occurring substances such as wood and metal, it is possible, with synthetics, to manufacture a substance that will meet a specific set of requirements by building up its chemical composition in a certain way. Thus the qualities of durability, flexibility, texture, translucency, impact strength, conductivity and so on are almost infinitely variable. Many plastics can be machined, most can be moulded through the influence of heat, and most can accept pigmentation during their manufacture so as to produce any desired colour. Commercial plastics are inert under normal day to day conditions, are non-corrosive, and are non-toxic unless subjected to chemical change.

Plastics are not complete substitutes for traditional materials, and in many cases must be regarded as complementary to them. They do not in general possess the strength of certain metals for example, nor the toughness of certain types of wood. However, the plastics industry is one of ceaseless technological development, and the adaptation of existing processes to meet an ever-increasing range of requirements has relegated many other substances to a position of inferior importance, a trend which is likely to continue into at least the immediate future.

THE COMPOSITION AND
CHARACTERISTICS OF PLASTICS

The chemistry and production of plastics is not a subject that needs concern the modeller in any great detail, although it is useful for him to have a background knowledge of their properties, be-

haviour and limitations insofar as these apply to his hobby.

Plastics are compounds of a number of different chemicals, principally hydrogen and carbon, although oxygen, chlorine, fluorine and nitrogen are common constituents as well. Moreover, all sorts of other matter may be mixed in with these elements to impart particular characteristics to the finished material. The basic elements combine together in different ways to produce molecules which in turn may be chemically modified into monomers, enabling them to be linked together to form larger molecules. This linking process is known as polymerisation, and the products so formed are called polymers. A polymer having a rigid chemical structure which, once formed, cannot be altered by heat or pressure is referred to as a thermosetting plastic. Included in this group are materials such as Bakelite, Melamine, epoxy and polyester resin, and polyurethane. A polymer which, because its molecular linkage is comparatively weak, can be reshaped by the application of heat or pressure is known as thermoplastic — materials such as nylon, perspex, cellulose-acetate, polystyrene and polyethylene are examples of this form of polymer— and this is the type of most concern to the modeller. The interchange of different elements making up the monomer can bring about different properties in the polymer thus formed, and the addition of various non-plastic ingredients can also affect its character and performance, and in these ways increased strength, resistance to heat and so on can be introduced to meet all manner of differing needs.

The thermoplastics of particular relevance to the modeller are polystyrene, polyethylene, acrylonitrile-butadiene-styrene (ABS), cellulose-acetate and cellulose-acetate butyrate (CAB), although other materials such as polyvinyl chloride (PVC) and polypropylene may also be encountered. Solvents for bonding components of the same chemical composition will be required, with or without a small amount of the material already dissolved in them, as may thermosetting polymers in an un-catalysed state to achieve the bonding of non-compatible materials or for casting or coating purposes. Although when initially manufactured these materials may take any one of a number of different forms — powders, granules, fluids, resins and so on — the modeller will require them to be in a prepared or semi-prepared condition before they can be of value to him. Polystyrene or ABS in granular form, for example, will be of little use, but when solidified as a contoured shape or a flat sheet they can be applied as his needs require them.

The preparation of polymers to produce solid materials that can be used by the modeller to build up structures involves four different methods, although there are several other forms of processing pertinent to the plastics industry in general which are not really of direct interest to him. The most basic method is known as calendering and entails the use of a system of rollers through which a continuous quantity of heated plastic is allowed to pass, thereby producing, when cooled, a flexible or rigid sheet of appropriate thickness. This sheet may then be subjected to further heating and pulled positively over a mould by mechanical means or, as with most commercially produced items, drawn positively over or negatively into it, assisted by vacuum pressure, thereby forming a contoured shape. The other two methods involve the heating of thermoplastic granules and introducing them into enclosed moulds. In one method, known as extrusion moulding, the molten plastic is com-pressed and squeezed through an outlet at one end of the mould, resulting in a continuous length of cooled material of constant cross-sectional area. Plastic rodding, beams and channels, and also sheet, are produced in this way. In the second method, known as injection moulding, a given quantity of granules is heated and forced by a ram into an enclosed cavity where it is allowed to cool and then released. Although the calendering and extrusion processes are relatively easy to under-stand and produce simple, straight shapes that are variable in two dimensions only, injection moulding and vacuum forming are rather more involved and require further elaboration.

INJECTION MOULDING

The underlying theory of injection moulding is not difficult to appreciate, but the factors affecting the transition of the plastic from a raw, granulated state into a hard, moulded component are numerous and extremely complicated. In an automatic injection moulding machine, a hopper feeds a measured amount of raw plastic into a chamber where it is heated through a temperature of around 250°C

CALENDERING

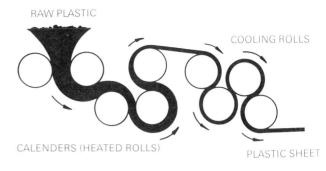

RAW PLASTIC

COOLING ROLLS

CALENDERS (HEATED ROLLS)

PLASTIC SHEET

VACUUM FORMING

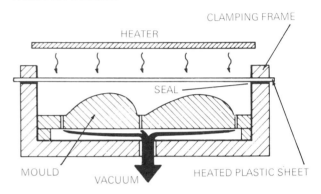

CLAMPING FRAME

HEATER

SEAL

MOULD

VACUUM

HEATED PLASTIC SHEET

EXTRUSION MOULDING

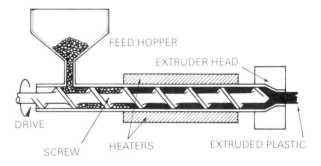

FEED HOPPER

EXTRUDER HEAD

DRIVE

SCREW

HEATERS

EXTRUDED PLASTIC

INJECTION MOULDING

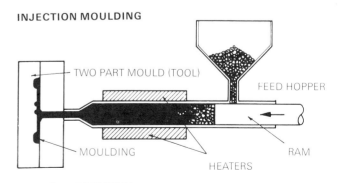

TWO PART MOULD (TOOL)

FEED HOPPER

MOULDING

HEATERS

RAM

THE FOUR PRINCIPAL
METHODS OF SHAPING PLASTICS

(480° F) into a fluid mass. A ram or plunger forces this mass through a nozzle into a mould which is in two or more parts, that incorporating the hole through which the plastic enters being fixed, the other or others being movable to permit the ejection and withdrawal of the moulded shape. In the moulding cycle, the parts of the mould are first drawn together and kept in position under hydraulic pressure, and the plastic granules enter the heating chamber. The ram then moves forward, first to consolidate the granules and then to inject a shot of the molten material into the cavity formed by the closed moulds. Dwell time then follows, wherein the ram is held still, permitting the material to consolidate, after which the ram is withdrawn and the plastic allowed to freeze into a hard mass. Fresh raw plastic enters the heating chamber while the mould is released and the moulding mechanically ejected and removed. The moulds are then closed again and the cycle restarts.

The vast majority of moulds used in the manufacture of plastic kits are in two parts, and may be designed to produce a single large component, such as the hull of a tank or a ship, whereby the molten material reaches the cavity for the moulded shape directly from the sprue, the entry hole in the fixed part of the mould. Alternatively, they may be of the multi-impression type, wherein a number of smaller, separate cavities are reached by means of a series of runners attached to the sprue, each cavity being connected to the runner system by a narrow aperture known as a gate. It is perhaps unfortunate that modellers seem to have made up their own minds about some of the terminology used in moulding thermoplastics and, for example, invariably refer to the runners as sprue. In actual fact, the sprue is rarely evident in an injection moulded kit, and even when it is present it cannot be utilised by the modeller in the way that runners can. However, in deference to popular taste, modelling rather than manufacturing terminology will be used in subsequent chapters of this book.

Quite apart from the design of the individual mould cavities, which will be considered in more detail later, there are several very important factors affecting the appearance of the finished moulding which, ultimately, concern the modeller in the construction of his model. The first determinant is that of temperature. The moulded shapes should be as stable as possible upon completion, and to achieve this it is important that the plastic is not degraded by heating it to too high a temperature, that it is melted to a uniform consistency so that the finished component may have an even density, and that the cooling of the moulding is undertaken evenly so as to reduce stress and distortion to a

minimum. The rates of heating and cooling are also of significance, necessitating a compromise between speed of production and complete consolidation of the material. Sinkage, a common flaw in plastic kit mouldings, is often caused by too rapid a cooling process, and short moulding, in other words the production of an incomplete component, is another type of flaw that may occur if temperature levels are incorrect.

The second factor relates to the pressure at which the molten plastic enters the sprue and fills the cavities. As well as to some extent determining the speed with which the moulding cycle is completed, the pressure exerted by the plunger, and the period of time for which the pressure is held, will affect the quality of the moulded shape. Again, consolidation is the principal consideration here, and sinkage, voids and short moulding may all occur if the injection pressure is insufficient or if dwell time is too short and permits a backflow of material into the sprue.

Time itself also influences the appearance of the moulding. The time required to complete one cycle in the injection moulding of plastic kits varies according to the size and complexity of the mould cavity system, the composition and viscosity of the molten plastic, and a number of other considerations, but a period of twenty to thirty seconds is typical. Roughly a quarter of this is dwell time, another quarter is freezing or setting time, and a further quarter is taken up by ejecting and withdrawing the moulding from the tool. Clearly, the quality of the cooled material will vary from shot to shot if the timing for each procedure is not regulated correctly.

The most important factor affecting the appearance and character of the finished moulding is flow. It is also the most troublesome to control, mainly because, occurring as it does unseen, it is so difficult to study in laboratory conditions. The physics of flow is a very complex subject whose niceties need not concern the modeller unduly, but there are a number of flaws which may arise as a result of flow problems and which may show themselves in kit mouldings. Short mouldings may be a product of flow difficulties as well as of temperature and pressure control since, particularly where there is an obstruction or a recess in the mould cavity, variable flow rates may cause premature cooling and setting. Differential flow rates may show themselves as marks on the surface of the moulding. Where these are identifiable merely as slight variations in colour, which is in the majority of cases, the painting of the component in question will render the flaws invisible. Occasionally, however, the fault will result in a physical surface deformity — this is most apparent at a weld line, caused by convergence of two relatively cool flow fronts which cannot fuse effectively, or where a phenomenon known as scuffing occurs, which brings about a change in surface texture, usually near the gates. These features are especially aggravating to the modeller where transparent mouldings such as canopies are involved, since their effects cannot be disguised. It follows that stresses, and consequently lines of weakness, will be set up within the body of a moulding as a result of flow patterns. The most obvious of these occurs inside the runners which, as modellers are aware, are frequently hollow for much of their length, on account of differential flow rates caused, amongst other things, by friction and drag. Plastic models are not normally subject to severe physical forces once built, but if care is not taken in the preparation and shaping of the components, fracturing can take place along lines of weakness, and there is evidence that the effects of stress can make themselves apparent over a period of time, especially if completed models are exposed to abnormal environments such as prolonged sunlight, excessive humidity or extremes of temperature.

The last major factor which produces an effect on the form of an injection moulded component is the nature of the material used in the shaping process. Clearly, different polymers have different properties and will behave during moulding in accordance with these. Additives will also affect the characteristics of a particular plastic. Polystyrene, for example, the most commonly used injection moulding material, is usually modified before it is supplied to the kit manufacturer by the addition of a lubricant to assist its flow, of styrene-butadiene rubber to improve its flexibility and impact strength, or of pigment to produce a particular colour. All these variables have to be taken into consideration when moulding is undertaken.

To complicate matters even further, the factors outlined above are all inter-related, as will perhaps have been noticed. The alteration of any one of them is likely to have a perceptible effect on the rest. It should be emphasised that strenuous efforts are made — and not inconsiderable sums of money spent — by the kit manufacturers to iron out as many of the problems that occur as possible, and this is one reason why the marketing of a kit may be delayed after it has been announced. Even then, strict quality control is exercised, and so the chances of a modeller receiving a poorly moulded kit are remote. Modellers should recognise, however, that the injection moulding process, though brought to a fine art, is nevertheless something of a compromise and that many of the minor moulding flaws for

Top: A typical large injection moulding machine. The ram mechanism and feed hopper are to the left, whilst to the right are the sliding safety doors through which the finished moulding is extracted by hand from the machine. At the extreme left are bagged polystyrene granules which will be loaded into the hopper as and when required.
(Photo by courtesy of Airfix Products Ltd)
Bottom: a large injection moulded kit – Airfix's *Cutty Sark* – which has just been eased from the tool but not yet completely removed. The huge size of the tool means that the complete kit can be moulded in one operation, but the moulding has to be divided by hand into several sections so that it may be packed into a box of reasonable dimensions. In the centre of the moulding, drooping and still in fact connected to the injection nozzle by its drawn out filament, is the sprue – not to be found in the kit when the customer purchases it.
(Photo by courtesy of Airfix Products Ltd)

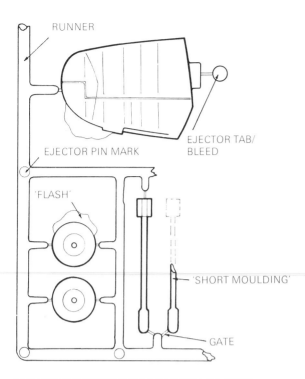

RUNNER

EJECTOR TAB/
BLEED

EJECTOR PIN MARK

'FLASH'

'SHORT MOULDING'

GATE

TERMINOLOGY (INJECTION MOULDED KITS)

which manufacturers are so gleefully taken to task in the review columns are unavoidable.

Of more direct importance to the modeller is the nature of the actual moulds used to produce the contoured and detailed components he requires to build his model. In order to manufacture a mould it is necessary first of all to undertake a lengthy programme of research, technical drawing, pattern making and resin casting. Once a particular subject has been decided upon, its detail appearance must be ascertained, and this will involve gathering as much information about it as possible. Plans, photographs, articles and scale drawings, plus a first hand acquaintance with the prototype if possible, are all of importance in this basic research, and from this a draughtsman produces a detailed set of design drawings, which entail a three-view plan of each component to be manufactured for the kit.

Patterns are then made up from these drawings, usually in wood although other materials such as metal and plastic may be utilised. Each pattern is larger than the plastic component to be produced from it — perhaps one and a half times or twice the size for major structural components and up to eight times the final size for small detailed parts such as aircraft undercarriage legs, machine gun mountings on tanks, and the like. The patterns are sealed and rendered perfectly smooth with several coats of polyurethane varnish, and a resin cast is taken from

each. A layer of wax representing the required thickness of the finished plastic is then aplied to the cavities in the resin casting, and further resin is poured in and levelled off with the top of the original mould. In this way a female mould (the first casting) and a male mould (the second casting) are produced, with the space in between corresponding to the kit component.

Each resin casting is then individually reproduced in a block of mild steel by means of a pantograph, which not only copies precisely the contours of each cavity but also scales them down to the required size. This die-sinking process consumes a considerable number of man-hours for each mould and involves a very high degree of skill since, although the pantograph stylus accurately traces the forms within the cavities, most of the fine detailing and all the final polishing is undertaken by hand. Runners and gates are cut into the moulds at this stage, and each individual tool is cut and fitted, jigsaw fashion, into the two main mould blocks.

The nature of the raw plastic and the operation of the injection moulding process have, as we have seen, an important bearing on the character of the mouldings produced, but the kit manufacturer is not fundamentally responsible for the performance of these requisites, although he will specify their function. He is, however, totally answerable for the precision and accuracy of the tools from which a kit is produced, even though the work may be done under contract by another company, and in some instances in another country. Perhaps the most basic consideration in tool design is the way in which the moulds fit together. The majority of those manufactured for plastic kits are composed of two parts, although it is possible to incorporate side - action tools or wedges so that components featuring prominent detail on flat surfaces which are aligned at severe angles to the main design may be produced as single mouldings, as with the 1/700 scale Waterline Series of ships issued by a group of Japanese manufacturers. Clearly, whatever the design of the tool, it is vital that its component parts fit together with great precision. If the alignment is poor, even to the degree of a fraction of a millimetre, the result will be plastic mouldings of bad register, which is much less tolerable in kit manufacture than in, say, the moulding of household products such as buckets or of cheap plastic toys, both because of the need for an accurate representation of a prototype and because complex, multi-part structures are being moulded. The male and female tools are provided with substantial slide bolts for locating them together accurately, but after the production of many thousands of mouldings from one set of tools natural wear will loosen the fit and register commonly suffers as a result.

Top: a fully automatic injection moulding machine, considerably smaller than the type illustrated previously. Note the chute down which the ejected mouldings emerge. The loading system is also automatic, the polystyrene granules being fed via pipes from a central store. Such machines as these are often fitted with equipment for colouring the plastic *in situ* – the 'black box' below and slightly to the left of the feed hopper is the regulator for this facility.

Centre: the patterns necessary for an injection moulded kit are usually made of wood and are considerably larger than the plastic mouldings which eventually result from them. Illustrated here are some of the limewood patterns for the Airfix 1/48 scale Messerschmitt Bf 109F, which are at $1\frac{1}{2}$:1, or 1/32 scale. Each pattern is made as a separate piece (as shown by the starboard wing upper half) and then mounted on a wooden block (fuselage half and engine cowling halves) before the two resin casts for each component are produced. The provision of internal detailing calls for an additional stage: an 'interim' resin cast is taken from the pattern and the required detailing worked on to it before the definitive cast is manufactured (cockpit detailing on starboard fuselage 'shell'). Note the highly polished surfaces of the patterns. (Photo by courtesy of Airfix Products Ltd)

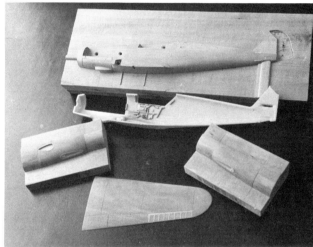

Bottom: the first piece of 'hardware' produced in the design process of an injection moulded kit often takes the form of a mock-up. This is essentially a hand made demonstration model, built to serve as a discussion point for a possible future project. The Westland Lynx helicopter depicted here is one such model: it is made principally from perspex but has its sliding door, rotor blades and rotor head made from brass. The scale in this instance is the same as that for the finished kit, ie 1/72. This is one mock-up that did evolve into a plastic kit – many do not! (Photo by courtesy of Lesney Products & Co Ltd)

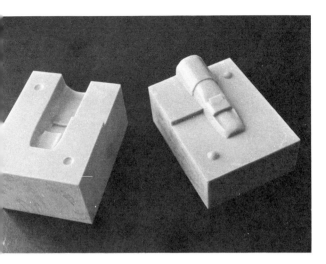

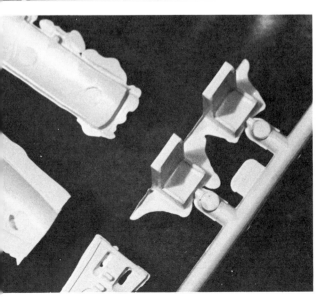

Top: male (right) and female halves of a resin cast for a Junkers Ju 87B kit component. The female is cast directly from the pattern, a layer of wax representing the scale thickness of the plastic component is then applied to the cavity, and the male cast is taken from that. Each casting will then be precisely copied and reduced into a steel block by means of a pantograph, the female block receiving panel line and rivet detail after completion.
(Photo by courtesy of Airfix Products Ltd)

Centre: two individual mould blocks for a 1/32 scale polyethylene French Grenadier. A multi-impression two-way tool will contain very many of these blocks fitted together with absolute precision, male moulds in one half, females in the other. The finished moulding, painted and posed on a polystyrene base, is shown alongside. Note the complex contours of the split line, necessary to overcome the problems of undercutting that are inevitably associated with an intricate shape such as this model possesses.
(Photo by courtesy of Airfix Products Ltd)

Bottom: the occurrence in an injection moulded kit of 'flash' — unusually prevalent around the components shown in this photograph — is generally caused by poorly fitting tool halves where the injected plastic can seep along the split line. Although the parts concerned are quite usable, their actual configuration being unaffected, some very careful work with a sharp blade is necessary before they can be used, and this can be especially tricky if the parts are of an intricate shape. Note also the presence of ejector pin marks on some of the components — further features requiring the attention of the modeller.

The necessity for complete flatness in non-cavity areas of the tools, particularly at the cavity rims, will be obvious. The split line will always be apparent on the finished moulding, especially where it occurs across a double cavity region, and shows itself as a seam. This cannot be completely eliminated in an injection moulded product since allowance has to be made for the evacuation of trapped air as the plastic enters the tool cavities, and venting may conveniently be directed along the split lines without detriment to the more noticeable surfaces of a moulded component. The viscosity of the molten plastic and the precision of the tool are such that the material will not normally be drawn into the split lines, but occasionally flashing will occur, resulting in thin wafers of plastic outside the main cavities. Whilst flash does not alter the shape of the moulding itself, it does require trimming before the affected plastic component can be used. Again, this phenomenon is more frequently associated with tools that have been in use for a considerable period.

The form of a moulded plastic component is very much dependent upon the manner in which the runners and gates are designed within the tool. Although production kits will rarely show direct evidence of an incorrect flow system, perfection is only achieved by a carefully thought out design and a method of trial and error whereby test shots of the mouldings are made before production runs are undertaken and any deficiencies put right. The design of runners varies somewhat from kit to kit, and toolmakers have differing opinions as to the form they should take. However, the chief determinants are that they should be as short as possible, and offer the maximum cross sectional area for their cross sectional circumference, consistent with flow requirements. Hence the majority are round or hexagonal and have their cavities machined in both the male and the female mould, although single depth runners are also encountered, usually where test shots have shown the need for an auxiliary feed system. Gating is also a very important consideration. Kit manufacturers do not, generally speaking, have to incorporate automatic degating mechanisms in their equipment as do companies mass-producing other types of consumer goods, but the design of the gates does reflect to some extent the philosophy behind plastic kit production. On the one hand, the requirement to make the individual kit components easily removable from their runners without causing them damage may be the most important factor in gate design, particularly when children, who may wish merely to break them off and not trouble about finishing them, are seen as the principal market. Gates of the minimum practicable size are in this instance necessary, and as few as possible are included in the layout. However, the problems of flow are more difficult to overcome, and the risk of a part being accidentally removed and possibly lost is heightened. On the other hand, where parts are to be removed with the aid of a craft knife or clippers, a number of gates may be led into a mould cavity from different directions and their individual size may be increased, both to obtain optimum flow conditions and to ensure complete rigidity and protection for the runner layout. The two approaches are clearly demonstrated by comparing a kit comprising a number of loose sections of runner bearing the various component parts with one consisting of a number of rectangular frames packed securely in the box.

The toolmaker has to work within a number of limitations in the design of the cavities themselves. The primary factor is that of draft, in other words the degree of taper that needs to be worked into the cavity to allow the moulding to be ejected cleanly. In general practice, a tool cannot incorporate cavities with sides at right angles to its face unless a complicated and costly system of wedges is introduced. Draft angles are kept to a minimum, of course, (although with some kits they seem unnecessarily exaggerated), but the production of, for example, a perfect cube is not technically possible with a two-part tool. It therefore follows that model kit components such as one-piece, constant diameter engine cowlings or one-piece 'blown' cockpit hoods for aircraft cannot be accurately portrayed.

Some degree of undercutting is permissible, provided this is restricted to fine surface detail — raised rivets or shallow longitudinal panel lines can be tooled along areas of deep draw, for instance — because of the natural shrinkage of polystyrene through cooling, which although only in the order of 0.006in per inch is enough to allow clean ejection. The problems of draft angles will need to receive the attention of the modeller, who may have to eliminate taper, modify the detail supplied or add it where it is absent, or disguise draw marks caused as the moulding is removed from the tool.

Perhaps the most serious limitation in tool design relates to the difficulty of producing thin wall mouldings. There are a number of reasons why components with a thickness of around 0.010-0.015in cannot often be moulded satisfactorily by injection, but all are connected with the problem of material flow. It will easily be appreciated that the viscosity of the molten plastic has to be carefully balanced, and if cooling takes place too rapidly within the mould, short moulding may result, a problem most likely to occur with thin wall cavities, where the effects of friction and drag are very much more evident. A process known as preplasticising, whereby the material in the injection nozzle is rendered more fluid, makes flow control easier to balance and goes some way towards solving the problem, and the majority of plastic kits are produced in this way. However, scale thickness with regard to such items as areas of clear glazing, wire wheels on vehicles, and material for the clothing on figure models, cannot be achieved, and it is perhaps this limitation more than any other which betrays the origin of a plastic kit model.

The last major design consideration concerning toolmaking relates to the means by which the mouldings are ejected on completion. Apart from tooling the individual cavities to facilitate the removal of the mouldings, it is necessary to incorporate an ejection mechanism so that the latter do not shrink on the male cores of the mould. With plastic kits, this mechanism takes the form of a platen fitted with pins which is attached to the rear of the movable part of the mould. The pins are so arranged that they give an even pressure that will displace the moulding without distorting it. The pins have each to be of a precise length, so that they lie flush with the mould cavities whilst injection is taking place, not only to enable a relatively flaw-free surface to be produced on the moulding, but also to facilitate optimum flow conditions for the molten plastic. In addition to permitting the removal of the mouldings, which must be perfectly timed so that the plastic is neither too cool to stick to the mould nor too soft to be disfigured, the pin

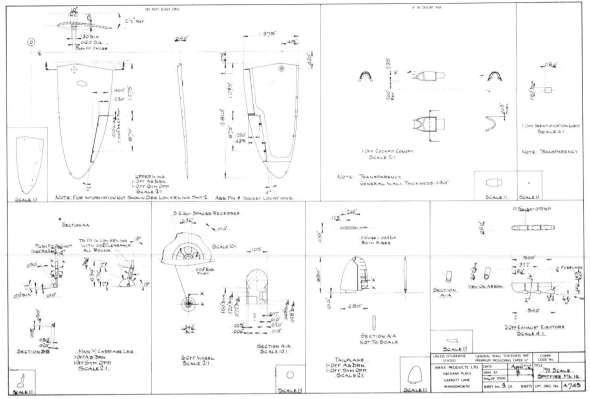

mechanism provides a venting system for the cavities.

Despite the care and attention that goes into the design of the ejector mechanism, economies dictate that flaws are unavoidable in some instances. To avoid spoiling the exterior surface of a moulded component, cavities are machined so that the pins act upon areas that will be unseen on the finished model, wherever this is possible; where this arrangement is impracticable, the pins may be so positioned that they impinge on adjacent runners or on special ejector tabs — which may, incidentally, serve also as bleeds or weld traps to overcome flow problems — in which case the gates must be strong. Sometimes, however, the manufacturer has no choice but to eject directly against the detailed surfaces of a moulding — aircraft undercarriage components and ships' fittings are especially vulnerable in this respect — and unfortunately the modeller's corrective work is often made more difficult by poorly machined pins. A fraction short, and they produce shallow cylinders of plastic which need to be removed; a fraction long, and the result is a circular recess which has to be filled; slightly loose, and flashing may occur.

As well as by physical ejection, mouldings are often separated from their tools with the help of a lubricant, especially if a particular cavity is giving trouble. The lubricant may take the form of an oil, a grease or a chemical agent (usually silicone), but whichever type is used, subsequent painting of the model may well be affected if steps are not taken to remove it. Occasionally it shows up as an obvious stain, brownish in colour, but more often it appears as a colourless film, and its presence may only be detected after careful inspection.

One problem that manufacturers — and modellers — have to come to terms with is the fact that moulds, even those made from steel, do wear out. The physical degeneration of a mould is a gradual, almost imperceptible process, but the stresses and strains of heat and pressure take their toll, and from time to time repairs and renovation have to be carried out. In addition, a mould may also become damaged either through accident or through day-to-day handling. Excessive wear may result in flashing, a thickening of the individual components, a loss of detail or poor component fit; a chipped or scratched cavity will cause minor deformities on the mouldings which will spoil the appearance of the finished model if left unattended. Renovation may be undertaken as often as necessary, but, in time, particularly if the tools are very old and do not reflect current technical skills, moulds outlive their usefulness and completely fresh ones are prepared. The process of producing a new kit starts over again.

16

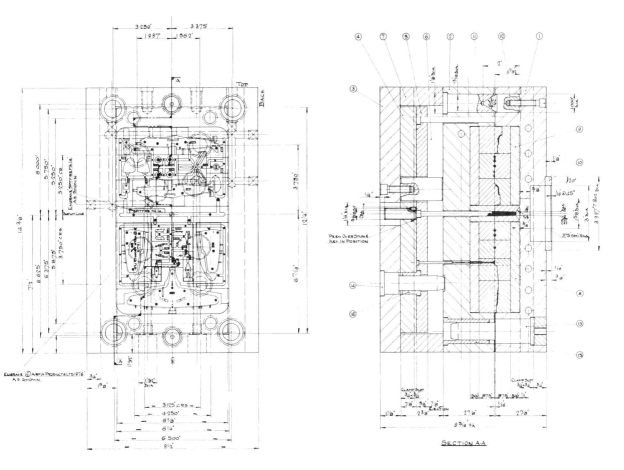

SECTION A·A

Opposite: component drawings for an injection moulded 1/72 scale Spitfire Ia kit, shown here about 1/25 actual size. The model which evolves from this particular kit is relatively small and simple; it will be appreciated how complex are the design drawings for a really large kit containing hundreds of parts. (Reproduced by courtesy of Airfix Products Ltd)

Above: a tool drawing for an injection moulded kit, again a 1/72 scale Spitfire Ia, reproduced about 1/25 actual size. On the left is the plan view of the tool showing the disposition of the cavities along the split line; on the right is a cross section through the centreline of the tool traversing fuselage (top), mainwheel and lower wing cavities. (Reproduced by courtesy of Airfix Products Ltd)

VACUUM FORMING

The principles of vacuum forming differ fundamentally from those of injection moulding, although in practical procedure with regard to kit production there are many marked similarities. It is a cheaper and quicker way of moulding plastic, but the raw material costs are higher, the thickness of the moulding is much more restricted and the sharpness of definition found with injection moulded products much more difficult to achieve. The process entails heating a piece of plastic sheet and then drawing it over a prepared mould by evacuating the air between the two. Once again, the theory

is simple to understand; applying the theory, however, is not so straightforward.

There are in fact four basic methods of vacuum forming, although only two of these are directly applicable to the production of plastic kits. All four methods require essentially similar equipment, and, compared with injection moulding machinery, this is very simple. It consists of a vacuum press into which the mould is fitted, a hinged frame on to which the plastic sheet is clamped, and a heater, usually of the infra-red variety, which may be swung into position over the press. The plastic sheet is fitted on to the frame and closed over the mould, making an airtight seal. The heat is then applied evenly over the surface of the sheet, and when the plastic is sufficiently soft the forming operation proper begins. Drape forming and air slip forming involve pre-stretching the plastic sheet before it is moulded, the first by drawing the heated sheet over a male mould before the vacuum is activated, the second by injecting compressed air below the heated sheet, causing it to balloon, and then drawing it over a male mould and evacuating the air. Negative forming requires the use of a female mould, and the heated sheet is forced into contact with it when the air between is withdrawn. The

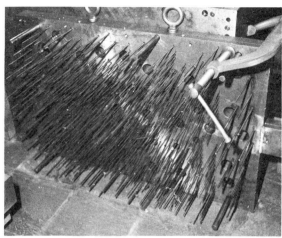

Top left and left: the moulding cycle in progress. The female mould (top) remains static while the male mould (left) has pulled clear and forced out the moulding by means of its ejector pins. The latter can clearly be seen projecting through the core. The polystyrene used in the manufacture of injection moulded kits may be 'general purpose' (GP), which is transparent and relatively fragile, 'high impact' (HI), which is toughened by means of additives, or 'medium impact', which is used for the AFV kit produced by this particular set of tools as it gives a fairly matt finish.

Above: looking for all the world like some kind of outsize brush, this is an ejector pin platen for a 1/24 scale aircraft kit. The platen fits on to the back of the male half of the tool – not, as it may be imagined, an easy task – and its activation permits the moulding to be freed when the injection cycle is completed. This is yet another instance where precision engineering of the highest order is required.
(Photo by courtesy of Airfix Products Ltd)

fourth method is really an extension of this process and is known as plug-assisted forming. A female mould is used as before, but the heated sheet is pushed down towards the mould by an appropriately shaped plug before the vacuum is applied. Drape forming and negative forming are the two methods generally used to produce moulded parts for kits and warrant more detailed consideration.

As with injection moulded kits, the production of a vacuum formed kit requires a great deal of preliminary research and the production of a detailed set of working drawings. From these, a master is made, but, unlike the system for injection moulded kits, this master is built to the same size as the finished kit. It is usually made from wood, waxed, polished and varnished to give a smooth, flaw-free surface, with fine details and small, complex components produced from suitable materials such as metals and thermosetting plastics. In the early days of vacuum formed kits, this master served as the tool and the plastic sheet was drape

formed over it. This method is still in use for the production of kits by some manufacturers, but nowadays the master is more commonly used to form a resin casting which is used as a female mould, the shapes being formed negatively into it.

Drape forming has several advantages over negative forming, the most obvious being the fact that the moulds are very much easier to make. In addition, the mould requires very little surface preparation as any small irregularities will be absorbed into the thickness of the plastic sheet as it is formed. The major drawback, of course, is that any sharp detail worked into the master will only be apparent on the inside surfaces of the finished moulding, and whilst this may be of no consequence in producing components like drop tanks and fuselage bulkheads which are comparatively featureless, it is far from ideal for major structural units such as wings and engine cowlings. There are other, more technical problems with positive moulding. One of these concerns draft, which must be of the order of 5° to ensure effective release; another is the possible occurrence of 'webbing' — vertical corrugations at corners caused by excessive stretching of the plastic sheet prior to the removal of the air beneath it, a problem of particular significance where several forms are placed close together on one mould; a third is the difficulty of producing a uniform distribution of the plastic sheet when the moulding has been formed.

In terms of the finished product, negative or female forming is more suited to kit production than drape forming, quite apart from the fact that finely executed surface detail can be transferred from the master to the moulded shape. Although, in general, draw depths achieved are considerably smaller than those that may be obtained with positive forming, there is far less tendency to webbing since no prestretching of the plastic sheet is required. Minimum draft angles are in the order of 1° — the permissible figure is much lower than for positive forming simply because the natural shrinkage of the plastic during cooling is away from the mould rather than towards it.

The production of a vacuum formed kit is, like its injection moulded counterpart, subject to a number of limitations and controlled by a number of interrelated factors. Perhaps the most obvious limitation is that parts can only be formed as hollow shells and, with the two methods described, only in one direction relative to the plane of the plastic sheet. Whilst this presents few problems with larger structures that one would expect to be hollow, delicate items cannot adequately be produced, which is the reason why some vacuum formed kits may include a number of injection moulded parts or suggest in their instruction sheets that alternative components be acquired from injection moulded kits, and why subjects requiring a high number of small, complex parts like ships and figures are not generally suitable for production.

A further problem concerns the nature and thickness of the plastic material used. Polystyrene sheet is normally selected since it is fairly easy to form, relatively cheap, and possesses properties that are familiar to modellers used to working with injection moulded kits. However, clear polystyrene cannot be used in vacuum forming processes since it clouds when stretched, and so materials such as PVC or, more usually, cellulose-acetate or CAB (toughened acetate) are employed, necessitating special adhesives or solvents when the models are built. The thickness of the sheet is also an important consideration. Generally speaking, the thicker the material the more difficult it is to reproduce detail on the mouldings, and, of course, the more heat is required to soften it and the more expensive it is in the first place. On the other hand, a certain amount

of structural strength is required for the finished components — one reason why early vacuum formed kits were flimsy was because of the uncertainty associated with drape moulding thick grades of polystyrene sheet — and so, in effect, a balance between cost, rigidity and practicability is struck, and 0.030 or 0.040in (30 or 40 thou) sheet is in general use now.

The thickness of the plastic directly influences the thickness of the finished moulding and of course represents the maximum that will be present on any part of it. Stretching a piece of plastic sheet, clearly, will reduce its thickness: the deeper the draw, the greater the stretching required, and the thicker must be the plastic sheet used in order to retain a rigidity suitable for the models that are to be made from the mouldings. The unavoidable thinning of plastic sheet as it is drawn over the mould is probably the most awkward problem affecting the production of a vacuum formed kit — and, from the modeller's point of view, one that is likely to cause him more trouble than any other — and depths of more than about 35-40% of the cavity diameter cannot adequately be moulded. It is only possible to encourage a more even distribution of the plastic by plug-assistance — wing root fillets are given better definition by one particular manufacturer by means of a quick prod with a screwdriver! — but unless an expensive mechanical system for this can be incorporated on to the press the problem persists. Holding a vacuum formed sheet up to a light source will illustrate the differing thicknesses produced. With some parts, for example spinner tips, the plastic may have become so thinned as to render the moulding unusable. In rare instances, actual perforation may have taken place.

Adequate venting of the mould must be provided to give a clear definition of shape in the finished product. This is usually done by drilling small diameter holes at suitable points through the mould, which accounts for the small rounded pips that are present on the surfaces of vacuum formed components and which have to be removed by the modeller. The vents are necessary to ensure that a complete evacuation of the air between the plastic sheet and the mould takes place as the material is formed and will thus be placed in every recess where air is likely to become trapped. Undercuts can be incorporated to more or less the same extent as for injection moulded tools, that is, natural shrinkage will permit very shallow undercuts to be released cleanly. For deeper intrusions, a movable core or wedge is required — a section of the tool is built as a separate part which slots into the main unit and has to be released with the moulding before it can itself be removed. The additional work required on the

THE FOUR BASIC METHODS OF VACUUM FORMING

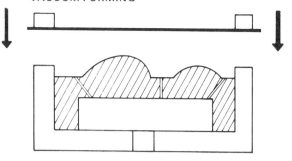

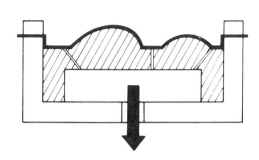

DRAPE FORMING

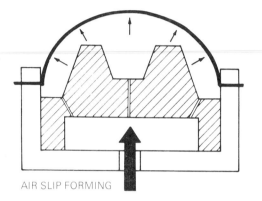

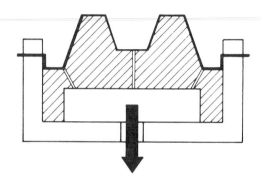

AIR SLIP FORMING

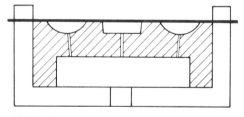

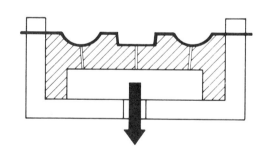

NEGATIVE FORMING

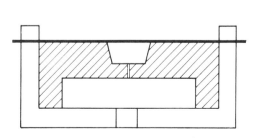

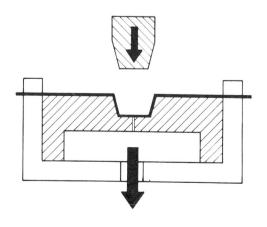

PLUG-ASSISTED NEGATIVE FORMING

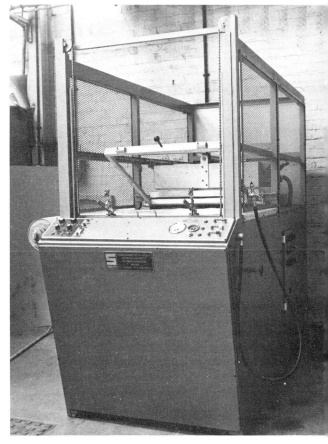

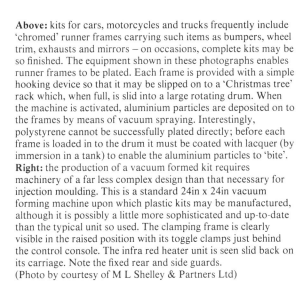

Above: kits for cars, motorcycles and trucks frequently include 'chromed' runner frames carrying such items as bumpers, wheel trim, exhausts and mirrors – on occasions, complete kits may be so finished. The equipment shown in these photographs enables runner frames to be plated. Each frame is provided with a simple hooking device so that it may be slipped on to a 'Christmas tree' rack which, when full, is slid into a large rotating drum. When the machine is activated, aluminium particles are deposited on to the frames by means of vacuum spraying. Interestingly, polystyrene cannot be successfully plated directly; before each frame is loaded in to the drum it must be coated with lacquer (by immersion in a tank) to enable the aluminium particles to 'bite'.
Right: the production of a vacuum formed kit requires machinery of a far less complex design than that necessary for injection moulding. This is a standard 24in x 24in vacuum forming machine upon which plastic kits may be manufactured, although it is possibly a little more sophisticated and up-to-date than the typical unit so used. The clamping frame is clearly visible in the raised position with its toggle clamps just behind the control console. The infra red heater unit is seen slid back on its carriage. Note the fixed rear and side guards.
(Photo by courtesy of M L Shelley & Partners Ltd)

part of the toolmaker, the greater precision of the tool and the extra time required to produce the moulded form all result in a more expensive product — another factor which the kit manufacturer has to weigh carefully.

Still other factors more directly concern the operation of the vacuum press. Briefly, these relate to the temperature of the heated plastic sheet, the speed at which it is drawn over the mould, and the speed at which the vacuum is produced. All will depend to a certain extent upon the thickness of the plastic used and the nature of the mould, but once again a careful balance has to be achieved. The heating system must provide uniform plasticity throughout the material being formed which means that the rate of heating and the temperature produced must be judiciously controlled — the plastic must be brought to its optimum temperature both across its surface and throughout its depth. Sophisticated heating equipment may even permit zonal variations in the distribution of heat to suit individual cavity requirements. Warping and the degree of shrinkage brought about during the moulding process present yet more problems for the manufacturer, particularly since they are not really measurable and thus are difficult to cater for. The speed at which the material is formed is vital to the appearance of the finished mouldings: if the shapes are produced too slowly, for example, cooling may take place too rapidly on those surfaces of the plastic that first come into contact with the mould, resulting in excessive thinning in areas of deep draw; if they are produced too quickly, uneven thicknesses of material may be produced over a single mould area.

The production of a vacuum formed kit is thus a very long and complicated business. Though nowhere nearly as expensive in terms of financial outlay as injection moulding processes, the necessary methods and techniques require a considerable amount of skill and time on the part of the manufacturer — who may well be one person working on his own. A vacuum formed kit may only take around a minute to mould on a press, but each unit may represent from one to two hours' work when all the preparation and ancilliary work is taken into account. Bearing in mind the production runs, which might be at best a couple of thousand units compared with perhaps hundreds of thousands for a commercially-produced injection moulded kit, their relatively high cost can begin to be appreciated.

MARKETING CONSIDERATIONS
Kit manufacturers are in business with one overriding motive — profit. Companies have produced kits that have not sold particularly well; they have been known to produce kits that have lost them

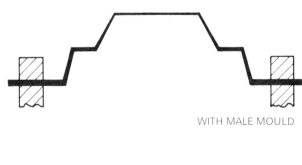

WITH MALE MOULD

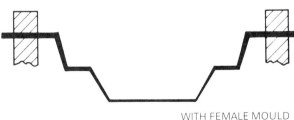

WITH FEMALE MOULD

THINNING OF PLASTIC SHEET IN VACUUM FORMING

money, but those that have done so consistently no longer *are* in business. The subjects chosen for translation into plastic kit form are selected merely because a manufacturer estimates that they will provide him with a good return on his investment. Despite what many modellers may like to think, this is the only reason why a particular kit is issued. Within these bounds, however, there is considerable room for manoeuvre, as will be seen in a moment.

The origin of a plastic kit is usually a suggestion — either a specific subject or sometimes a particular type of model — as to what might constitute a worthwhile venture. Whether it is in fact worthwhile is determined by defining or interpreting, to the best of the manufacturer's ability, a number of circumstances, facts or influences, most of which concern the market for which it might be produced. The type of market is particularly important, since it will affect the complexity, and therefore the cost, of the finished product. If children are seen as the principal customers, as is the case with a great many manufacturers (perhaps the majority), there is very little point in producing a kit of an unfamiliar subject, since the volume of sales is unlikely to realise a fair profit, if any. Producing a kit specifically for enthusiasts does have the attraction of offering rather more latitude in the choice of subject, but on the other hand the comparatively low volume of sales will dictate a higher retail unit price, especially if the kit is to be of the same degree of complexity as more popular lines. These two approaches, in fact, reflect in general terms the respective philosophies behind the production of injection moulded and vacuum formed kits, the one requiring a huge capital expenditure by the manufacturer and thus relying on mass sales, the other needing relatively little financial outlay and catering for the specialist modeller.

The strength, location and purchasing capacity of the potential market must also be taken into account by the manufacturer. The strength of the market is usually indicated by the familiarity of the subject that is being considered. Kits of Spitfire aircraft, Sherman tanks or the battleship *Bismarck* will always sell well simply because the prototypes are virtually household names and an enormous number of people can identify with them — clearly, the less well known the prototype, the fewer kits are likely to be sold. The location of the potential market must also be taken into account, although this is seemingly of little importance to certain manufacturers who perhaps place less reliance on exporting their products than others. What may loosely be termed the American, the European and

Right: the manufacture of vacuum formed kits is, with most concerns involved, something akin to a latter-day 'cottage industry'. Apart from the high degree of skill involved in the production of the actual moulded shapes, very careful thought has to be given to the choice of subject: the availability, or the possible future availability, of an injection moulded kit of a particular prototype precludes its consideration as a vacuum formed product since the sales of the latter would be so badly affected as to make it an uneconomic proposition. Hence vacuum formed kits tend to be 'gap-fillers' – subjects which do not perhaps have the mass appeal necessary for the large investment an injection moulded kit would require – and such a subject is represented here by the somewhat exotic McDonnell XP-67, built from the 1/72 scale Rareplanes kit.
(Photo by courtesy of Gordon Stevens)

the Japanese markets are the most lucrative, and whilst ideally a kit might be produced to satisfy the interests of all three, in practice this is not easy to achieve — if market location were the sole criterion, very few different subjects would be produced as plastic kits. Therefore a particular kit may be designed with one specific market location in mind, any popularity that may be generated elsewhere being regarded as a bonus. This is especially true of vacuum formed kit ranges, where a large proportion of the subjects are obviously chosen with the American market in mind, but it is also detectable in ranges of injection moulded kits, for example 1/72 scale aircraft kits originating from France and Italy and 1/700 scale warship kits produced in Japan, and of course in individual subjects. The inclusion of a decal sheet offering a range of choices as to how a model may be finished is not, as some modellers think, a move designed to incline a manufacturer favourably towards them as individuals, although this may indeed be an incidental effect. It is good sales policy in a much broader sense since the product will then appeal to the parochialism or nationalism of a very large number of modellers. A plastic kit of, say, the Hawker Siddeley Harrier will sell well everywhere because it is a familiar aircraft, even if it is supplied only with decals for RAF markings, but its sales are likely to be increased dramatically, and especially in the USA, if US Marine Corps markings are also provided. The purchasing power of a market is of course related to its average age, standard of living, and so on, and indirectly to such factors as its country's economic health and even political policy. Children have limited financial resources, and so a kit directed towards them must be appropriately priced — the manufacturer's choice of subject is in this instance somewhat limited since, as noted earlier, the volume of sales must be large

enough to keep the unit cost realistic. Catering for enthusiasts, again, permits a wider choice in terms of retail price alone, since these modellers, being generally adults, have more money available and are prepared to spend larger sums for particular kits. Even so, there is a theoretical limit to what a customer will pay for a given product, and a careful estimate of this has to be made before a kit is committed to production.

A further set of influences affecting the choice of a kit subject concerns the nature and strength of its actual or potential competition. This is perhaps most graphically illustrated by the tendency for kits representing a really up-to-date combat aircraft to be released at the earliest opportunity in an attempt to forestall the efforts of other manufacturers. The effects of this policy may be unfortunate: from the modeller's point of view, it can mean a hastily designed and possibly poor quality kit, or the representation of, for example, a pre-production aircraft with comparatively limited scope; from a manufacturer's point of view, it entails considerably more risk than might be associated with other subjects since his competitors are likely to be working along the same lines and may release their versions first. To the disinterested, the results occasionally border on the comic — a few years ago, three 1/72 scale F-15 Eagle kits were issued almost simultaneously, and for many modellers the only consideration affecting their purchase was one of price. However, the fact that competing manufacturers have not included a particular subject in their ranges is not in itself a good reason for producing it. All the other factors must be taken into account, and only if each is favourable may a kit be proceeded with. Somewhat paradoxically, a particular kit may be issued simply because it *is* included in the ranges of those companies which are regarded as direct competitors. The market here is more or less guaranteed, and the product should prove to be a sound and steady seller over a long period of time. Manufacturers will also talk in terms of having a 'balanced range' — again, with a view to a mass market rather than the individual demands of enthusiasts — so that perenially popular items such as German tanks and aircraft of the Second World War, or individually famous machines such as the P-51 Mustang or the Hawker Hurricane, are bound to be incorporated into their lists. Some scope is often offered in an effort to promote sales, for example by issuing a kit with a well known name but providing parts to complete a relatively obscure sub-variant, but this implies a certain level of sophistication with regard to the modeller, and again involves a degree of risk on the part of the manufacturer.

One other important factor influencing the choice of kit subject is the effect on the potential market of short-term fluctuations and trends, and, obviously, the manufacturer who can anticipate these and produce accordingly is likely to reap the reward. Particular events such as a much-publicised space venture or the release of a well-promoted and highly popular film are often accompanied by an appropriate plastic kit. Whilst such a kit might be expected to sell in reasonable numbers long after the impact of its progenitor has faded, the fundamental reason for its existence is its initial topicality. The launching of the kit should, ideally, coincide with the period of maximum publicity accorded to the actual subject, but the necessary period of research and development usually precludes this. However, the delay is as short as possible, and manufacturers will frequently defer production of other new kits in order to concentrate their efforts on the one whose success depends upon early release.

The explanation that a particular subject is not represented in plastic kit form because it is not technically possible to mould it is one of the myths that surround the hobby of plastic modelling. Whilst this contention may have been true in the early days of plastic kit technology, it is now no longer valid, and the only limitations imposed by the forming process are those outlined in previous sections of this chapter. It may surprise many modellers to know that virtually all the subjects that they require but are not produced in kit form have been carefully considered at one time or another by most of the manufacturers, and have been either shelved temporarily or rejected out of hand according to the factors mentioned above. There is a good deal of argument amongst kit producers as to the relative importance of each factor — this is partly responsible for the vast amount of subject choice

offered to the kit modeller — but it cannot be denied that successful companies know their own business best. The more successful they are in selling their products, the more adventurous they are likely to be in their selection of subject matter.

The question of scale occupies the thoughts of both modeller and manufacturer. Insofar as generalisations are valid, it can be said that conformity of scale throughout the plastic kit industry becomes more apparent with the decreasing size of the models produced. Thus there tends to be a small range of scales for small models and a larger range for big models. This is mainly because small models may conveniently be displayed together as a collection and the kits for them are cheaper to manufacture, thereby encouraging the expansion of one or two scales instead of many different ones. Kits for model armoured fighting vehicles (AFVs) may serve to illustrate the point: small models are available as either 1/76 or 1/72 scale kits; those of what may loosely be described as intermediate size are produced as 1/48, 1/35 or 1/32 scale kits; whilst really large 'showpiece' models may be found in 1/25, 1/24, 1/21, 1/16, 1/15 or 1/9 scales. Sometimes a manufacturer will very successfully introduce a completely new range of kits to a scale not hitherto tackled, or only in piecemeal fashion, but the gamble is undeniably great. Two of the best known instances of this were the pioneering 1/32 scale range of aircraft kits produced by Revell, who saw the need, or what turned out to be the need, for a collection of large, well-detailed models of this type, and the 1/700 scale series of waterline ship kits which saw the release of a vast number of subjects over a comparatively short period of time as a result of a collaborative venture by four Japanese companies. It might be argued that Revell's project succeeded because there was an obvious gap in the market whilst the Japanese created a demand by sheer weight of numbers, but in both instances an immense investment was required, far greater than would be called for by merely adding to existing ranges. The success of these schemes, it might further be argued, lends weight to the old maxim that the consumer does not know what he wants, only what he thinks he wants.

As well as the need to invest in research, tooling and kit production, a manufacturer will also have to turn his attention to the manner in which his product is presented to his customer. Aside from the well known psychological advantages of using yellow on the outside of the packaging and featuring dramatic artwork on the kit box top, there are some more fundamental considerations. A plastic kit will generally consist of the parts required to build the model, a leaflet giving guidance about its construction and painting requirements, a decal sheet providing coloured designs that would normally be too difficult for the average modeller to paint successfully, and a colourful box or other system of packaging serving the dual purpose of keeping the contents of the kit together and attracting the customer to it. Vacuum formed kits usually dispense with the decal sheet and offer only rudimentary instructions and packaging in the belief that the real enthusiast is interested only in the mouldings provided and will be able to solve all the other problems himself. Whether this is sound commercial policy is a matter for debate; at least one company engaged in the production of these kits thinks otherwise and provides in each kit detailed instructions, a carefully researched decal sheet and injection moulded parts for those areas of the kit that cannot adequately be represented by means of the vacuum forming process, the only obvious economies being concerned with the method of packaging. However, such a policy is at present the exception to the general rule, and so any consideration of the overall presentation of a plastic kit is much more relevant to injection moulded products.

In formulating the design of the structure of a plastic kit, a manufacturer takes into account not only the limitations of the moulding process,

but also the degree of complexity that is required in the finished product. From a purely economic point of view, the manufacturer will wish to use as few parts as necessary, and if he could produce all his kits with half a dozen parts each and maintain his profit margins he would do so. However, the demands of his customers, reflected in the products of his competitors, are such that this is not practicable, and so the minimum number of parts commensurate with ease of construction and the provision of the required amount of detail are supplied. How this is interpreted varies somewhat from kit to kit and from company to company, and it is also influenced of course by such factors as cost and potential market, but the levels of sophistication apparent in kits designed at around the same time are more or less comparable.

Whether or not the colour of the plastic used in a construction kit is an important influence in its sales is largely a matter for conjecture, but there is evidence to suggest that the psychological effects of certain colours may be quite strong. White — one of the most difficult colours to work with from a manufacturer's point of view — is very well received by modellers, ostensibly because it is neutral and offers a good surface for the coverage of paint, but possibly also because its visual association is one of cleanliness. Light grey is another neutral colour, and it permits an easy visual appreciation of moulded detail. Kits moulded in strong primary or secondary colours, or in black, may well succeed in attracting children; they might well assist sales if the colours resemble those found on the prototype, as in the case of tanks moulded in sand or green coloured plastic, because they convey an immediate impression of realism; and they may have a psychological impact by subconscious relation — the sinister connotations of black would certainly seem

Below: 1/32 scale aircraft kits, pioneered as a series by the American company Revell, first appeared in the early 1960s and reached their peak of popularity some ten years later. The range is still being extended by Hasegawa and Matchbox, but although most Revell 1/32 kits are still in production the company is now issuing new items only infrequently. The example featured here is their Hawker Typhoon Ib.

to be suited to the role of the bomber aircraft, for example. However, it could well be that unless the pigments for a plastic moulding are carefully chosen there may in fact be sales resistance from some sections of the market — a warship moulded in red and white, for instance, would immediately imbue the kit with a toy-like quality in the eyes of some.

The provision of optional parts is nowadays a common feature of the plastic kit. These may either serve the purpose of permitting a choice of natural attitudes to be shown on a model, as for example with an aircraft kit which perhaps may give the modeller the option of finishing it in flying or parked configuration or offer a number of inter-changeable offensive loads, or they may allow different variants of a basic prototype to be built, such as two distinct versions of one particular type of tank. This policy is usually only followed if the necessary extra components are few in number and can readily be incorporated into the design of the tool. The additional cost is therefore relatively small and is likely to be well rewarded in the form of increased sales. There are instances where one kit provides sufficient parts for two complete models to be built, usually two very different and separate, but nevertheless complementary, subjects; one Japanese company has even issued kits of aircraft containing parts to enable two separate, slightly different models of what is basically the same airframe to be completed. These approaches are not so much a case of optional parts as one of providing a supplementary model, and a development of this form of thinking, and one which is common practice, is the utilisation of a set of mouldings to provide the parts for more than one kit. One method of doing this is to reissue the mouldings, after a suitable time lapse, with revised packaging, thereby giving the impression of a completely different kit. Modifications to the components may or may not be made, but the re-released kit will usually contain fresh decals, recommend a different paint scheme and appear with a new title. The other method of using the mouldings from one tool for entirely separate kits is a system much favoured by Japanese manufacturers whereby kits are issued in pairs, or even in threes or fours, usually with a short time lag between each, the subsequent kits containing a large proportion of the parts found in the first. Each kit is in general sufficiently different in character from its companion products to make impracticable the inclusion of all the necessary parts in one package. Ships, aircraft, tanks and trucks are particularly suited to this treatment.

A manufacturer's approach to surface detailing is one of the more contentious issues amongst model-lers. The usual complaints are that the detailing is incorrectly positioned, inaccurate in style or too prominent, and they are generally well-founded. The most common grievance concerns the portrayal of rivet heads as random domes which, scaled up to full size, would look quite extraordinary. (Strangely enough, the representation of panel joints by means of raised lines is hardly ever adversely criticised, although it is equally unrealist-ic.) Manufacturers are also heavily censured for providing 'fabric' and other textured designs, again for the most part with good cause. This ornament-ation is purely an attempt to convey a visual impression which will appeal to the customer; the fact that it is frequently overscale may generally be attributed to the need for economy. Rivets may conveniently be machined into mould cavities by using a solenoid, textured surfaces may be etched mechanically by spark erosion, and it is far easier and less time consuming to engrave a line into a cavity, thereby producing a raised line on the moulding, than to furnish it with raised detail in order to produce a recessed effect on the plastic. It is quite possible to produce a kit showing all its detail perfectly in scale, but whether modellers would be prepared to pay the necessary price is another matter.

One other method by which the component parts of a kit may be engineered in an attempt to influence the customer favourably is by providing some form of operable device. This might involve a simple tooling exercise to enable the wheels of a vehicle to revolve, the gun of a tank to elevate or the propeller of an aircraft to rotate, and will normally have no appreciable effect upon the overall fidelity of the finished model. Provision for motorisation is frequently made with the larger and more expensive kits, and a few are fitted to accept radio control equipment. On occasions, however, some really startling gadgets are devised, the operation of most of which is achieved at the expense of accuracy. Three examples which spring readily to mind all relate to aircraft kits. Possibly the most ingenious involved the fitting of a network of interconnected threads within the body of the model, and by depressing the arrestor hook all manner of interesting pieces were simultaneously raised, lowered or swung out. Rather less pretentious, but nevertheless of equal fascination, was the provision in one kit of a clever little device which when activated emitted a noise which, it was claimed, imitated the engine sound of the proto-type. Arguably the most preposterous was a mechanism whereby a simple switch in the vicinity of the cockpit enabled a miniature plastic bomb to pop neatly out of the tailpipe. However, such delights are largely a thing of the past, much to the chagrin, it must be said, of a certain number of modellers.

The design of a kit instruction leaflet provides perhaps the best clues as to the kind of market for which the kit itself is basically produced. In setting down the recommended sequence of assembly, the majority of European manufacturers adopt a system of drawings illustrating the progress of the kit's construction, supported by a part numbering arrangement and a series of symbols indicating the type of operation that needs to be carried out. There tend to be very few instructions in the form of text, and those that are included are multi-lingual in nature. Kits from Japan and the USA, on the other hand, are usually accompanied by detailed descriptive directions as to how best the model may be built, the probable reason for this being that a large proportion of the kits produced are destined for their respective home markets. Two numbering systems are in general use to enable parts to be

Top: in order to attract custom, several manufacturers provide optional parts in their kits to give the modelmaker a choice of two or more slightly different configurations of the same basic subject. One of Heller's Saab Draken kits, for example, will provide enough components to enable the 35F interceptor (shown on the left), the 35XT two-seater (right) or the 35E reconnaissance version to be produced. Whether this policy is more lucrative to the manufacturer than providing the choice in two or more completely separate kits is a matter – apparently – for some debate; zealots are likely to buy enough kits to enable them to build all the versions on offer anyway.
(Models: Geoff Prentice)

Bottom: many modellers regard with some scepticism kits that feature moving parts, since many of the latter are incorporated only at the expense of authenticity. This 1/72 scale Airfix F-111E for example, a demonstration model built without modification although finished with Modeldecal transfers, illustrates the point: the overall impression is convincing, except for the fact that the fuselage apertures for the wing sweep, which on the real aircraft are automatically sealed as the wings move forward, have to be left as open slots if the facility is to remain operable as the manufacturer intends.
(Model and photo: Ray Rimell)

identified, one based on the stages of construction, the other keyed to the parts on the runners. In the first system, the parts are assembled in strict numerical order, the manufacturer clearly having organised his sequence before the mouldings are finalised. Although the logic of this approach is easily appreciated, it can mean that the modeller has to spend some time locating the parts he requires before he can proceed with the assembly, which in the case of a large kit might be a very time consuming business. The other method, favoured particularly by Japanese companies, allows the manufacturer to prepare his instruction sheet at any stage in the design of the kit since the parts are numbered in sequence along the runners. Whilst permitting the modeller to locate each part with ease, especially if, as commonly happens, a runner diagram is provided for him as well, there is always the chance that he may omit a vital component. Each system has its merits and drawbacks, but the younger modeller is perhaps better served by the first. Modern practice is to tool each part in a kit with its number, either on a surface of the component that will be hidden once the model is completed or, more commonly, on the runner close to it. Identical parts are normally allotted the same number, which is useful inasmuch as it saves space on the instruction sheet since assemblies that are duplicated need only to be shown once as diagrams. However, where every part is given a different number irrespective of whether the moulding is repeated, a procedure followed by one British manufacturer, there is, again, less chance of any part or sub-assembly being overlooked during the construction of the model.

Although errors do occur from time to time in manufacturers' recommended assembly sequences, the clarity and general presentation of such information is by and large of an excellent standard, and newcomers to the hobby of plastic modelling will find little difficulty in the construction of any kit. Sadly, the same cannot be said for many of the painting guides that accompany them, although it is true to say that recent years have witnessed a marked improvement generally. A modeller wishing to produce a convincing model requires guidance that is clear, comprehensive and, as far as possible, accurate. He will need to know the principal colours for the exterior surfaces of his models; unless he is producing figures or very small scale models he is likely to require information about interior finishes; and he may well wish to know which paints he should use for certain less obvious details that may only be apparent under close scrutiny. Few instruction sheets satisfy all these demands. The shortcomings are too numer-

ous to enable them to be discussed in depth, but typical examples are a set of drawings showing aircraft camouflage with only one side elevation, drawings that individually are far too small for clarity, a complex camouflage scheme shown by means of half-tone textures that are virtually indistinguishable from one another, a recommendation for the use of vague colours such as 'grey' or 'green' or a completely inadequate instruction such as 'refer to box top painting for colour scheme'. In many kits, no information at all is provided about certain areas of a model, notably cockpit interiors for aircraft, small decks and platforms for ships and engine details for vehicles, and on occasions what is presented proves to be incorrect. The main reason for these failings is presumably economy, meaning both the cost of researching the necessary information and the cost of printing it on the instruction leaflet. It might be argued that the majority of modellers do not require detailed guidance for painting their models, and that the real enthusiasts will regard finding out the information as part of the hobby anyway, but it is nevertheless true that the high degree of sophistication found in the mouldings of most plastic kits is rarely matched in the painting instructions that accompany them.

An instruction sheet will usually include some historical and technical data relating to the prototype which forms the subject of the kit, and this will doubtless prove interesting to the younger modeller, although enthusiasts are likely to have a good knowledge of the subject before the kit is purchased. A few sheets provide some extremely useful close-up photographs of the prototype, enabling those interested enough to incorporate additional detail on their model, and one manufacturer makes a practice of offering information as to how an appropriate diorama might be tackled.

Kits representing aircraft, AFVs, and road and racing vehicles will almost always include a decal sheet to enable the modeller to show badges, insignia, lettering and so forth on his model without having to apply them with a paintbrush. More will be said about decal technology and application procedure in a later chapter, but in general terms, the quality of manufacturers' decal sheets nowadays is very high indeed, and it may fairly be reasoned that this is yet another example of a response to market requirements. The improvements over recent years have in fact been quite far-reaching, attention having been paid to accuracy and intensity of colour, comprehensiveness of detail and quality of adhesion and surface finish. A choice of markings is more often than not offered to enable the modeller to produce his model in one of two or three different schemes, even where no option of configuration is permitted in the kit mouldings.

Above: some moving components, however, can readily be incorporated into a kit with little or no detriment to its overall scale fidelity, as the optional-position turrets and control surfaces on this Airfix 1/72 scale Handley Page Halifax BIII (built to represent the famous *Friday the 13th*) testify. However, the increased tooling costs involved in producing some types of moving parts have resulted in the inclusion of such items in a plastic kit becoming less common than it was.
(Model and photo: Ray Rimell)

Of paramount importance to the marketing of plastic kits is the method in which the unsold product is first presented to the public. A significant proportion of kits sold are bought on impulse, and even more are purchased without any assessment of their contents having been carried out, and it is therefore hardly surprising that manufacturers spend a great deal of money in ensuring that their products are packaged in the most attractive way possible. An injection moulded kit is generally marketed in a full colour box with eye-catching artwork on its lid accompanied by secondary information as to its subject matter and manufacturer. The scale of the model is stated on the box top in most instances, and additional information such as the number of parts the kit contains and brief details about any special features may also be present. The box ends will show most of this information in condensed form — most import-

antly, since the storage of kits on retailers' shelves means that these are often the only surfaces of the box that are immediately visible — and may include a small reproduction of the main box art, whilst the sides may advertise other products available from the manufacturer's range, historical data about the kit subject, details of relevant colour schemes, etc. If the packaging is of the one-piece box type with pull-out end flaps, a full colour painting guide may be provided on the base. For very small kits, the packaging may be in the form of a stiff piece of card on which is mounted a clear plastic moulding containing the kit components and decals. The contrast with the method in which vacuum formed kits are presented could hardly be more striking.

Although the packaging of a vacuum formed kit tends to be very basic, in some instances consisting only of a polythene bag, it still constitutes a relatively high proportion of the total cost of the product since it involves a labour-intensive process. It is not therefore strictly true to say that such kits are marketed in elementary packaging only because the buyer, who is presumed to be an enthusiast, does not require it to be otherwise. However, it is important to the modeller that he receives his kit in good condition, and one function of packaging is to protect the goods for which it is designed, and this is where there is room for improvement. Very many customers buy their kits by means of mail order, and it is really the responsibility of the company sending out the goods to ensure that as far as possible they are received by the purchaser in satisfactory condition, since this is usually a service for which payment is made. It is probably true to say that most vacuum formed kits are sold in this way, in very many instances directly by the manufacturer, and few are afforded even the basic protection of a cardboard box. Although more adequate and more attractive packaging would add considerably to the retail cost of a vacuum formed kit, it is a matter for some conjecture as to whether sales would be adversely affected if this policy were adopted. To date, there seems to be no evidence either way, since no such kit company appears to have had the resources — or the courage — to try to find out.

The introduction to the market of a new kit is made known in a number of different ways. The first official announcements of kits produced by the major companies are usually made at the various Trade Fairs that are held at different times during the year in a number of countries throughout the world. Although modellers are made aware of the announcements at the earliest possible opportunity through the pages of modelling magazines, the function of a Trade Fair is primarily to enable manufacturers to advise retailers of which kits will be forthcoming in the months to follow and to attract their custom. Contact between manufacturer and modeller is effected by means of catalogues, for which a nominal charge is usually made, and advertisements which are placed via the appropriate media. The catalogues are generally well in keeping with the highest concepts of consumer relations, being in the majority of cases highly colourful and very professionally produced, and often containing supplementary information relating to the broader aspects of plastic modelling. Advertisements often seem much less flamboyant by comparison, because they tend to promote a single kit, almost always a new release, which by itself will probably not generate a vast profit. A catalogue will illustrate a manufacturer's complete range of products and is likely to be referred to at frequent intervals by the prospective customer, thus representing a much sounder investment.

Modelling enthusiasts will learn more about particular kits through reading articles and reviews in magazines. Whilst these fulfil one advertising requirement in that they bring to the attention of the customer available products, it is questionable whether they have any appreciable effect, good or bad, on the sale of these products, unless no other notice of availability is published. Whilst there are doubtless many modellers who will not make a purchase until they have read an objective appraisal of a kit in which they are interested, reviews are generally read only by enthusiasts (because modelling magazines are generally read only by enthusiasts) who may well buy the kit as soon as it is released, which is, more often than not, some time before the review appears.

There is one other method by which news of forthcoming kits is made public, and this is the strictly unofficial vehicle of rumour. Plastic modelling is one of those hobbies where enthusiasts can quite easily become fanatics, and it does not take a great deal of imagination to suppose which particular subjects might be considered suitable by a manufacturer for translation into kit form — a plausible subject is announced in convincing fashion, and before long the report has spread amongst the intended audience. The rumour may indeed be well-founded, but needless to say it can cause annoyance to a manufacturer, who quite obviously has better things to do than confirm or deny hearsay. Companies understandably take steps to protect their interests, and most would prefer to make no announcements whatsoever prior to the release of their products if this were commercially practicable, such is the competitiveness of the industry. If a rumour reaches the wrong ears, and comes from a reliable source or is convincing enough to be believed, financial loss may be the result.

TRENDS

Many of the changes that have taken place over the years in the manufacturers' approach to the production of a plastic kit have already been noted, and if a single observation can be made, it can be said that the product of today is much more refined that it was twenty-five years ago. Accuracy and scale fidelity are now very much better, the number of parts a kit contains is generally very much higher, instruction sheets are much more comprehensive, decal sheets have improved beyond all recognition, the provision of optional parts is now commonplace, gimmickry is not often found, the enthusiasm amongst modellers for scenic presentation has encouraged companies to include appropriate parts in their products, and of course with the vast increase in the size of their ranges and the large number of new companies in direct competition, manufacturers have been forced to look for more esoteric subjects. In addition, vacuum formed kits have brought a new dimension to the hobby. These trends are easily discernible, and it is interesting to turn the mind as to where they might lead in the future.

Interest in plastic modelling continues to grow, and while this is sustained it is reasonable to expect that the improvements seen over recent years in

Right: same subject – different treatment: the moulded components for a vacuum formed (top) and an injection moulded 1/72 scale kit for the F-86D Sabre. Both, if built with care, will produce neat, convincing models, but the greater appeal possessed by the packaging of the injection moulded product with its full-colour box, comprehensive decal sheet, display stand and separate instruction sheet is readily apparent. 'Overlapping' such as this is rare: the vacuum formed kit normally provides the modeller with the opportunity of building a model of an unusual subject not otherwise available, although he must expect to pay rather more than he would for a comparable injection moulded product. The injection moulded Sabre, incidentally, also illustrates the practice whereby one established manufacturer acts as the overseas distributor for another – the kit is designed and produced in the UK by Airfix, but this example is a repackaged set of mouldings distributed by Tomy for the Japanese market.

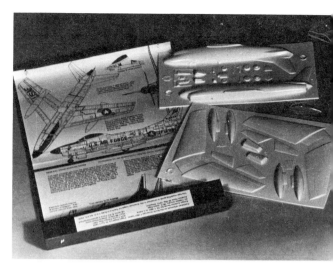

plastic kit technology will continue to grow as well. Manufacturers will claim that this trend is in response to the demands of the market; modellers may venture the opinion that they can only show interest in what is available to them. However, it is perfectly true that modellers are very much more informed than they used to be, and so their requirements, which become more and more exacting, will presumably continue to be met. The consequent higher cost of producing a kit, allied to the ever-increasing costs of raw materials and labour, is likely to result in higher retail prices, but it should also mean that manufacturers will utilise their resources to an even tighter degree. This may be done by re-issuing more old kits in 'modernised' form (perforce in many instances, since moulds for popular kits become unusable in time), by including more and more options to encourage the customer to buy twice instead of once, by producing different kits of one or more sub-variants of a prototype in order to use the same tool for several items, by dispensing with moving parts, and by economising on packaging. In any event, the number of marketable subjects is decreasing steadily, and even though manufacturers will look anew at subjects previously rejected, the rate of issue of completely fresh subjects is bound in time to slacken off. It is always possible, of course, that a new scale will come into vogue, perhaps 1/100, and this will enable manufacturers to start afresh with all the established subjects. To give a kit wider international appeal, both national and international, decal sheets may well provide an increased number of choices, despite the fact that it even now may cost as much if not more, kit for kit, to print the decals as to produce the set of mouldings. The size of the sheet is in fact of much less importance than the number of colours used on it, and so, provided careful selection is carried out, this is a quite feasible proposition.

It is not beyond the realms of possibility that co-operation rather than competition will become a feature of kit manufacturers' relationships with each other. Quite apart from conformity of scale, which might be construed as a form of co-operation as well as one of competition, the seeds have already been sown. It may come as a surprise to some modellers to realise the number of marketing deals that have been struck — Frog-Hasegawa, Airfix-MPC, Revell-Italaerei, Monogram-Bandai, Tomy-Airfix, Tomy-Heller, Hasegawa-ESCI and Aurora-Heller are just some of those that have operated in recent years — and of course tools from companies that have ceased trading are usually bought up by others and kits produced from them, Kitmaster-Airfix, Frog-Revell, Frog-Novo and Aurora-Monogram being examples of this arrangement. In years to come, as the oil gradually runs out, there may be no option but to pool resources. We shall have to see.

Chapter 2
Aids, materials and equipment

Human nature being what it is, most people who build models on something other than a casual basis will at least attempt to produce a result that demonstrates their highest level of workmanship, and most will endeavour to improve their standards of execution in relation to previous achievements. This may involve the neatness with which the model has been assembled, the degree to which the model's accuracy has been improved, the amount of additional detail that has been incorporated, the care with which the paint finish has been applied, or the originality in the way the model has been presented. Some will concentrate their efforts on one of these aspects of the hobby, whilst others will try to combine all of them in the building of one model, each aspect requiring a rather different attitude on the part of the modeller and a different approach as regards technique. However, each will also require a certain inspiration in the first instance, so that the modeller is provided both with a stimulus to improve his own standards and with reliable reference sources so that his discoveries can be put into practice. In addition, a range of tools, materials and accessories is needed so that ideas and techniques can be applied directly to the model.

REFERENCE SOURCES
Precisely what constitutes a reliable reference source will depend very much upon the sort of standard to which the model in question is to be produced, in other words how particular the modeller is about detail accuracy in his work. Most modellers will refer exclusively to secondary source material since this is generally more accessible and frequently easier to understand, but a few, the dedicated enthusiasts, will dismiss this as being too risky a business and will use only primary references to guide them.

Primary source material consists of first-hand information and pictorial evidence and, for the modeller, is limited to four principal types. Firstly, there are official documents. These may be in the form of the written word and include such things as paint specifications and directives concerning the application of paint, official handbooks, pilots' notes, drivers' manuals, and the like, or they may be in the form of plans — the original builder's plans for aircraft, ships, tanks, and so on. Secondly, there are first hand accounts. These may be found in books as eye witness accounts or descriptive passages, or may be picked up in conversation or from speakers giving lectures. Thirdly, there are photographs, which faithfully record details of their subjects' configuration and surroundings and may give an indication of the colour scheme they display. Fourthly, there is the actual prototype itself, although the instances where this is available for inspection are comparatively rare.

Whilst primary sources are the most reliable form of reference, it would be idle to suggest that they are invariably flawless. Official directives, for example, are often ignored, usually of necessity rather than flagrantly and especially under the exigencies of war. The author was interested to learn that a wartime RAF maintenance crewman, with whom he was talking on one occasion, frequently applied paint that 'looked about the right shade' rather than complied with official specifications, to aircraft at his station. Official plans, too, are often at variance with the actual hardware for which they are prepared, simply because modifications tend to be made to machines in the light of experience. A case in point concerns the Frog Armstrong Whitworth Whitley kit, which, following official plans, has the bomb aimer's glazing in the nose of the aircraft offset from the centreline. In fact, the Whitley design was modified whilst the aircraft was in production and the glazed panels were fitted symmetrically.

The deficiencies of the human memory and the

natural tendency to exaggerate are the principal reasons why first-hand accounts cannot always be taken as entirely accurate. In substance, such accounts relate a generally truthful picture, but details are apt to become lost or uncertain. On the other hand, the unusual is clearly remembered — if a witness, or more especially a group of witnesses, recall seeing a warship painted entirely in red for example, then red it certainly was.

Photographs are generally very reliable primary sources, although they can of course be tampered with — the activities of wartime censors spring readily to mind — and tonal values are often misrepresented. Further, official labelling can be vague, misleading, or on occasions incorrect. Colour photographs, of course, should not be used to match colours for a model since the effects of light and the problems of colour reproduction in the printing process may create distortions, although they can certainly be useful as a guide.

The best form of primary source material is undoubtedly a first-hand acquaintance with the model prototype, such as may be formed at a museum, an air display or a motor-racing circuit. However, even here there are difficulties. Some sort of pictorial record will usually be needed by the modeller who visits his real-life subject, and thus his own skill and thoroughness are of importance. Additionally, he should take care that the prototype he is looking at is itself accurate — this may sound somewhat absurd, and indeed is if his model is to depict the prototype as it appears when he sees it, but many museum specimens are repaired, reconstructed and repainted (they may even be full-size models themselves) and may not retain their original appearance. Anyone wishing to produce a really accurate model of the USS *Texas* as she appeared during the Second World War, for example, would find a visit to San Jacinto, where the ship is preserved, extremely helpful, but he would still need to undertake a good deal more research.

Below: scope for improvement. A comparison between a model and a photograph of its prototype will often reveal at a glance the work that needs to be done to improve a standard injection moulded kit if one is attempting to make the latter look realistic. Ship kits are notorious in this respect, principally because of their necessarily small scales although there are frequently other less explicable errors evident. The model of HMS *Exeter*, which is merely assembled from a kit, indicates the problem in telling fashion. Apart from its general lack of finesse, its over-simplification, and the presence of visible joints, several inaccuracies of configuration become apparent when one compares the model to the real thing. Among these are the 'spread' of the tripod masts, the line of the hull scuttles, and the shape of the bridge block. (Ship photo: IWM)

Above: reliable references or sources of confusion? These photographs show features which, if translated on to a model, might well cause a few raised eyebrows, and illustrate the dangers of being dogmatic about what is 'right' and 'wrong'. Kit manufacturers are frequently taken to task for providing decals featuring RAF insignia wherein the shade of blue is too light, but the 611 Sqn Spitfire I in the foreground of the top photograph shows as a very pale colour. The contention that camouflaged WWII aircraft were invariably matt finished is not supported by the evidence in this photograph either – the aircraft on the left has caught the sun in no uncertain fashion. The glossy nature of the exhaust pipes on the machine in the foreground is also noteworthy. This photograph is dated 11 January 1940. (Photo: Popperfoto)

Below: Obviously a 'posed' shot but nevertheless of considerable interest is this photograph of a Spitfire I taken on the same day and at the same place (RAF Digby) as the previous one. The absence of an individual aircraft code letter, the red centre of the fuselage roundel being 'too big' (the roundel itself being 'wrong' in other respects as well), and the 'hard' camouflage demarcation lines (except for that immediately in front of the cockpit), are all points which show how unwise it is to generalise about the painting and marking schemes of wartime aircraft. (Photo: Popperfoto)

Secondary source material may loosely be defined as second-hand reference data and includes such items as redrawn plans, sketches made from photographs or from the actual model prototype, and written accounts wherein original documentation has been interpreted. This form of source material is usually much more readily available to the modeller, appearing as it does in books, journals, magazines, kit instruction sheets, and the like. Needless to say, the accuracy of such information depends to a large extent upon the skill, thoroughness and integrity of the person responsible for it, and it should be said straightaway that a good deal of secondary source material is utterly reliable.

The major problem with written information appearing in books and journals, however, is that a good proportion of it is drawn itself from other secondary source material and not from primary sources. Thus errors are not only perpetrated, an excusable and inevitable literary failing, but they may also be perpetuated and their number increased. These shortcomings may result from a simple printer's error or they may be derived from haphazard research on the part of the author responsible, and they may or may not be important, but the modeller should recognise the fact that they exist.

A similar situation arises with scale drawings, many of which purport to be accurate plans. These may be taken directly from official builders' plans, and if so — and provided they are prepared by a skilful draughtsman — they may be considered generally reliable. But very many are not, and one's suspicions are immediately aroused if the source from which a particular drawing is taken is unquoted. It must be remembered that, however conscientiously they may be prepared, a set of scale drawings is only an interpretation. This is especially relevant with regard to the problem of curves, which are a complex mathematical subject in themselves and not merely any smooth lines, other than straight ones, between two points. A further consideration is that the smaller the scale of the drawing, the more exaggerated any discrepancies are likely to be. The modeller should also beware of scale drawings which are claimed to be 'measured from the real thing'. It is difficult to perform this operation in a thorough manner without totally dismantling the subject whose proportions are to be ascertained.

Camouflage patterns pose similar dilemmas for the modeller. A pattern prepared by direct observation of the prototype will at best be a close approximation, in particular where compound curves are involved, such as along the fuselage of an aircraft, and, again, much reliance is placed upon the ability of the artist responsible for the camouflage guides. Even where schemes are reproduced from official master drawings, the assumption is often made that these drawings were always meticulously followed 'in the field', whereas in fact they rarely were.

Two other sources in which a great deal of faith is sometimes put are the kit instruction sheet and the kit review. Pictorial information included with plastic kits varies enormously in the standards it attains, but for a number of reasons, principally time and the need for economy, such information is often gleaned from secondary sources, and the problem of interpretative error crops up again. Kit reviews are sometimes useful inasmuch as they may present an informed opinion about a particular product, but too often they are superficial in coverage, descriptive rather than analytical in content, and destructive rather than constructive in approach. Too frequently they pronounce dogmatically, with observations backed up by evidence drawn from secondary sources which, as we have seen, are more often than not flawed. The circle is neatly completed when the comment is passed that the configuration of a kit is accurate because it matches precisely a particular set of scale drawings — in all probability the very drawings from which the kit was originally prepared.

What, then, is the modeller to do if he wishes to produce an accurate model? The answer is that he must compromise and compare. Although the preceding paragraphs have drawn attention to some of the dangers of relying on one particular reference source, a collection of sources, such as a set of scale drawings, a selection of photographs and a detailed kit review, will enable the modeller to form his own opinions as to how accurate his model can be. The more information he can gather around him, the more successful he is likely to be in his quest for complete authenticity. Some questions will always remain unanswered and so the modeller must be prepared to accept compromise. Ultimately, he is his own judge.

TOOLS AND MATERIALS
The increasing popularity of the hobby of plastic modelling has paved the way for the introduction of a very extensive range of tools, equipment and materials designed to assist the modeller. Exactly

Below: photographs of this kind are a model enthusiast's dream but unfortunately they are all too rare. This picture of the prototype Fairey Battle (K4303) shows to good effect the configuration of its two-pitch de Havilland metal airscrew and a lot of useful points about the airframe detailing, notably the nature of the panel joints, the fastenings for the removable engine panels, and both 'flush' and 'mushroom head' rivets. Note also the 'sooting' caused by the exhaust gases and the finish of the natural metal used in the aircraft's construction. (Photo: Popperfoto)

what he acquires will be determined by the amount of labour he puts into his models, how particular he is about the appearance of his work, and how much money he is prepared to spend, and so it is somewhat impractical to discuss which tools and materials are essential and which are not. All are useful, to a greater or lesser degree. Some of the available equipment, usually relatively expensive, merely reduces the time taken, or the level of skill required, to complete a task which may be undertaken by a far less pretentious tool, and such equipment may therefore be considered a luxury rather than a necessity. There are also unfortunately a number of fashions which pervade the hobby from time to time and in which modellers tend to get caught up. The most prominent in recent years has been the acquisition of an airbrush which, according to some opinion, immediately transforms a kit builder into an expert modeller. Properly used, an airbrush is an invaluable piece of equipment, but it cannot be reckoned as a complete substitute for the paintbrush. Another fad of a few years ago was the application of gleaming foil to surfaces of models in order to represent any form of natural metal. Needless to say, such a finish could look quite preposterous if little thought were given to the type of surface it was supposed to represent.

What sort of jobs does the plastic modeller need to undertake in order to achieve a neat, realistic result? Basically, he needs to do two things — shape his medium and then embellish it with colour. To produce a shape he needs to fit together component parts, remove unwanted material and add extra where it is absent; to give it colour he needs to apply some sort of pigment to the finished form.

The binding together of two pieces of polystyrene, the plastic most commonly used in modelling, may be simply effected by the application of polystyrene cement, a somewhat misleading term since the substance involved is more accurately a chemical solvent. This solvent can take two different forms — a rather viscous liquid supplied in a tube, or a more fluid substance supplied in a bottle. Broadly speaking, the tube variety is more useful where strength and rigidity of construction are required, consisting as it does of liquid cement in which a little polystyrene has already been dissolved, but it does have a tendency to string, particularly if kept over a period of time, and it is rather too clumsy for delicate work. There is not a great deal to choose between the various brands available, and prices appear to be comparable, so one particular variety cannot really be recommended in preference to another. Liquid cement does vary much more from brand to brand, mainly because it may be composed of a number of different substances, including methyl-ethyl-ketone (MEK), acetone, or various chlorinated hydrocarbons. The most important variables are its viscosity and its powers of solvency, which are usually in proportion to each other. Liquid cement such as that marketed by Britfix (Humbrol) and Gloy is rather stronger than, for example, Mek-Pak (G N Slater Ltd). All these solvents by definition react with the surface of a piece of polystyrene, and the stronger the solvent the stronger the reaction, and the greater the damage if accidental spillage occurs or over-enthusiastic application takes place. Solvents for other plastics materials may be required, such as acetone for cellulose-acetate and butyl lactate or butyl acetate for CAB, but special care must be exercised when joining dissimilar materials as the solvent may not be effective.

Adhesives, too, have their place in plastic modelling. It may be desirable on occasions to employ materials other than plastics in the construction process — metal, wood, paper and card are just some of the more common substances that may need to be used — and of course plastics themselves can also be bonded together with agents other than solvents. There is a variety of adhesives available to suit each material, including cyanoacrylate and the so-called universal adhesives, and it is largely a matter of personal preference as to which particular one is applied. However, there are three which seem to be favoured more than others. The first is epoxy resin, an expensive adhesive prepared by mixing together a resin and a setting agent, and this has the ability to bond together a wide range of otherwise non-compatible materials, with the added advantages of great strength and fast setting time. The modeller will find it invaluable whenever he has occasion to use metal components, and plastics other than polystyrene. The second widely used adhesive is white PVA glue, which is useful for materials derived from wood. Where a bond of no particular strength is required but where there is a danger of irreparably damaging a plastic component by using solvents, such as the fixing of cockpit canopies or vehicle windscreens, PVA glue again has its advantages. The third adhesive is in fact not marketed as such but nevertheless has the properties necessary for a satisfactory bond. This is ordinary matt varnish such as that produced by Humbrol, and this substance is particularly useful where tiny deail is added to a model. It possesses no great strength, and its drying time is relatively long, but it is very fluid and virtually undetectable when set.

There are occasions when some device is necessary to clamp together the component parts of an assembly, particularly where mating surfaces do not align perfectly with each other, in order to ensure that the bond formed between them is completely welded before it has had a chance to set. A number of different items may be employed in this situation, but adhesive tape is probably the most versatile. However, rubber bands and various forms of clips or mechanical clamps are also favoured by many modellers, and each is useful in its way.

In order to produce a given shape in plastic it is necessary both to remove material and to apply it. In order to remove it, three basic methods are employed, cutting, gouging and abrading, and there is a wide selection of tools available for these tasks. Perhaps the most useful general purpose cutting tool is the craft knife, which can be obtained in a variety of styles, including lightweight and heavy duty, and may feature such contrivances as snap-off blade shafts or even retractable blades. However, the basic requirements are that the knife should be comfortable in the hand, able to withstand reasonable pressure, and able to provide the correct type of blade for the job being undertaken.

Polystyrene quickly blunts a razor sharp cutting edge, and so it is desirable to have a number of unused spare blades available. The blades themselves may be of three basic configurations, straight, convex or concave, of which the first two can be used for precision work. The convex type is generally preferable since by design it can afford a smaller surface contact line to the material being cut, which therefore offers less resistance, and it gives a greater choice of cutting angles. It is perfectly possible to use a razor blade as a basic cutting instrument — although handling the doubled-edged variety can be a very hazardous affair and is not to be recommended — but for delicate work such a tool is somewhat unwieldy.

Where relatively thick sections of plastic need to be cut, a more practical tool is a saw, and of the types available the most useful is the razor saw, which has been developed with modellers in mind. The teeth are extremely fine, and cuts may be achieved with strokes in either direction. Other types of saw, such as a small tenon saw or a coping saw, certainly have their uses, though these are somewhat limited by comparison.

Double-bladed cutting instruments will be useful to the modeller from time to time. A small pair of nail scissors is handy for a wide range of jobs, and a place might also be found for a pair of nail clippers and a small pair of pointed, general purpose pliers.

Gouging tools will be found to be invaluable for a wide variety of tasks involving the piecemeal removal of material from a portion of plastic, and most can be utilised for scraping operations as well. The convex craft knife blade is particularly useful

Made entirely from plastic strip and assembled exclusively with liquid cement, this 1/48 scale Bailey Bridge was built in conjunction with plans drawn up by the modeller from numerous photographs of the prototype. A model of this nature, consisting as it does of delicate components and best constructed by cementing the various pieces *in situ*, really precludes the use of tube cement. (Model: Dave Williams)

for general work, but jobs calling for greater precision may successfully be accomplished by using tools such as craft lino cutters and some of the more elaborate or expensive modelling gouges. Precision work of a rather different nature can of course be undertaken by using a drill, and miniature jewellers' drills are available in a good selection of gauges for this purpose. A pin chuck will give the modeller good control over these tools, although many modellers claim success merely by rotating the drills between thumb and forefinger. A few pins, or other, more manageable instruments such as an old pair of dividers, will also be found useful.

The third principal method by which material may be removed is abrading. This will require the use of a number of rigid and non-rigid abrasive surfaces which, ideally, should be of a number of different grades ranging from coarse, for rough work, to the finest possible, for final preparation of the model prior to painting. A very serviceable item, and one that can be obtained relatively cheaply, is the abrasive board, which may be purchased as a manicure accessory from the chemist or alternatively made up by the modeller by gluing appropriate grades of abrasive paper to appropriately shaped extemporary tools such as thick pieces of card or sections of dowelling. More expensive, but at the same time more able to withstand constant use, are the different types of file. Mouse-tailed files and needle files, available from most hobby shops or handyman's stores, are to be found in the inventories of most modellers and may assume a variety of cross-sectional shapes. Again, none is without its advantages, but of most assistance are the flat, round and half-round types.

Abrasive paper is itself an indispensable item, and in addition to the standard glasspaper, emery paper (neither really necessary in plastic modelling, however) and wet-and-dry paper, there are a number of more specialised products which offer considerable advantages. One of the most useful — and durable — is a product widely available in the USA known as Flex-i-Grit. This is offered in a selection of grades, ranging from the equivalent of about 200 down to what becomes virtually a polishing cloth, and consists of polyester sheet coated with particles of silicon carbide, chromium oxide, etc. The beauty of this product is that it can be rolled and folded without causing cracking, and it is therefore of great assistance in smoothing out awkward angles and intricately contoured surfaces. Another fine finishing film, which, although produced in the UK, does not appear to be stocked in very many places, is Crocus, which is available both as a cloth and as a paper, and metal polish or toothpaste may also be used for final surface preparation of the model. However, wet-and-dry paper, used either way, will suffice for most purposes and may be economically used and easily wielded if cut into small rectangles before use.

No plastic model, whether made up of preformed or hand-made components, is without its initial flaws, and perhaps the most basic of these are the gaps which inevitably occur when parts are fitted together. In addition, it is often desirable to build up the contours of a model in order to achieve a required shape. Some form of pliable compound is therefore needed to fulfil these tasks. There are innumerable such products available; some are produced specifically for the modeller and tend to be fine-grained, setting without too much shrinkage, whilst others are manufactured for a more general market. Relatively coarse-grained fillers, such as Plastic Padding, Humbrol Body Putty, Tetrion, Milliput and Polyfilla, have the advantage of being comparatively cheap, and they are to a point water soluble in that the substance can be removed from the surface of a model, provided it has not completely set, with a damp rag, without detriment to any moulded detail. Finer grained products, such as Holt's Loy, Rinshed-Mason's Green Stuff (both car body filling compounds) and Tamiya Putty, set more quickly but, once applied, can only be removed by abrasion. The ideal filler is thus very much a matter of personal choice, influenced by the type of task it is required to perform.

There are a number of ways in which a home-made filling compound may be prepared. An old favourite, and one that still has its uses, is made up by mixing polystyrene filings with a small amount of plastic solvent. A pliable modelling material of similar characteristics may be prepared by allowing small sections of scrap plastic to dissolve in a bottle half full of brush cleaning fluid. This concoction, generally referred to as 'liquid sprue', is widely used by figure modellers for shaping their models, and can be both easily moulded on application and shaped with a file when hardened off. Tube cement on its own can also be used as a filler, particularly along gaps which are readily accessible and where loss of moulded detail is not a consideration.

For some gaps, particularly those of a hairline nature, ordinary gloss enamel paint is often a more effective filler than any of the compounds mentioned, and certain cellulose-based fillers such as Green Stuff may be diluted with cellulose thinners and used in much the same way.

Some form of tool is obviously required for applying these substances, and the choice will clearly depend on the type of job in hand. A household putty knife is useful where large areas of filler have to be applied, but for more intricate work an old, well-worn, pointed nail file or a small screwdriver are ideal. Liquid fillers such as those described in the previous paragraph are more effectively administered with a thin brush.

There are a vast number of miscellaneous tools which modellers tend to acquire for a variety of jobs, and a brief discussion of some of the most useful of these is perhaps appropriate at this point. For handling and positioning small parts, a good quality pair of pointed tweezers is of considerable assistance. Dental tweezers, with hooked points, are particularly useful, and a number of other dental tools such as probes, descalers, excavators and

EXTEMPORARY TOOLS FROM
WOOD AND ABRASIVE PAPER

Top: the use of filling compound is not restricted to plugging the gaps that may show themselves as the assembly of a model progresses. This 1/72 scale Martin-Baker MB5, for example, has its entire fuselage made from the substance: a stout plastic card framework has been overlaid with Milliput epoxy putty and then shaped by abrasion. Producing a bulky structure by this method requires much patience since most fillers need to be applied in fairly thin layers and a great deal of sanding and 'making good' is involved as the outline takes shape. (Model: Jim Charlton)
Bottom: a 1/35 scale US T-23 Medium Tank, about half way to completion. The hull uses the suspension from the Italaerei M4A1 Sherman, but most of the hull proper is sheet polystyrene, or plastic card. Note how the kit hull sides have been incorporated into the body of the model, thereby simplifying the attachment of the running gear. This model also illustrates another use to which filling compound may be put: thinned lacquer-based putty has been carefully dabbed on to the turret to give a 'cast' effect. (Model: Greg Bieszczad. Photo: Donn Buerger)

dental spatulas, if they can possibly be obtained, are very handy for adjusting the positions of small parts in awkward places on a model. Pins, toothpicks or wooden cocktail sticks may be used for applying tube cement or small areas of filler. Those who produce hand-made components for their models will rely a great deal on basic mathematical equipment such as a pair of dividers, a steel rule and a steel set square, whilst for more general modelling purposes a small vice might be considered a worthwhile purchase.

Brushes are useful for a number of jobs other than painting. A thin, long-haired brush is required for the application of liquid cement along joints and a broader one might be available for coating larger areas of plastic with liquid cement should this be necessary. A broad, soft brush may be used for general dusting and cleaning purposes, whilst a stiffer brush with cut down bristles is helpful in clearing clogged areas such as may result after the application of abrasives to a model.

It is neither possible nor necessary to describe in detail every conceivable tool that may be useful to the plastic modeller, but methods of using those mentioned, together with details of general modelling techniques, will be outlined later. In addition, equipment more specialised than the basic instruments described above will be considered in a separate section of this chapter and, when appropriate, in subsequent chapters.

PAINTS, BRUSHES AND ALLIED EQUIPMENT

It has already been mentioned that the second major task confronting the modelmaker is the application of colour to his subject, so as to transform it from a dimensionally convincing shape into one of overall realism. There are, once again, a large number of options open to him in pursuing such a course, including paints of varying types,

pastes, powders, inks, metallic skins and printed transfers, whilst the continuing popularity of the hobby has resulted in the availability of a wide range of specially designed accessory equipment.

Paint technology in general has improved dramatically over the last couple of decades, and the benefits have not passed the modelmaker by. Enamel paints, the most popular media for finishing plastic models, now possess extraordinary covering capabilities and extremely fast drying times and are available in a vast array of different colours giving both gloss and matt finishes. Some of the larger plastic kit manufacturers, such as Airfix, Revell and Heller, produce their own ranges of enamel paints, but a larger choice is offered by specialist manufacturers like Humbrol, Testors, Pactra and Modelcolor.

Enamels are probably, for modellers, the most versatile of all painting media, and many will use these exclusively in their work, but there are a number of other types of paint which enjoy popularity, especially where the surface finish represents a non-metallic material. Artists' oils are much favoured by figure modellers, and, although far from quick-drying, they can, with experience, give an excellent finish in a range of sheens and can be intermixed with any oil-based paints, including enamels. Oil-bound poster colours are still in use, again principally by figure modellers, although this particular type of paint appears to be almost unobtainable now, at least in the UK. Water-based paints such as designers' gouache, casein, Rowney's Cryla, Pelikan Plaka and various other acrylics are all in widespread use and produce intense, quick-drying colours. However, these paints require a matt enamel base before they can be effectively applied to polystyrene surfaces, and the non-acrylic varieties need waterproofing before the painted models can be safely handled.

A satisfactory paint finish is not only as good as its workman, it is also as good as the brushes used to apply it will permit. To a certain extent, different types of brush are peculiar to different types of painting task, but all should be of the best quality possible. This may be a truism, but it is unreasonable to expect a defective brush to produce a flawless finish. Sable haired brushes, though undeniably expensive, are in general to be preferred to other kinds since they are softer, more paint-retentive and with careful husbandry very long lasting, and chisel-shaped as well as pointed brushes might be needed, the former to cover large, unimpeded surfaces, the latter both for general and for more intricate work. Small, complex designs might more easily be managed by using instruments such as pens or ink bow compasses, and modellers who eschew decals will rely on these a great deal.

Cheap brushes of lesser quality do have their place in modelling — certain painting techniques dictate the need to have available one or two expendable brushes — and colouring substances other than paint may from time to time be used to produce special effects such as weathered finishes, staining, dust, dirt, and so forth.

There are a number of materials associated with the painting of models that will be required by the modeller. The most obvious of these are media with which to thin paints and fluids for cleaning brushes. Ordinary white spirit is normally adequate for both jobs if enamel paints are being used, although there are proprietary thinners and cleaners available. Artists' oils, too, can be managed by using white spirit, though linseed oil and turpentine are the principal media for thinning this type of paint. Water- and polymer-based paints may be both thinned and cleaned with water.

Varnishes may be used for sealing the painted surface of a model, for modifying the reflectance of the painted finish, or for producing a particular degree of sheen. Polyurethane varnishes are readily available both as specific modelling accessories or as standard household products, and are suitable for all types of paint surface. They may be either applied by brush or sprayed, and can be obtained as both gloss and matt finishes. Lacquers such as Frisk-Lac may successfully be applied to enamel surfaces and, indeed, are particularly useful if cellulose paint is to be sprayed on to a plastic model, a method much favoured by car modellers. Krasel Industries' Micro Gloss and Micro Flat are varnishes originating in the USA that have proved very popular with plastic modellers, and Testor's Gloss-cote and Dullcote, marketed as aerosol sprays, are other much-used products.

It is possible to regulate the sheen of a finished model by careful preparation of the varnish — matt and gloss may be intermixed, provided the varnishes used are compatible with each other. However, it is also possible to reduce the sheen of a gloss enamel paint by mixing in a flatting agent such as that developed by Humbrol. Artists' oils, too, may be similarly modified by using Paris's Marble Medium as an additive, or by reducing the amount of natural medium in the paint prior to its application.

Masking materials, which take two principal forms, are an important painting aid without which few modellers can manage. Adhesive materials such as masking tape or Sellotape will be required for producing hard, straight lines and may also serve to a limited extent as the basis for home made adhesive stencils. Adhesive film such as Friskfilm and Trans-paseal is suitable for the preparation of stencils of larger dimensions. Masking fluid, available under such brand names as Micro Mask (Krasel) and Maskol (Humbrol), (although PVA glue is as effective and generally cheaper), is of assistance for closing off transparent areas such as cockpit canopies and windows if models are to be sprayed. The fluid sets as a rubbery substance which may easily be peeled from the model without affecting the surface over which it is applied.

The simulation of different types of bare metal is a problem which many modellers encounter, and one that has received some attention from the model accessory firms. Silver-based paint, carefully prepared, may be used to represent natural metal quite effectively, but it does have its limitations, particularly with regard to application and surface texture. A number of foil-like substances have been developed in an attempt to overcome these drawbacks — Metalskin and Bare Metal are perhaps the best known — and, with care, a considerable degree of realism can be achieved with these. Liqu-a-Plate and Real Met'l are fluid preparations much in vogue in the USA, whilst Rub 'n Buff, a form of metallic paste, is equally popular and may be mixed with enamel paints and other colouring media to produce a wide range of metallic effects.

The external surfaces of models frequently demand the application of very intricate designs such as lettering, numerals, insignia and trim stripes, and to assist the modeller a plastic kit will include these designs in the form of printed transfers, or decals. The desire for a certain amount of individuality on the part of the modeller is to some extent met by the availability of proprietary decal sheets bearing other alternative designs from which the modeller may select his preference. Such sheets may offer conventional waterslide decals or, more unusually, may carry decals of the pressure-sensitive type which are applied to a model by careful burnishing techniques. It is also possible, for

Top: the cockpit of this 1/48 scale model of a Gloster Meteor F8 (from the Slipstream kit) includes a parachute harness made from masking tape, seat straps from Lasso draughting tape and some painstaking work with fuse wire and fine slivers of plastic. It will be quickly appreciated how invaluable a pair of tweezers is in adding such intricate detail – few modelmakers manage without them, even if they are simply assembling a kit. (Model: Geoff Prentice)

Centre: artists' oils are ideal where subtle variations in colour and texture are called for, and because of this they are very popular with figure modellers. Their long drying time and their complete compatibility both with polystyrene and with oleoresinous paints such as enamels gives them a degree of versatility unmatched by any other painting media, although skilful technique is required since they can only be applied by hand. This 54mm scale model of a Chasseur d'Afrique (Historex, with some Airfix components) has been finished entirely in artists' oils. (Model: Alan Edwards)

Below: the paints available to modellers have changed beyond all recognition over the last twenty years or so, and today there are several large ranges that have been developed specially for small-scale finishing work, most particularly of enamels. Quite apart from the choice of colours that is offered, the quality of the paints manufactured by companies like Humbrol, Pactra and Testors is such that, if applied with reasonable care, one thin coat is usually of sufficient density to render further applications unnecessary; the moulded detail on a model may also be preserved in sharp definition, as this photograph of a 1/72 scale Hawker Hurricane (Heller kit) shows. (Model and photo: Ray Rimell)

Top: deeply textured surfaces cannot realistically be moulded in small scale plastic kits because of the inability of the process to cope with undercutting and because of the fragility that would be necessary for correct scale appearance. Certain intricate effects, however, can be achieved by using a pyrogravure or electrically heated needle. The headgear, hair and epaulettes of this 54mm scale 5th Line Lancer, together with the horse's mane, demonstrate the capabilities of this useful tool. (Model: Alan Edwards)

Below: few would dispute the contention that an airbrush is capable of producing effects that would be inordinately difficult, perhaps impossible, to create by using only a paintbrush. The soft edges and subtle colour blending evident on this model of an Opel GT illustrate the point. Careful masking is mandatory to achieve effects such as these – in this particular instance self-adhesive heart shapes from a stationery shop were applied at various stages during the painting process. The model is built from the 1/24 scale AMT kit. (Model: Reg Hale)

those possessing the required skill, to produce home-made transfers by applying pressure-sensitive designs to, or by painting directly over, waterslide film.

One other essential painting requisite is a soft, fluff-free cloth which is of course necessary for brush-cleaning purposes. However, it is useful also in the application of pastes such as Rub 'n Buff, as are pieces of synthetic sponge, for producing certain paint effects such as mottling and feathering, and for applying waterslide decals.

SPECIALIST EQUIPMENT

There are some items of equipment which, whilst considered indispensable by many, may conveniently be regarded as specialist in nature since they are beyond the aspirations of a great number of people who build plastic models. These are mainly power-operated or power-assisted tools, and the majority are priced in such a way that very careful thought needs to be given before they may be judged a worthwhile purchase.

Comapanies such as Dremel and Precision Petite market a large range of miniature power tools and associated equipment, including drills, routers, engravers, sanders, polishers and even lathes, and there is no denying the usefulness of these implements, especially if the modeller is working with basic plastic materials of a robust nature. Thermal tools such as soldering irons, welders and pyrogravures are also of considerable assistance, the last-mentioned being favoured particularly by those building figures from plastic since they are fundamentally needles which can be electrically heated and thus used to produce engraved lines and to soften plastic to facilitate reshaping.

Specialist equipment is also of value in painting models. The most humble power tool helpful to the

CHECKLIST SPECIALIST EQUIPMENT – 1

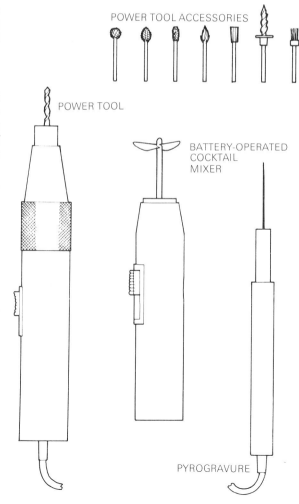

POWER TOOL ACCESSORIES

POWER TOOL

BATTERY-OPERATED COCKTAIL MIXER

PYROGRAVURE

modeller is a simple paint stirrer, which may be easily adapted from a battery-operated cocktail mixer; the most exotic piece of painting equipment is undoubtedly the airbrush, manufactured by such firms as Badger, DeVilbiss, Paasche and Humbrol, which in recent years has completely altered the attitudes and approaches of a great many modellers towards the painting of their models.

The chief advantages in using an airbrush are that, by its ability to impart a fine spray of paint, it may be used to produce an evenness of finish and a softness of definition that are much more difficult, if not impossible, to achieve with a paintbrush. Its major drawbacks are that its acquisition demands a considerable financial outlay on the part of the modeller and its use involves a lengthy preparatory procedure. In addition, it is a tool that calls for a high degree of manipulative dexterity to produce good results. The airbrush may be of two basic designs: the least sophisticated type is principally a miniature spray gun and normally produces its spray by mixing air and paint outside the confines of the instrument through separate nozzles; more complex are the needle airbrushes, which incorporate the means to control both the paint flow and the air flow, either individually or via a single button. The degree of control provided with an airbrush will dictate the degree of finesse that can be achieved with it and will also generally dictate its retail price.

Some form of air supply is of course vital to the operation of the airbrush, and this may originate from a compressor, a replaceable aerosol unit or a car tyre inner tube. Again, the more sophisticated the equipment the better and more consistent will normally be the results achieved — the total cost of a complete set of airbrushing equipment can easily approach three figures.

STRUCTURAL MATERIALS AND MODEL ACCESSORIES

The concept and anatomy of the plastic construction kit was considered in Chapter 1, but another important aspect of the hobby of plastic modelling is the modification to individual requirements of the pre-formed shapes supplied in a kit. The progression from this approach to one where relatively few kit components are incorporated into a model, or even none at all, can readily be appreciated. To help satisfy these designs, there are a number of products and materials available.

The primary plastic modelling material is polystyrene sheet, obtainable in a wide range of sizes and a variety of thicknesses from 0.005in (5 thou) up to 0.1in (100 thou). There are several different colours available, although white is the

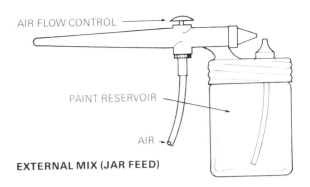

AIR FLOW CONTROL

PAINT RESERVOIR

AIR

EXTERNAL MIX (JAR FEED)

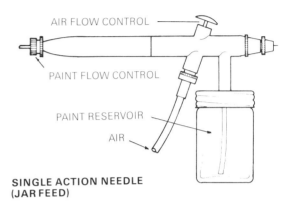

AIR FLOW CONTROL

PAINT FLOW CONTROL

PAINT RESERVOIR

AIR

SINGLE ACTION NEEDLE (JAR FEED)

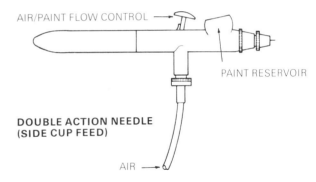

AIR/PAINT FLOW CONTROL

PAINT RESERVOIR

DOUBLE ACTION NEEDLE (SIDE CUP FEED)

AIR

CHECKLIST SPECIALIST EQUIPMENT – 2

most popular and will be adequate for the majority of the modeller's needs. Transparent plastic sheet will certainly be required if windows are to be represented, although it should be remembered that adhesives or special solvents will be needed if this sheet is not polystyrene.

Skilled modellers can apply a variety of techniques and produce practically any shape they require using plastic sheet, but there is available a range of accessories manufactured from this material which can obviate much of the preparatory work necessary to achieve such objectives. Simple vacuum formed textures such as cobbles, tiles, stonework and brickwork are some of the variations produced, and more elaborate creations such as gun emplacements, ruined buildings and natural landscape features, originating from companies like Bellona/Micro Mold and Deauville, are extremely useful for dioramas and scenic models. Vacuum formed accessories of greater precision are the various structural mouldings that enable a standard plastic kit to be adapted to a different configuration. Most of these concern models of aircraft, mainly because of the difficult contours that generally need to be produced with these subjects, but also because of the greater popularity of such models. These so-called 'conversion kits' may consist of fuselage sections, car body shells, moulded transparencies, drop tanks for aircraft and the like, and companies involving themselves in such work include Airmodel, Horizon and Tandair. The mouldings supplied in a product of this nature are often sufficiently comprehensive to prompt the manufacturer to describe it as 'complete', and such kits were discussed in the first chapter of this book.

A limited number of injection-moulded accessories have appeared on the market. These are for the most part related to military vehicle modelling, although certain components for other subjects are available. Armtec produce a good selection of these items, including miniature machine guns, tools, jerrycans and sandbags. Certain of the principal kit manufacturers, such as Italaerei and Tamiya, carry similar accessory packs in their ranges.

Extrusion-moulded materials also have their place in plastic modelling. Perhaps the most basic is plastic rodding, sold under a number of different labels and in various thicknesses from 0.01in upwards. A more recent introduction is Plastruct, a range of sheets, beams, channels, columns and angles of varying sizes and ideal for building models of structures composed principally of straight sections, such as vehicle chassis, buildings, frameworks, and so on. These items are produced in ABS plastic and require a strong solvent, for example MEK or Plastruct's own product Plastic Weld, to ensure effective bonding.

A number of other materials may conveniently be mentioned at this juncture, including the contents of the oft-quoted 'spares box', which, dependent upon how many plastic kits the owner has built (or how many he has consigned *in toto* to scrap), can be a very productive source of parts for building models. Many advocate that every scrap of plastic left over after a kit has fulfilled its function — indeed, every scrap of plastic that comes to hand — should be put by in case it is needed at some future date, and this policy, according to individual whim, can result in the solution to a modelling problem or so much space-consuming litter. Discretion must obviously dictate one's course of action. Sections of

sprue frame, both clear and opaque, can however be usefully stored since these, cut to suitable lengths, make excellent disposable paint stirrers and may also be used for producing fine polystyrene filament, a technique which will be described later.

The modeller who uses plastic as his medium may frequently need to employ other kinds of materials, and moreover should if they perform a particular function more satisfactorily. Typical examples are metal articles such as rod and wire, useful where structural strength or fine, pliable filament are required, and fine chain and mesh, which cannot easily be represented using plastic substances.

STORAGE AND MAINTENANCE

Common sense will prescribe the need to organise reference material and arrange tools and equipment to the best advantage. It is also prudent for the modeller to pay some attention to the condition of his equipment and keep it in the best repair possible. To these ends, various methods may be devised and some simple procedures followed.

Most serious modellers will attempt to build up a personal reference library reflecting their own particular interests, and will purchase books and subscribe to magazines in order to do this. It is helpful to organise some sort of indexing system so that articles, plans or photographs may be readily located. This might take the form of a loose-leaf file, with entries listed under appropriate headings, or alternatively a card system, with subjects arranged according to personal preference. However, producing a detailed and comprehensive index can be an extremely time-consuming operation, and perhaps a more sanguine approach, and one favoured by many whose fields of interest are very specific, involves the physical removal and rearrangement in files of selected magazine features.

Above right: a fairly recent introduction to the field of plastic modelling accessories is the Plastruct range, which includes a variety of extruded shapes, as well as sheet, all in ABS. The potential of Plastruct is illustrated in this photograph of a 1/16 scale Traction Engine which is built entirely from it, but of course its use demands a high level of modelling skill since each component used in a model has to be shaped by hand. (Model: Ted Taylor)

Right: tools, techniques and painstaking research are the keys to the production of a truly accurate scale plastic model – and all these ingredients have gone into this Lotus 49C. The model is based on the 1/12 scale Lotus 49B kit from Tamiya, but only about 25 per cent of the model uses components from it. The complete underside and interior of the monocoque is made up of hand-built parts, as are the 'wishbone' suspension detail and most of the engine components. The car represents that driven by the late Jochen Rindt to win the 1970 Monaco Grand Prix. (Model: Dave Patrick. Photo: George Tanner)

The storage of tools is again largely a matter of personal convenience, but modelling and painting equipment should at least be kept completely separate, and the latter should be stored in a dust-free container. Modelling implements such as files should be periodically cleaned, and this may be done by pressing adhesive tape over clogged surfaces and then peeling it off and by the application of a stiff brush. Should the file be seriously clogged, as may happen if filler is abraded before being completely set, it should be left for several hours and then carefully cleaned by picking out the unwanted material with a pin. Blades may be honed in much the same way as carpenters' chisels, and saws may be sharpened by the judicial application of a suitable abrasive tool. Abrasive paper such as wet-and-dry and Flex-i-Grit may be brushed clean and then washed if required, a move which enables the modeller to take advantage of its tendency to become progressively finer as it wears. Tools and equipment used for painting require careful maintenance, since failure to observe this can quickly lead to problems and even render such equipment unusable. More will be said on this subject in Chapter 4.

HAZARDS

It is perhaps fitting to conclude this chapter with a few words about the less obvious dangers associated with plastic modelling. The hobby involves the use of a number of toxic chemicals, and certain modelling procedures may create noxious fumes. It is essential that both prolonged breathing and accidental spillage of these substances be avoided. Simple precautions include the necessity to keep liquids tightly sealed when not actually being used, and the need for the modeller's surroundings to be well ventilated. Many advocate the use of a face mask for spraying operations, and this is sound advice. Naked flames should be kept well away from modelling materials, except when techniques dictate their use.

Ignoring such safety precautions may have no immediately apparent effects, but the long term consequences are very uncertain. Industrial processes involving the use of similar substances are subject to stringent regulations, and many plastic modellers would be surprised at the measures that are taken to obviate, or at least reduce, any possible risk to health.

Chapter 3
Construction techniques

There are a variety of reasons why a particular prototype may be selected as a model subject. It may be that the modeller has a close personal association with it, he may be attracted by its visual impact, he may have a very high regard for its fame or notoriety, he may wish to give himself a greater understanding of it, or he may look upon it simply as a subject without a model of which his collection would be incomplete. In any event, he will have a certain familiarity with it, and this provides the initial motivation to produce a model. Provided this motivation is maintained, the modeller will sustain his involvement with his subject, and the model will be completed. The standards to which the model is produced will be determined by his own experience and abilities, which might in turn be influenced, consciously or unconsciously, by a knowledge of the capabilities of other modellers, or by the stimulus of competition. Thus, from a very early stage in the building of a plastic model, in fact before the building process is actually begun, care and skilful technique will need to be applied. To what degrees these attitudes are developed is very much a personal affair, but the more developed they are, the more realistic the finished model should be.

PREPARATION
Whatever methods are to be used in the making of a plastic model, it is important that the modeller, before construction begins, has a clear image in his mind of the appearance of the completed model. A very young modeller might be attracted initially, and very often solely, by the art work displayed on the packet or box in which a kit is presented. If the interest is more fully developed, the fact that the kit offers greater scope than its mere contents suggest will be appreciated, and a certain amount of appraisal will take place, either before a purchase is made or, if perhaps the modeller is an avid kit collector anway, before a start is made on actually

producing the model. This preliminary survey work may take any or all of a number of forms.

Assuming his starting point to be a plastic kit, an initial inspection will tell the experienced modeller a great deal about the work he may wish to undertake. The general quality of the kit may be assessed at this stage, and it may be ascertained what sort of features are included, whether any options are offered as to how the model may be completed, and whether the overall effect is likely to be convincing. Any areas obviously requiring additional work may be detected, and the sort of techniques needed to achieve a satisfactory result may be noted. A more thorough scrutiny might show whether any parts are damaged or missing, and if repairs cannot be effected or substitute parts found or fabricated, a note to the manufacturers will usually rectify matters, although this course of action is rarely necessary.

Familiarisation with the general layout of the kit, more easily carried out with the assistance of the construction sheet or booklet, will determine whether or not the sequence of assembly suggested by the manufacturers is logical. Quite frequently, in order to conserve space and because the manufacturers may assume that painting will take place only after construction is complete, a different procedure is more satisfactory. For example, it may be better to attach aircraft canopies at a very late stage in the building of a model in order to prevent accidental damage occurring or to facilitate painting, or perhaps numerous sub-assemblies such as bogies on tanks, gun mountings on warships or undercarriage systems on aircraft need not be undertaken right at the beginning. However, any deviation from the recommended order should be accompanied by a check to ensure that no difficulties arise as a result and no parts are left out.

Reference material might next be gathered and made ready, and a more detailed comparison made between the shape and definition of the kit and its prototype. Depending upon the comprehensiveness and reliability of these references, a fuller opinion might be formed as to the general accuracy of the kit, but this is an exercise best undertaken as building proceeds and, as already noted, one in which the final decisions can only be taken by the modeller himself.

Moulding processes dictate that kit parts, of course, are attached to some sort of carrier, and the first step in the building of a kit is the removal of the individual parts from this carrier. Injection moulded components, which may be attached by one, two, three or more gates or spigots, should be removed by using a craft knife blade — simply breaking them off may damage the parts and create unnecessary repair work. The sprue, or more correctly runner, immediately adjacent to the spigot should first be supported in some way. One method of doing this is to position a hard, flat surface beneath it in the form of a step, so that the component to be removed overhangs it. The initial cut should be made a short distance away from the actual part, leaving a piece of spigot still attached. The part can then be manoeuvred into a convenient position for final trimming, again ensuring that good support is given beneath it — fragile parts are easily fractured or broken if this is not done. In some cases, for example if the component being removed is extremely small or if the edge to which the spigot is attached is convex in character or very thin, difficulties may be encountered and the spigot stump may have to be removed by paring or sanding it away in the hand. In these cases, it usually intrudes on to the outer surface of the component, and great care should be exercised in disguising it. The use of a file is not recommended for such purposes — the grain of the plastic means that the spigot is considerably more resistant to abrasion than the remainder of the component, and damage may inadvertently be caused. In certain kits, the spigots are rather substantial, and the use of a knife demands the application of considerable pressure to cut through it. The risk of damage here is again very real, not only through the blade slipping but also because the pressure required may break the spigot, not cut it. A razor saw can be employed instead to detach the part, and the stumps trimmed away as before.

Anything formed by a system of two or more moulds will obviously show a seam around it, betraying the position of the split line. If the moulds are poorly-fitting, plastic may be forced out along the split line during the injection process, resulting, as we have seen, in flash. All excess material of this nature should be removed from the kit components, the methods employed being determined by the

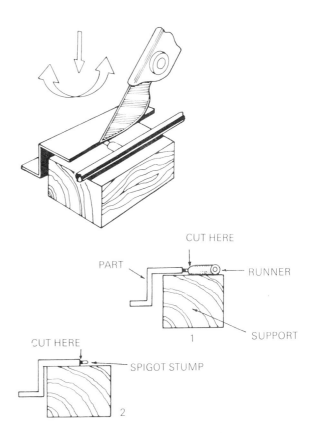

DETACHING INJECTION MOULDED COMPONENTS

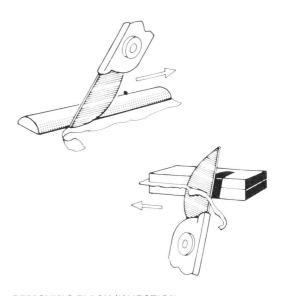

REMOVING FLASH (INJECTION MOULDED COMPONENTS)

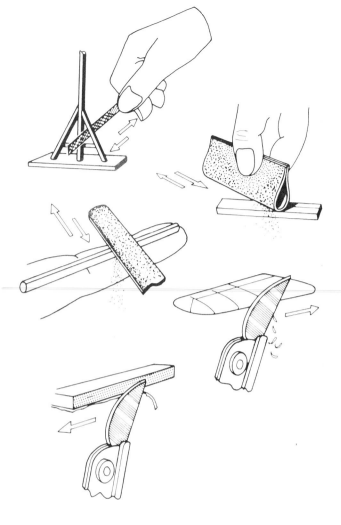

REMOVING SEAMS (INJECTION MOULDED COMPONENTS)

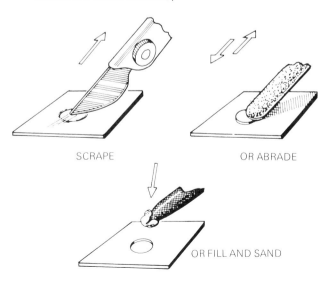

SCRAPE   OR ABRADE

OR FILL AND SAND

ELIMINATING EJECTOR PIN MARKS

shape of the surface on which they appear and by the seriousness of the problem. Despite the observations put forward by kit reviewers on occasions, every single piece in every single kit produced by the injection system needs this sort of preparation, although where the seam forms part of a major joint such as along a fuselage half or wheel half it may be dealt with during the assembly stage.

Seams may occur along the edge of a component, along the body of it, or, with complex shapes, in both these places. Generally speaking, the coarser the seam, the coarser the grade of abrasive needed to eliminate it. A sharp convex blade may be used to pare away flash and to reduce the prominence of a seam, or, where the seam is very fine, directly remove it. Final rubbing down should be administered to each part, using the finest grade of flexible abrasive possible. Special problems may occur where the seam lies along the centre of a flat surface, such as may be found with small superstructure blocks on model ships. Files or sanding boards are not really suitable here, since the adjacent surfaces may become disfigured. The seam may be reduced using a knife, as before, but a convex sanding face such as may be formed by gently curving abrasive paper should be used, and the seam removed by gentle strokes both across it and along it, taking care not to touch the edges of the part. Seams occurring in awkward places, such as across the cooling gills of a radial engine, warrant special treatment, and a sharp pointed blade or even a razor saw may be of assistance here. Where a seam crosses an area of considerable fine detail, a sharp blade may be the only practicable tool to use. Fragile parts such as ships' masts, gun barrels for small-scale tanks and exhaust systems for vehicles should always be carefully supported, either with a block on the working top or with the forefinger.

Seams may also occur within the body of a kit component where an opening has been moulded. Typical instances of this are undercarriage bays in lower wing halves of aircraft, apertures in road wheels of tanks, and the inner rims of radial engine cowlings. Access may be a problem, but the tip of a blade usually solves it. Alternatively, semi-rigid abrasive paper may be cut into thin slivers and used.

On the few occasions when non-polystyrene components are used in a plastic kit — PVC tank tracks and vehicle tyres, and polyethylene figures for example — trimming must always be carried out with a very sharp blade. Filing and sanding should be avoided since these will only roughen the surface and render the parts unusuable.

Seams are by no means the only flaws to be found on plastic kit components moulded by the injection process. Two other problems to which the modeller must set his attention concern ejector pin marks, caused by the device on the moulding machine which assists the release of the sprue frame from the mould, and sinkage, which occurs during the cooling of the plastic. These features are not, it should be said, found on every kit component, and where they do occur they only need disguising where a surface visible on the finished model is affected.

Ejector pin marks appear on plastic kits as small rings on one side of a sprue frame. They may be flush with the surface of the plastic, recessed, or slightly proud, depending on the degree of technical finesse with which the moulding equipment has been manufactured or, if it has been in use for a considerable period, its condition. Thus, where they need attention, they may have to be lightly touched out with a blade, filled and sanded, or filed away. An ejector tab, used, it will be recalled, where a pin pushing directly on to a component would completely spoil the latter's appearance or where the part is simply too thin for the pin to engage it, can be regarded as a spigot and attended to accordingly.

Sinkage is a common feature in a plastic kit, usually occuring where an unusually thick section of material has been moulded. Typical positions are directly over locating pins, on hubs of one-piece wheels and along wing trailing edges where upper and lower surfaces have been moulded as one. These flaws require filling, but since the depressions are for the most part shallow and fairly gentle, a fine-grained, well-bonding filler such as Loy or Green Stuff is necessary — other varieties may simply shrink and fall out. Keying may be assisted by drilling angled holes inside the depressions prior to filling. In order to determine the extent of the sinkage, it is helpful to pass a piece of very fine abrasive paper over the surface under scrutiny; the natural sheen of the plastic is thereby removed except in the area requiring treatment. Careful filing and sanding after the filler has set will produce a good, even surface which blends with the surrounding contours of the component. Fine surface detailing often has to be sacrificed, unfortunately, although there are ways of restoring it, as will be discussed later.

The preliminary preparation required for vacuum formed components is altogether different from that necessary for injection moulded parts. The physical removal from the carrier — in this case flat plastic sheet — demands a great deal of careful application, although, as in all modelling techniques, experience will improve the modeller's skill. The individual parts may first be separated from each other using a sharp craft knife — scissors are not recommended since their cutting action tends to warp the plastic. Next, excess plastic may further be

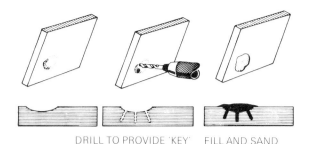

DRILL TO PROVIDE 'KEY'   FILL AND SAND

ELIMINATING SINKAGE MARKS

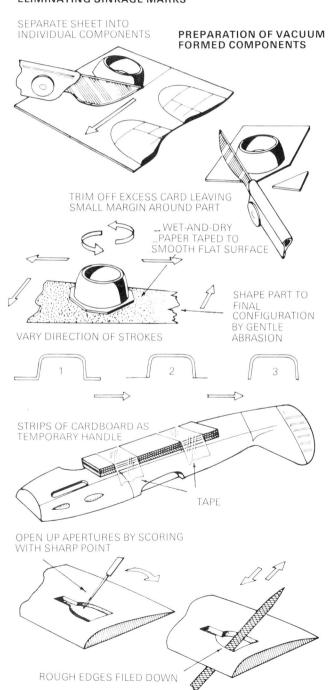

SEPARATE SHEET INTO INDIVIDUAL COMPONENTS

PREPARATION OF VACUUM FORMED COMPONENTS

TRIM OFF EXCESS CARD LEAVING SMALL MARGIN AROUND PART

WET-AND-DRY PAPER TAPED TO SMOOTH FLAT SURFACE

SHAPE PART TO FINAL CONFIGURATION BY GENTLE ABRASION

VARY DIRECTION OF STROKES

STRIPS OF CARDBOARD AS TEMPORARY HANDLE

TAPE

OPEN UP APERTURES BY SCORING WITH SHARP POINT

ROUGH EDGES FILED DOWN

removed by trimming a little more closely to the part, but still leaving a thin border around it. A sheet of 400 grade wet-and-dry paper can then be taped securely to a smooth, flat, rigid surface such as a table top, and the remaining excess plastic cleaned off by moving the component back and forth over the paper. There is a danger, however, of removing too much material from the edges of the parts, and a few simple guidelines can be followed to advantage. It is important first of all not to apply too much pressure during the sanding process — this will make the task rather time-consuming, but it is a helpful precaution against subsequent repair work. The sanding must also be done evenly. One way of facilitating this is to alter the position of the part in the hand every so often, or altering the direction of the strokes relative to the hand, sometimes sanding with a rotating motion. Progress should be checked at frequent intervals by holding the part up to a strong light to ensure that the thinned plastic card margin appears evenly translucent. Ideally, the excess plastic should fall away as a single, very thin wafer of material — the point at which it does begin to fall away indicates that sanding has been completed. It may sometimes be necessary to finish off this sanding in the hand, and where the edges of a part do not form a continuous straight line, as with a one-piece lower wing featuring dihedral, it may be the only way of trimming the part effectively, although various sanding jigs may be prepared to assist the modeller. Small parts may be more conveniently handled by preparing a small sanding board that can be held in one hand and using a wetted forefinger to move the part across its surface. Alternatively, a temporary handle can be taped to the part to assist grip. All such abrading operations with these kits may be carried out with wet paper or dry.

Once the outline of a vacuum-formed kit component is satisfactorily achieved, there is not a great deal more to do regarding basic preparation, unless the mouldings are bereft of detailing or unless the detailing is lacking in refinement, and these problems will be discussed in another section of this chapter. However, openings such as wheel wells, cockpit areas and engine cowlings may have to be made. As before, unwanted material should always be removed in stages if a knife is used, but by using the point of an old pair of dividers and continuously scribing around the edge of the material to be removed, the excess plastic can be taken out in one piece, leaving only a roughened edge to be carefully sanded back. This technique is especially useful if there is an adjacent moulded ridge, such as occurs with a recessed wheel bay on a lower wing surface — and the risk of accidental damage to the outer surface of the part is considerably reduced.

There are a number of very minor flaws which may require the modeller's attention before a kit component can be considered fully prepared. Parts produced by either of the two principal moulding processes may show small blemishes such as tiny nodules of material, which may result from a damaged mould, or thin surface scratches, which may occur because of a defective mould or simply because of rough handling after the kit has been packaged. In addition, vacuum-formed kit parts will have a number of small bumps on their surfaces because of the evacuation holes necessary on the original tool. Such irregularities may be carefully sanded off or, in the case of scratching, attended to alternatively with filler, although if the marks are of a negligible nature they may become undetectable beneath a coat of paint. In any event, a careful inspection of each part should be carried out.

As a final preparatory procedure, components may be washed carefully in lukewarm water laced with a few drops of washing-up liquid. This will remove unwanted plastic dust and filings and also clean off any traces of releasing agent that may be present on the parts. If no further assembly work is to be carried out with the parts, they may be allowed to dry and stored in a box ready for painting.

It may be appropriate here to mention the well-known modelling tip of painting parts whilst they are still attached to the sprue. The one drawback of this recommendation is that it is extremely difficult — in some instances virtually impossible — adequately to prepare the parts beforehand. Seams may perhaps be cleaned up if the attachment spigot is a sturdy one, but access is nearly always a problem and the spigot still has to be cleaned off afterwards. There are a number of methods of mounting small parts in order to carry out painting, and these will be considered when painting techniques are discussed.

BASIC ASSEMBLY PROCEDURE

Once the component parts of a plastic kit have been prepared, attention can be turned to their assembly. Which particular parts are assembled, and in what order, will be determined principally by the painting requirements of the model, and some deviation from the construction sequence recommended by the manufacturers is often desirable, especially if the modeller wishes to make the best use of his time.

The assembly of any model, whether it be derived from a plastic kit or from other, more basic materials, usually involves the fitting together of a number or previously painted units — rarely is it practicable for the construction to be completely finished before any paint is applied. In the case of a plastic kit, these units may consist of single parts or a group of assembled parts, the total number of which will vary according to the scale and complexity of the kit. The modeller must decide at which stage each unit can be regarded as complete and ready for painting, since manufacturers' directions in this respect tend to be lacking and range from a vague suggestion that 'small parts should be painted prior to assembly' to a more informative but still inadequate indication of the colours to be used for certain small details. As well as deciding at which point a unit is ready for painting, the modeller must also make up his mind when assembly work on a unit should cease in order to enable him to carry out any tidying up or reshaping that may be necessary.

Having planned his construction procedure in outline, the modeller will then direct his energies to the physical assembly of the model. Although commercial kits are generally produced to very high standards these days and component fit is usually of

a high order, some small adjustments here and there may be necessary; if the kit is relatively old, or if it has been in continuous production for a long time, the fit of the parts may be very poor. The problem of ill-fitting parts is rarely so serious as to make it insuperable, but it can involve the modeller in a great deal of extra preparatory work.

There are three reasons why plastic kit parts, injection-moulded and vacuum-formed, may not fit particularly well. It may be that the kit has a basic design fault that has somehow escaped the attention of the manufacturer's quality control system, which would be very unusual in the case of an injection-moulded product, or has been deliberately left unattended to, which unfortunately is fairly common with some ranges of vacuum-formed kits. Poor fit is also caused by a deterioration of the moulds, whose edges may become damaged and worn with increasing use, allowing, as we have seen, an excess of plastic to develop on the parts. A third possibility, and one which applies particularly to larger components such as aircraft fuselage halves and two-part hull structures for ships, is that the plastic becomes warped on cooling after being released from the mould. In order to rectify these shortcomings if they are present, the kit parts should first be test-fitted — a procedure known in modelling parlance as 'doing a dry run' — to ascertain the extent of the necessary corrective work. In many cases, poor fit can be disguised by careful application of filling compound, but because this can damage the external surfaces of a model, as much as

Below: component exchange, a form of remodelling well known to figure enthusiasts, can be applied to all types of model, often in a major way. This partially built tank model is based on the Monogram M48A2, but the engine deck, air cleaners, track and suspension from Tamiya's 1/35 scale M60A1 kit have been incorporated, thus producing an M48A3. The versatility of liquid cement is also demonstrated in this model – the 'cast' effect of the turret was made by coating its surface with the solvent and then dabbing it with the finger. Note the use of plastic card for the track guards.
(Model and photo: Donn Buerger)

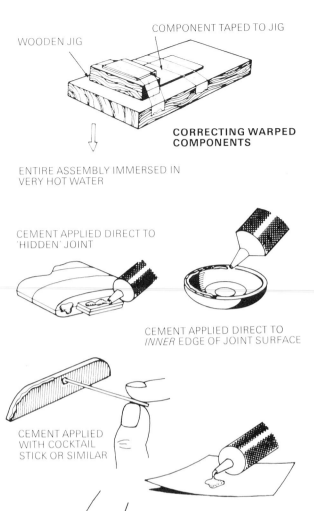

WOODEN JIG

COMPONENT TAPED TO JIG

CORRECTING WARPED COMPONENTS

ENTIRE ASSEMBLY IMMERSED IN VERY HOT WATER

CEMENT APPLIED DIRECT TO 'HIDDEN' JOINT

CEMENT APPLIED DIRECT TO *INNER* EDGE OF JOINT SURFACE

CEMENT APPLIED WITH COCKTAIL STICK OR SIMILAR

LOCATING PEG DIPPED INTO CEMENT AND POSITIONED

APPLICATION OF TUBE CEMENT

possible should be done to obviate the need for it, at the same time thereby ensuring a stronger joint at the outset.

Where difficulties of alignment are likely to present themselves, or where the precise positioning of a part is called for, manufacturers usually provide a number of locating pegs, with corresponding holes to receive them, moulded on or adjacent to the mating surfaces. Occasionally, the male and female locators do *not* precisely correspond, or they may not fit each other satisfactorily, in which cases the pegs should be removed. Many modellers habitually remove all locating pegs as part of their preliminary preparation. Where poor fit is caused by an excess of material along the mating surfaces, some trimming with a craft knife or filing will generally cure the problem, provided periodic test-fitting is carried out as work proceeds. Warped components can usually be put right by careful bending, but if the warpage is really serious there is a simple technique which will in most cases save the job of sending to the manufacturer for a replacement part. The component is securely taped in its correct attitude to a jig made up of odd pieces of wood, and the whole assemblage may then be immersed in very hot, but not quite boiling, water. When removed from its jig afterwards, the part should retain its required shape.

The choice between tube and liquid cement as a solvent for bonding together polystyrene components will depend upon the nature of the surfaces to be mated and the strength of the joint required. Liquid cement is generally cleaner to use, easier to apply and more suitable for small detail work, although its ability to penetrate deeply into a clamped joint is of course limited. Tube cement, on the other hand, is ideal for dissolving broad areas of relatively thick plastic and for assembling parts which are subject to stress in the finished model. Thus one might use liquid cement for fitting the weather decks to a ship's hull, assembling the elevating mechanism for a small-scale artillery piece or adding epaulettes to a 54mm figure, whilst tube cement might be more appropriate when fitting the locating tongues of an aircraft's wing into its fuselage or when positioning its undercarriage.

It is not advisable to apply tube cement directly to a plastic component, except where there is no risk of damaging its external surface or where it is definitely easier to do so. A large block built up from laminations of thick polystyrene card, for example, is more easily constructed with cement applied straight from the tube, and the fitting of a lower wing panel such as might be provided for a model of a jet aeroplane may also be more conveniently achieved in this way. In most other cases, the cement is better administered with a small tool such as a pin, wooden cocktail stick or sharpened matchstick, although if the tube is fitted with a nozzle that has to be pierced before use rather than one with a screw cap, the flow may be fairly easily controlled. The cement may be picked up on the pin directly from the nozzle or from a pool formed on a piece of scrap cardboard. The latter method can be rather wasteful, but it is also convenient for cementing parts which require a small drop of solvent on a long locating peg, as the peg can be dipped into the solvent. Tube cement sets very quickly — even if a thick drop is applied it will soon form a skin in contact with the air — and so it is necessary to work fairly rapidly when using it. Where practicable, both mating surfaces should have a thin layer of cement applied since a much stronger bond is likely to result.

Liquid cement requires the use of a slim, long-haired brush for its application, and is more suited to assemblies where the edges rather than large surfaces of parts are mated together or where a unit needs to be carefully positioned before it is cemented. It is thus ideal for the construction of vacuum formed kits and, indeed, should be the exclusive solvent for any polystyrene parts formed by this process. Although assemblies may be tightly clamped together before the cement is allowed to flow along the joint, it is often helpful to grip the parts less firmly between the fingers whilst it is applied since this permits more extensive capillarity and therefore a deeper penetration of the liquid into the joint, and consequently a stronger bond when set. To assist penetration further, the parts may then be gently squeezed together and firmly clamped. For affixing delicate parts, the brush should be very lightly loaded.

The solvent nature of polystyrene cement dictates that great care should be exercised when it is used, since a thick layer of tube cement or the flooding of joints by the liquid variety can cause the plastic to become softened and deformed. However, weak solutions such as Mek Pak may be used to restore the sheen to a plastic surface that has been mildly roughened by abrasive action, and it may also be used to reinforce existing joints. For these applications, the loaded brush should be passed evenly over the surface being treated in a single stroke.

The use of adhesives, as opposed to solvents, for modelling purposes, calls for slightly different techniques, but all types should be applied very sparingly to a plastic model, and the makers' general instructions should at all times be followed. Epoxy resins such as Devcon or Gloy's Fast-Set are much in favour with some modellers for applying cockpit canopies to aircraft, metal axles and 'chromed' parts to vehicles and so on since it is a strong general purpose adhesive suitable for use on most non-permeable surfaces, and is transparent when set. Its major drawbacks are that it has to be mixed with a hardening catalyst before it can be used and, since more resin than is needed has to be prepared, much may easily be wasted. Moreover, it sets hard within a few minutes, which in certain circumstances may not be a helpful thing. The adhesive is usually supplied as a complete package containing both the resin and the setting agent, which must be carefully mixed following the manufacturer's directions. A disposable container such as an old jam jar lid may be used as a mixing palette, and a clean piece of scrap sprue, sharpened to a point at one end, makes a good, if primitive, tool for both stirring and application. Only one of a pair of matching surfaces need be smeared with the adhesive, and it is essential to mate the parts being glued together perfectly at the outset, since adjustments after the adhesive has cured are not normally possible.

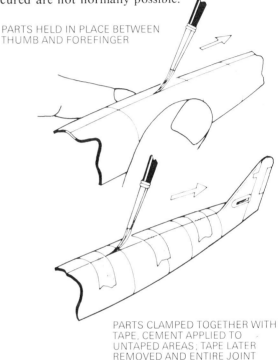

PARTS HELD IN PLACE BETWEEN THUMB AND FOREFINGER

PARTS CLAMPED TOGETHER WITH TAPE, CEMENT APPLIED TO UNTAPED AREAS; TAPE LATER REMOVED AND ENTIRE JOINT BRUSHED

APPLICATION OF LIQUID CEMENT

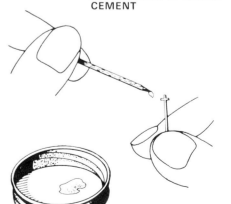

APPLICATION OF EPOXY RESIN AND OTHER ADHESIVES

The same general guidelines should be followed for the application to plastic surfaces of ready-to-use adhesives such as Bostok, Evostik, Permabond, Seccotine, Loktite and PVA white glue. It should be remembered that many adhesives are mildly flexible when set and do not take kindly to a file or abrasive paper, leaving a rough, pitted surface. Excess glue may be pared away with a sharp blade after it has hardened off, but a perfectly smooth finish is not always possible.

Now and then it is necessary to introduce some sort of reinforcement to a joint, for example where considerable structural strength is required or where the components are too thin or their mating surfaces too small to effect a satisfactory joint merely by cementing them. Models of mounted figures displayed at precarious angles on their bases, an aircraft model where a flimsy nosewheel leg has to support a well-weighted forward fuselage, a structure produced by assembling edge to edge two very thinly moulded parts, and topmasts on ship models under stress from rigging are typical instances where some additional support is often necessary. The joints may generally be made more secure either by adding some form of bracing, or by fitting a rigid support within the body of the components concerned.

Butt joints, bulkheads, spacers and gussets are terms that modellers working with vacuum formed parts or with flat plastic sheet will be familiar with. Plastic card and plastic strip may themselves be used to good effect for reinforcing potentially weak joints. Strips may be placed beneath a lengthy butt joint such as may be found along the fuselage of an aircraft model, the hull to deck junction of a ship, or any other similar location where extra strength is

Above: the occasional need to reinforce a plastic model is amply demonstrated by the 'action' pose of this 54mm scale model of Joachim Murat (a modified Historex kit). Rigid steel rod was introduced into one of the horse's back legs and inserted into a prepared location in the granite base, thereby effecting a very strong joint.
(Model: Alan Edwards)

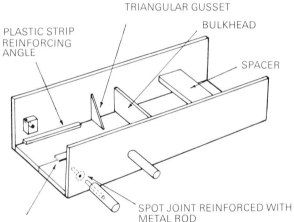

TRIANGULAR GUSSET

BULKHEAD

PLASTIC STRIP REINFORCING ANGLE

SPACER

SPOT JOINT REINFORCED WITH METAL ROD

BUTT JOINT REINFORCED WITH PLASTIC STRIP

METHODS OF JOINT REINFORCEMENT

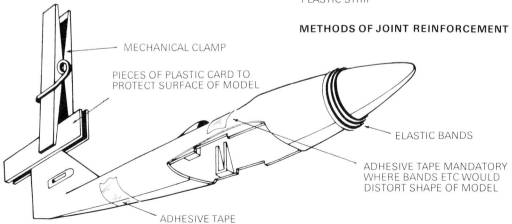

MECHANICAL CLAMP

PIECES OF PLASTIC CARD TO PROTECT SURFACE OF MODEL

ELASTIC BANDS

ADHESIVE TAPE MANDATORY WHERE BANDS ETC WOULD DISTORT SHAPE OF MODEL

ADHESIVE TAPE

CLAMPING JOINTS

required. Triangular gussets may be prepared from plastic card to reinforce an angled joint, and spacers or bulkheads may be positioned if an obstinate warpage problem persists. Vacuum formed kits used all to be produced in very thin plastic, and these techniques had to be applied to each joint made. Thicker card is normally employed nowadays, but there is nevertheless still great merit in using a system of reinforcement, and similar measures are frequently helpful with injection moulded kits.

Spot joints may effectively be reinforced by introducing a length of wire, needle or steel rod connecting each part. Holes to receive each end of the rod should first be drilled in the two parts to be joined, and the metal fixed with a suitable adhesive. This technique may also be used for repairing broken parts such as undercarriage legs, ships' masts and vehicle axles, where something more than a basic cemented joint may be required. Precise alignment is usually a problem, but a simple aid is to introduce a tiny spot of gloss paint into the drilled hole on one half of the broken part, place the other half carefully in the correct position and shake the unit with one flick of the wrist. The paint will be transferred to the other half of the broken part and indicate the exact location for the second drilled hole.

Once a joint has been made with polystyrene cement, maintained pressure is usually required to enable the solvent to act effectively. Small detail parts such as ships' anchors, fuel filler caps on model cars or antennae on aircraft can generally just be pressed gently into position. Similarly, parts which present a large surface area in relation to their size may be merely cemented, applied to their location points and safely left to set. However, where large structural units need to be assembled or added to others, a clamping device is usually required to keep the cemented surfaces tightly together whilst the solvent hardens. The best general purpose clamp is probably a simple strip of adhesive tape such as Sellotape, which may be stretched across a joint to hold it together. As well as clamping such joints, the tape may be of assistance in ensuring alignment, for example along a fuselage spine where the edges of two components may not automatically present a perfectly flush contour.

Elastic bands are used by many modellers, especially for keeping two halves of a cylindrical unit such as fuel tank tightly together, but there is a danger of distorting the shape of the assembly if bands are used at any point where the circumference is incomplete. Mechanical devices such as Bulldog clips, G-clamps, bench vices and even suitably modified clothes pegs are useful from time to time where really sturdy components are being cemented and where there is the need for a very tough joint, but the potential for this sort of equipment, is, as far as the plastic modeller is concerned, comparatively limited.

There are a number of minor perils involved in using clamps on plastic models, the most obvious being the ability of some types to exert too much pressure and crush the components they are supposed merely to clasp. But even tape and elastic bands can cause problems, mostly associated with the cement or adhesive used along the joint. If cement is to be used along a joint before it is clamped, it is vital that none is allowed to ooze out, since the application of tape over the bond will cause the

Below: a basic requirement for a neat plastic model – and one that is not always given the attention it deserves by the modeller – is the correct alignment of the various component parts as the latter are added during construction. All models, with the possible exception of figures, require a careful 'truing-up' of their parts before the cement is allowed to harden off – the 1/700 scale *Gneisenau* model illustrated here, for example, needed its masts, platforms, funnel, gun barrels, directors, etc all carefully checked from three directions as its assembly progressed. In many cases, such a check may be carried out by line of sight 'in the hand', but a setting jig is a very helpful aid and ensures complete accuracy.

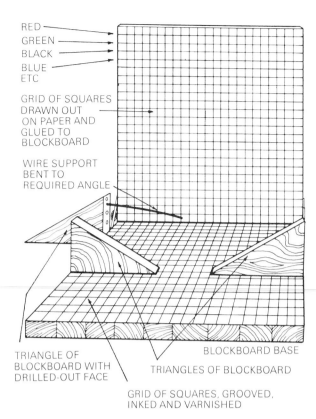

RED
GREEN
BLACK
BLUE
ETC

GRID OF SQUARES
DRAWN OUT
ON PAPER AND
GLUED TO
BLOCKBOARD

WIRE SUPPORT
BENT TO
REQUIRED ANGLE

TRIANGLE OF
BLOCKBOARD WITH
DRILLED-OUT FACE

BLOCKBOARD BASE

TRIANGLES OF BLOCKBOARD

GRID OF SQUARES, GROOVED,
INKED AND VARNISHED

A SETTING JIG

cement to spread out beneath it and spoil the surface of the model, and if the plastic is softened through using too much cement a band might cut into it, causing scars that are difficult to repair. Where tape is applied across a joint prior to cementing, there is a danger that the liquid, by capillary action, will flood across the plastic surface directly under the tape and completely ruin the model. If a long, difficult seam has to be negotiated, the work is best tackled in two stages. The tape is applied at intervals of a couple of inches or so along the joint, and a very small amount of liquid cement is brushed along the sections of bare seam visible in between. When the solvent is completely hardened off, the tape may be removed and the remaining sections cemented. An alternative method is to devise some form of temporary jig so that the tape, whilst still firmly clamping the joint, does not actually come into contact with it. Strips of plastic card or flattened sprue may be fashioned to provide jigs of this sort.

More complex jigs are frequently required for aligning major structures as they are added to a model. Aircraft models may require vertical fins, precisely horizontal stabilisers and wings set at a

certain angle of dihedral, ships will require masts that are perpendicular to their decks (at least, when viewed longitudinally), trucks and cars will need to have wheels that are truly vertical, and gun barrels of tanks may need to be set at certain angles, and, whilst these assemblies may be convincingly and accurately accomplished by reckoning, it is still very easy to make an error of judgement. It is doubtful whether a jig could be designed to cater for every modelling problem of this nature, but a few pieces of wood and a little care and attention will go some way towards solving a large proportion of them.

A useful home made jig may be prepared in a couple of hours and is composed principally of two pieces of half-inch blockboard 18in by 18in (45cm by 45cm) hinged together and provided with stays to allow one to be locked in an upright position. The baseboard is carefully scored at right angles to its edges with a grid of half-inch (1cm) squares and thoroughly varnished. The grooves are then stained with black enamel paint and the whole base is varnished again. A sheet of paper 18in by 18in is prepared and marked out with vertical lines ½in apart, using Indian ink. Horizontal lines are drawn ½in apart using a selection of coloured inks in regular series, for example red, green, black, blue. The paper is glued on to the other piece of blockboard and covered with adhesive transparent sheet. Identical pairs of right-angled triangles of a variety of forms and sizes are prepared from blockboard, at least one of the larger pairs having a series of small holes at equivalent heights drilled along one of the edges forming the right angle.

A model requiring precise alignment such as described above may be placed — taped if necessary — on to the base with its centreline matched to the grid scored out, and the triangles may be slid beneath wings, stabilisers, gun barrels and so forth until they are correctly aligned in relation to the coloured grid on the vertical board. Dowel, sprue, or wire bent to a precise point may be inserted into the drilled holes to help the true alignment of masts, yards, aerials, wheels, fins, etc. The undercarriage rake of an aircraft model or the wing stagger of a biplane can also be checked for accuracy, in fact the whole device is as versatile as its builder's imagination. The supporting blocks may be held in position with double-sided Sellotape if required, although this should only be necessary with really large models, and the cement may be applied either before or after the model is set up. The quoted dimensions of the jig are suitable for the majority of plastic models, but of course some modifications may need to be carried out by those who build, for example, large-scale aircraft or sailing ships.

After the joints are firm, it is usually necessary for

the modeller to disguise them in some way. Even those which may on first impressions seem perfect are likely to benefit from his attention, and those which coincide with a noticeable seam or panel line on the full-sized prototype will also generally need some treatment. As much as possible should have already been done before assembly to render the joints of a model less obvious, but there is a limit to what can be achieved in this preliminary work, especially where two components are assembled in order to produce a flush surface such as with ships' hulls and funnels, wheel halves, gun barrels, aircraft fuselages, and the like.

The importance of not tackling a joint until the cement has thoroughly set throughout should be stressed. This will mean leaving it for at least twelve hours, preferably longer, before any work is done on it — attempting to sand or file plastic that is still soft will only lead to more work later on. Should any excess cement have been squeezed out of the joint during assembly, it may be pared or sliced away using a very sharp blade. This will probably reveal more softened plastic, and so work should again be suspended for several hours. However, if the joint is neat, it may be smoothed with a file or abrasive paper, or scraped with a blade, taking care to remove as little of the surface detail immediately adjacent to it as necessary. It is often possible to render a joint lying along a flat or convex surface totally invisible merely by abrasion, but if it is still detectable, some making good will obviously need to be undertaken; quite frequently, a definite gap will appear between two supposedly mating components. In these circumstances, the joints will need to be filled in order to make a good finish possible.

The choice of material to be used as a filler will to some extent depend upon the type of gap requiring treatment, its position in relation to its surroundings, its width, and the nature of the surface it represents. Before any filler is used, however, one preliminary step needs to be taken. The joint to be filled should be bridged along its length in some way so that the gap does not penetrate through to a hollow interior. This bridging may already be present because of the nature of the joint — for example, with the assembly of two solid components — but if not it will have to be introduced. Gaps of up to about 0.5mm can normally be bridged by applying a fairly generous brushful of liquid cement at intervals along its length and allowing it to close the gap by capillary action. Larger spaces may be bridged by inserting slivers of plastic card of a suitable thickness and then brushing over liquid cement to fix them. The card strips will normally need to be pushed well inside a gap, but if the latter is easily accessible and the surrounding surfaces of

the model are featureless, the card may be built up proud and later trimmed and sanded to match the contours of the model.

Whichever filling compound is selected, it is important that as little as possible should be allowed to stray on to the surface of the model. Where there is a danger of spoiling a transparent area or a particularly important piece of fine detailing, it is possible to confine the filler to the place where it is required by masking off the surrounding surfaces of the model with one or two layers of adhesive tape. The tape should remain in place until sanding and general finishing work has been completed on the joint.

Where gloss paint is used as a filler, as it may be for fine hairline gaps, a thin brush should be used and strokes made across rather than along the gap. This will ensure that the maximum amount of paint is built up. A rag dampened — not soaked — with white spirit may be stretched across the forefinger and immediately wiped over the joint, again at right angles to it, to remove any excess. The use of paint as filler does have obvious limitations. It will of course only be effective where its surface tension permits, and it will not bring about a perfectly flush finish, also because of its surface tension, although building up several applications, each time after the previous one has completely dried, will to some extent overcome this.

Polyfilla mixed to a very thin consistency can be

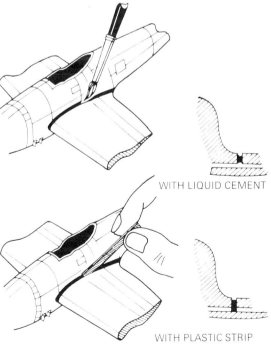

WITH LIQUID CEMENT

WITH PLASTIC STRIP

BRIDGING GAPS

Above: an example of an extensively reworked kit, this 1/48 scale Focke-Wulf Ta 152H was produced using Otaki Fw 190A components. The major alterations concern the fuselage, which has been considerably lengthened, the wings, which have been greatly increased in span by using plastic card, and the fin, which has been extended in area.
(Model: S Inazuka. Photo: Susumu Yoshida)

applied in much the same way as paint, but when drying out it is liable to shrink and crack. If mixed to a stiffer consistency, or if Fine Grain Polyfilla is used, a spatula will be required for its application. Fillers and putties of other types should similarly be applied with a spatula, at all times keeping the compound within the confines of the gap being treated. Small amounts at a time should be applied, since the substance generally remains workable only for a short period, and the tool should be wiped clean regularly. The filler should be worked quickly and thoroughly into the gap; if the seam is shallow, the filling may be finished off flush with the surrounding contours of the model, but if the gap is deep it may have to be treated in two or more stages, allowing ample drying time in between.

One frequently comes across photographs of half-built models showing filler piled up in great layers along seams and joints, but it is very questionable whether sound advice is really being offered. Not only is this an unnecessarily wasteful method of applying an expensive material, although admittedly it may be quick; it also involves the modeller in a great deal of work to renew the correct finish and may destroy any moulded detail that is present.

Most proprietary filling compounds may be filed and sanded quite safely when set, and many can be pared or scraped with a knife if necessary. However, as with solvent, it is essential to ensure that the hardening off process is complete before any attempt to shape filled areas is begun. This process will vary according to the type of filler used and the thickness applied, but most are ready within twelve hours. Interference with water-based cellulose fillers before they have set will not normally cause any irremediable damage to a plastic model since polystyrene is non-absorbent of water and indeed, as

noted earlier, excess filler can be removed with a damp rag, but the true cellulose fillers will react with a plastic surface and bind with it — which is the reason they make such efficient compounds for plastic models — and if abraded before they are set will present a very unpleasant spectacle.

The choice of abrasive needed to smooth down any filled joint is dependent upon the nature of the filler that has been used, the amount of material to be removed, the accessibility of the joint and the form the latter takes, and, clearly, common sense will determine how best these requirements may be met. However, there are a number of points to which attention might be usefully drawn. 'Hard', fine-grained fillers do not take too kindly to abrasion by narrow, rigid instruments such as files, since the pressure needed to remove material entails the risk of making a false stroke which could seriously damage the adjacent plastic surfaces, especially if access to the joint is awkward — the reduction of a filled joint to the required contours generally means transforming an uneven surface into a smooth one, which increases the risk. A semi-rigid abrasive such as wet-and-dry paper, or a completely flexible one such as Flex-i-Grit, is often to be preferred since the breadth of the abrasive surface in contact with the model can be controlled, the pressure can be more easily regulated, and sharp edges such as a file possesses are eliminated. Smoothing will usually need to be finished off with these materials anyway since, for a delicate plastic model, metal files, even jewellers' files, are of a rather coarse cut.

Mention has already been made that abrasive paper may be glued on to home-made tools of various configurations, cut into small rectangles for general use, or sliced into strips. It may of course also be mounted on various types of miniature template and held with tweezers to clean out difficult angles, or fitted to larger pieces of wood to form sanding blocks.

Whether to use abrasive paper wet or dry is a problem that perplexes some modellers, and, indeed, either method has its advantages. The ultimate objective in sanding joints is to produce surfaces that are texturally indistinguishable from the rest of the model, which being plastic has a hard, and usually smooth and shiny, finish. It therefore follows that all traces of abrasion and its associated debris need to be removed. A sanding sheet dipped periodically in a basin of water will generally enable this objective to be reached more easily since the particles removed from the surface of the model are held in the lubricant and themselves act as a mild abrasive, which guarantees a smoother surface and the elimination of the dust problem. On the other hand, the abraded surface can become obscured during the sanding process, and there is a paste-like residue to be cleaned from the model afterwards. Using abrasive paper dry will result in a great deal of fine dust being deposited over a wide area of the model — and a more extensive cleaning task — and requires the use of progressively finer grades of paper to eliminate scratches. There is thus not a lot to choose between the two methods in terms of the finished result, but the time taken to achieve it might be an important consideration.

Once a joint has been filled and sanded to the modeller's initial satisfaction, there still remains a little more work. Quite frequently, a joint that seems good might betray its presence when the model is later painted, especially if it is to carry a single colour. To help avert this possibility there are one or two ways in which a check may be made. A thin coat of matt white enamel paint can be brushed over the joint and its adjacent surfaces, and when the paint has dried a careful inspection may reveal flaws previously unnoticed. If the area is lightly sanded with a fine abrasive paper through to the model surface, any tiny cracks or depressions will show up since the paint will not be removed from these areas. Alternatively, a coat of liquid cement may be applied, giving the surface a definite sheen and a filled area possibly a slightly darker hue, and gentle abrasion later when the solvent is hard will similarly reveal areas requiring further treatment.

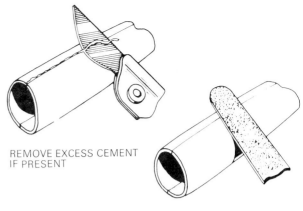

REMOVE EXCESS CEMENT IF PRESENT

ABRADE DIRECTLY

FINISHING 'GOOD' JOINTS

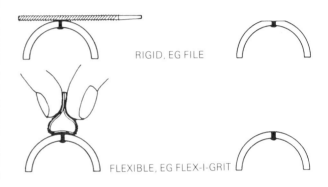

RIGID, EG FILE

FLEXIBLE, EG FLEX-I-GRIT

ADVANTAGES OF REDUCING FILLED JOINTS WITH FLEXIBLE ABRASIVE

ETC

NOTE RECESSES FOR POINTS OF TWEEZERS TO GRIP

MINIATURE SANDING BLOCKS

Filler may once again be touched into any offending areas, and the sanding and checking procedures carried out as before. The whole operation may be repeated until a completely satisfactory result is obtained.

REMODELLING
The building of a plastic model may merely involve the assembly and painting of a number of pre-formed shapes, and there are a great many people who derive a lot of enjoyment, and produce very attractive and interesting work, by doing just this. There are others, however, whose interests lie in

Top: the natural progression from altering a kit's components to show some measure of individuality in the finished model is the utilisation of kit mouldings only as part of the structure. Shown here are two *Skylab* space vehicles. The larger (1/48 scale) model represents the actual 'Wet Lab' design and is built from perspex tubing, plastic card, metal rod and Revell's Command Service Module kit; the smaller (1/144 scale) model, showing the original 'Dry Lab' design, is built from Airfix Saturn S4B components and plastic card.
(Models and photo: Mat Irvine)
Bottom: aircraft modellers are very well served by 'conversion kits'. These consist of a section or sections of model aircraft – usually vacuum formed – which may be used in conjunction with an available injection moulded kit to give a variation of the original configuration. This photograph shows a de Havilland Vampire NF10, produced from a Frog 1/72 scale Vampire FB5 but incorporating the forward fuselage nacelle and canopy from the Airmodel 1/72 Vampire NF10 'conversion kit'. The Airmodel kit in fact provides a complete nacelle and a choice of canopies so that a model of either the NF10 or the T10 may be produced.
(Model: Geoff Prentice)

building models which possess a greater degree of accuracy and realism than can be achieved by using unmodified kit components, or who look upon a plastic kit as a basis for something other than the subject denoted by the manufacturer's packaging. A more demanding aspect of plastic modelling, therefore, is the alteration of the moulded components supplied in a kit in order to satisfy the modelmaker's individual requirements.

Remodelling the overall configuration of a plastic kit will involve changing the character of certain of its parts or substituting specially tailored components for those supplied, or both; the work required will be determined by the appearance the finished model is to assume, and may be simply and speedily accomplished, with perhaps just a few carefully judged strokes of a craft knife, or extremely time-consuming and complicated, demanding the production of so many hand-made units that the contribution to the model made by commercially-produced components is relatively insignificant. There are, however, a number of factors which will affect the modeller's opinions as to how best this work may be approached.

The first factor relates to basic economics. Magazine articles describing the construction of a particular model frequently refer to the inclusion of components obtained by purchasing either specially-designed 'conversion kits' or complete injection moulded kits. Alternatively, they may suggest that the modeller finds the required parts by recourse to his supply of spares left over from previous kits, most of which are not in fact spares but components derived from unfinished or redundant models. In extreme cases, the purchase of an expensive kit is advocated for the sake of one small piece. In all these instances, an additional outlay is implied, and this may well entail a sum of money so large as to be unrealistic, and a cheap method of acquiring a given part may therefore be of paramount importance.

Another factor concerns time. If the modeller's principal interest is building up a representative collection of models as quickly as possible, he may not be favourably disposed towards spending many hours producing intricate components such as engines, wheels, and so forth. If he specialises in one specific category of model, there is less likelihood of wastage if kits are purchased purely as sources of useful parts, and any additional expenditure to these ends may be more easily justified.

A third and in many ways the most important factor is the skill and experience of the modeller. Whilst many people are discouraged from deviating too far from the components supplied in a plastic kit by a lack of confidence in their own abilities, it is at the same time true to say that many exponents of the finer arts of modelling do not appreciate that they may be fortunate in possessing a rare talent. A technique that is easily mastered by some may be inordinately difficult to learn for others.

Nowadays, many kit manufacturers recognise the fact that some modellers may wish to change the character of a basic kit model to their own liking, and go some way towards meeting these requirements by offering a choice of configurations in the components they supply. Options may consist simply of such things as a choice of underwing stores for an aircraft model, provision for full hull or waterline models in a ship kit, or a choice of stowage equipment for a model of a tank, but these considerations do not really change the overall concept of the finished miniature. More enterprising is the offering of optional parts which enable models of completely differing characteristics to be built, and examples of these might include alternative arm components for a figure, alternative turrets for a tank model, or a choice of fuselage components to enable different marks of an otherwise similar aircraft to be represented.

For the most part, the options offered within one particular kit will demand only those basic constructional techniques essential for assembling a kit that provides no choice of configuration since the component parts are directly interchangeable, but occasionally some other simple skills are called for. The most common amongst these is the ability to remove a section of plastic from one or more of the kit parts, a technique which, incidentally, is more and more often required for basic constructional procedure, as in the separation of individual aircraft undercarriage doors from a group consisting of a single unit. A moulded channel is usually provided to help the modeller remove the necessary sections with the aid of a sharp blade, and the methods of detaching and preparing the mouldings are the same as those related previously.

A much greater variety of choice, albeit a choice principally amongst aircraft model subjects, is offered by the availability of vacuum formed components. These are produced by small specialist companies, often comprising only one or two enterprising individuals, who see the need for providing moulded shapes that may be difficult for the modeller to produce from basic materials himself, and the opportunity at the same time for a profitable commercial venture. Because of their limited market, these products tend to be relatively expensive, and unfortunately their quality still varies somewhat. In the early days of commercial accessory kits such as these, there were innumerable 'back street' vacuum-forming businesses whose

efforts, though very probably spurred by good intentions, left a great deal to be desired in terms of accuracy, fit and general presentation. However, many have since fallen by the wayside, and, generally speaking, those that remain have built up interesting ranges and a good reputation.

Injection moulded parts fulfilling a similar role are also produced, although the increased costs involved in producing such components is higher and their commercial viability consequently reduced. Kits consisting wholly or partly of parts cast in resin are available on a very limited basis too, but production methods here are less straightforward and more time-consuming, resulting, again, in high retail prices.

All these mouldings may be treated as normal kit components and prepared accordingly. Where construction work calls for the drastic modification of an existing kit part, such as the removal of a section of fuselage, this should be done whenever possible before any assembly takes place. A razor saw is generally the most useful tool for such surgery. The line of severance should be carefully marked out with a hard pencil, and if necessary a cutting guide may be prepared from plastic strip and held or taped to the part being treated. The initial saw cut should take the form of a groove along the pencilled line, the section being removed by gradually and evenly increasing its depth — cutting right through the plastic in one place only at a time can make following the guideline difficult. A firm cutting surface is essential, and for some types of work a simple sawing jig is useful. This may be fashioned from odd pieces of wood. The saw should at all times be kept perpendicular to the surface of the plastic, and to assist this a mitre block can be incorporated into the jig.

Difficulties may arise when these accessory components are amalgamated into the principal structures of a model. Although the parts to be integrated may have been meticulously designed and produced to quite accurate dimensions, the kit, or kits, in conjunction with which they are supposed to be used may not conform precisely to reality, and problems of component fit may well arise. It is just as possible that the special mouldings are inaccurate and the kit correct. Perhaps both are wrong. Whatever the cause, the modeller has a problem to overcome and a difficult joint to negotiate. The first task, after ascertaining the extent of the fault, is for the modeller to form an opinion as to where the error lies and establish whether it may be easily corrected. Thus two halves of a fuselage section which form an assembly that is too narrow might benefit from the introduction of a fillet of plastic card inserted along the joints; one that is too wide

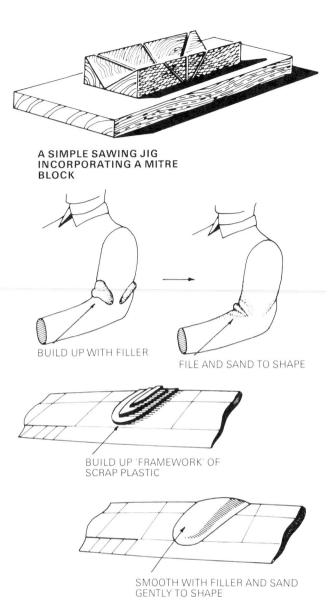

A SIMPLE SAWING JIG INCORPORATING A MITRE BLOCK

BUILD UP WITH FILLER

FILE AND SAND TO SHAPE

BUILD UP 'FRAMEWORK' OF SCRAP PLASTIC

SMOOTH WITH FILLER AND SAND GENTLY TO SHAPE

BUILDING UP CONTOURS WITH FILLER

Top: remodelling can sometimes quite successfully be achieved solely by filing and filling the contours of the moulded kit components. Here, a 1/72 scale Hawker Siddeley Gnat, shown (background) more or less 'straight' from the Airfix kit for the Red Arrows T2, has been quite drastically altered in fuselage, wings and tailplane simply by removing unwanted material with a knife and a file, building up new nose and fuselage contours with filling compound and adding a new canopy adapted from another kit. The result represents a quite different aircraft, the Gnat F1, completed here in Finnish Air Force markings.
Bottom: an example of plastic card modelling on a major scale, this incomplete 1/32 scale M6A1H, a kit for which has not yet been produced, has its hull and skirt armour made from polystyrene sheet. Although of course less complicated than curved surfaces, structures such as these nevertheless demand some very precise measuring and shaping in order to realise a result that is both neat and accurate. The track for this model has also been produced from plastic card.
(Model: Paul Giltz. Photo: Greg Bieszczad)

sheet. The work will also ask of the modeller a considerable knowledge of his prototype and demand greater skills and more time-consuming effort than that required when using ready - moulded parts

Reducing the contours of a pre-formed shape is perhaps the most basic technique that may be necessary to produce an accurate form, and this may generally be achieved by file, sanding board or abrasive paper, progressively reducing the grade of abrasive as work nears completion. Where there is insufficient room to wield such tools, the tip of a convex blade might be more effective in removing excess material, either by slicing or scraping it away. These methods are suitable only for subtle changes of contour, since the components in most kits are moulded to a thickness that will not permit the removal of very much plastic.

Complementing these techniques, in a way, is the application of filler to model structures in order to build up their size. This method is particularly useful for achieving contoured surfaces, and is applicable particularly to figure modelling for emphasising folds and creases in clothing. It is also handy for building up fuselage shapes on model aircraft, modifying hull contours on model ships, representing Zimmerit anti-magnetic paste on German AFVs, and so on. Care should be exercised to make sure that the compound keys successfully with the surface to which it is applied. The latter must be absolutely free from dust and grease, so it needs to be carefully washed, and it can be scored or drilled to help the filler grip. If a considerable thickness needs to be built up, irregularly shaped pieces of scrap plastic can be attached to the model before the compound is applied — laying on thick quantities of certain cellulose-based fillers leads to trouble

may have each mating surface sanded back a little; one whose contours are incorrect might be put right by reshaping it with a file. If the error cannot be isolated or if, once found, it cannot easily be attended to, some compromise will have to be accepted and the joint made good by trimming, filing, filling and sanding in the usual way.

Variations to the shapes offered in commercially-produced kits — and accessories — may be achieved by more basic means. Such work might merely involve abrading a contour to reduce its prominence, but it may also dictate the use of fundamental materials such as filling compound and plastic

with the drying-out process, and may even cause a softening of the plastic beneath, which can have dire consequences. The filler may, however, be quite safely built up in a series of wafer-thin layers, allowing ample drying time in between each, but the plastic framework ensures a good bond and is more economical. When completely hardened off, the filler may be filed, sanded and otherwise shaped in the normal manner.

HAND-MADE COMPONENTS
The versatility of polystyrene as a modelling medium is nowhere better demonstrated than on the workbench of a modeller who builds his own components for use in the assembly of a model. It is a light material, and one that is very easy to work, and, as we have seen, it may be shaped using a variety of tools and methods. Being a thermoplastic, it can also be heated and moulded at a temperature of about 105°C (220°F), and when cool will retain the shape thus formed. Its major disadvantage is that it lacks rigidity and strength when produced in thin sections, but the availability of ABS plastic in accessory form goes some way towards making up for this deficiency.

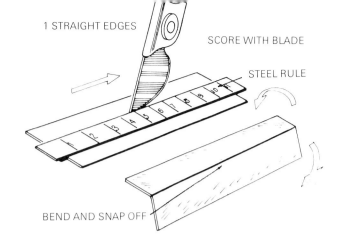

1 STRAIGHT EDGES

SCORE WITH BLADE

STEEL RULE

BEND AND SNAP OFF

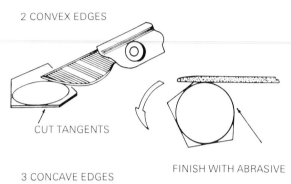

2 CONVEX EDGES

CUT TANGENTS

FINISH WITH ABRASIVE

3 CONCAVE EDGES

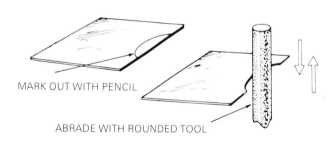

MARK OUT WITH PENCIL

ABRADE WITH ROUNDED TOOL

**PREPARATION OF FLAT
SURFACES FROM PLASTIC
CARD**

Opposite: the advantages of preparing components from laminations of plastic card are realised in this 1/48 scale Westland Whirlwind. The complex contours of this particular aircraft make the production of a set of wings using any other method very difficult; laminating also eases the task of modelling the radiator intakes since each layer of card can be profiled before it is cemented to give the required recesses. The wheels, tailplane and rudder are also made from laminated plastic sheet, but the fuselage and engine nacelles are thermo-formed. Laminated card needs to be left for a very long period of time before it is shaped so that the effects of the solvent used disappear totally – several months were required in this instance. (Model: Tony Woollett)

Three basic types of surface are required for producing hollow-section components for a plastic model. Flat surfaces are the most straightforward, since polystyrene and ABS sheeting is readily available in this form, and will be required for most types of model, but particularly military equipment, ships and commercial vehicles. Simple curves, that is, those contoured in one dimension only, are less common but may be necessary for some areas, including ships' funnels, barbettes and gun tubs, sections of tank hulls and cowlings, and simple mudguards. Compound curves, the most difficult to reproduce, apply to all types of model but part-icularly aircraft and modern vehicles such as saloon cars.

Before a part consisting of one or more flat sides is prepared, it is obviously necessary to ascertain the dimensions and shape the finished component will require. The size may be scaled from a drawing or from the model being built, or in some cases may be computed with reference to a photograph. The shapes may then be drawn out on a piece of polystyrene card of appropriate thickness. Thin card (0.005in and 0.010in) can quite easily be sliced with a sharp blade, but although it is possible to cut through thicker material the blade quickly becomes blunted. The separation line, however, may simply be scored with a blade, a sharp, pointed instrument or a razor saw, and then snapped section by section with the fingers. Thin strips may be snapped using pliers which have had the jaws padded with a couple of layers of adhesive tape to prevent any damage to the plastic. Breaking the material in this way will leave a ragged, uneven edge which will have to be cleaned up with a sanding board, and so it is advisable to draw out the part fractionally oversize. Parts with convexly curved outlines may be prepared by cutting a series of tangents around the edge and then smoothing it off with an abrasive, but concave perimeters will have to be worked almost exclusively with abrasive equipment since access with a knife is difficult.

The joining of two flat pieces of plastic card may adequately be achieved by butting them against each other, and, clearly, precision of fit is of paramount importance here. Mitred corners, though needing considerable care to produce neatly, will reduce the amount of filling and sanding that will be necessary after the joint is set. Reinforcement is not usually needed unless comparatively thin card is used or unless particular strength is required, but if it is added, strips of plastic along

the interior of the joint will provide adequate support, and gussets and more extensive bracing will be of benefit if large structures such as tank hulls are being prepared.

Simple curves may best be produced by rolling the card with a cylindrically-shaped former on a slightly resilient surface. Thin strips of plastic may be worked quite conveniently on the forefinger, using a paintbrush handle; larger pieces may be prepared on a thick layer of cardboard with dowelling. The curvature may be controlled by the amount of pressure applied and by the diameter of the instrument used to roll the plastic, and the formation of tight curves is also assisted if the instrument is moved across the plastic, under pressure, in one plane. The plastic will be found to uncurl initially, but sustained movement of the rolling instrument will gradually stretch the outside surface of the strip and make the whole thing very pliable, and after a few minutes' work it will be found that the desired shape may be formed with the fingers and retained.

Permanency of shape may also be achieved by subjecting the plastic to heat. The piece being worked on can be firmly taped on to a wooden jig and immersed in hot water, as described in the previous chapter. In certain instances, for example with a small strip of plastic, it is possible to tape the part to its former and pass it close to a naked flame, though not too near so as to melt the plastic. It should be stressed that this technique takes practice to perfect and should be the subject of much experimentation with odds and ends of material to ascertain the optimum distance between the part and the heat source and the length of time necessary to set the plastic.

As well as lending permanency to a curve already prepared, a heat source can also be used to induce a curve, and with experience a considerable degree of control can be exercised and predetermined shapes

1 ROLLING

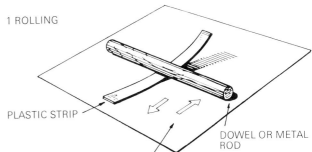

PLASTIC STRIP

DOWEL OR METAL ROD

THICK CARD OR BLOTTING PAPER

2 IMMERSION METHOD

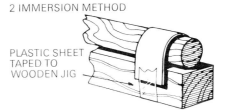

PLASTIC SHEET TAPED TO WOODEN JIG

ENTIRE ASSEMBLY IMMERSED IN VERY HOT WATER

3 FLAME INFLUENCE METHODS

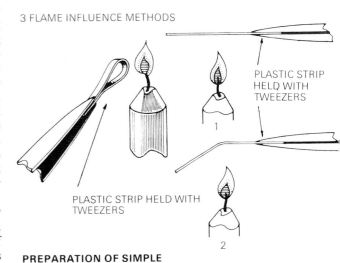

PLASTIC STRIP HELD WITH TWEEZERS

PLASTIC STRIP HELD WITH TWEEZERS

PREPARATION OF SIMPLE CURVES

produced quite accurately. Again, thin strips of plastic are the only materials that may be shaped in this way, and single bends rather than continuous curves are more applicable to this particular technique. The plastic strip is held with tweezers, or if of sufficient length with the fingers, a distance of about 1in (2cm) above a steady flame and allowed to droop as far as required. The speed at which the plastic is heated and the amount of heat applied are quite critical, since local melting may commonly occur. Both these factors can be controlled by the distance between the flame and the plastic. A candle will provide an adequate flame, but it should be set up in a draught-free environment. A further variation of this technique is to soften a section of the

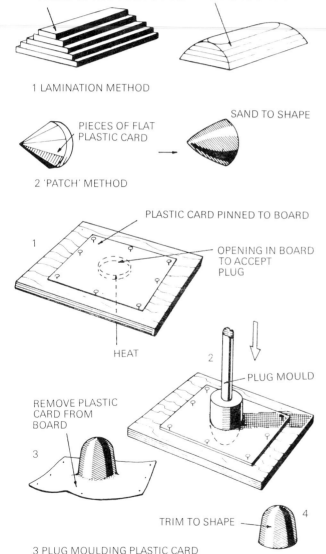

1 LAMINATION METHOD

2 'PATCH' METHOD

3 PLUG MOULDING PLASTIC CARD

PREPARATION OF COMPOUND CURVES

plastic strip by passing it back and forth over the heat source and then draping it over a prepared jig. This method is useful if several pieces of identical shape are required.

The thickness of the plastic is of course a vital consideration with all these techniques, and the thinner the gauge used the more readily can the material be shaped, since uniformity of heat distribution is easier to accomplish. However, few problems should be encountered with thicknesses up to 0.03in, which will suffice for most modelling requirements.

Small parts which need to combine rigidity with permanancy of contour can sometimes more conveniently be produced by laminating appropriately shaped pieces of polystyrene card together and then carving and sanding to achieve the desired form. Parts involving compound curves can of course be produced following this method. Polystyrene lends itself admirably to this 'bread and butter' approach, but a few words of caution should be sounded. The plastic used should always be of the thickest gauge possible to prevent any chance of warpage or other deformities arising whilst the layers are being built up. The joints between each section should also be very thoroughly bonded. The entire mating surface of each pair of matching parts should be covered with a thin coat of tube cement, or a thick, well-brushed coat of liquid cement, and the two layers immediately clamped together under the greatest possible pressure. This is to ensure that all the air is evacuated — if it isn't, problems may occur when the shaping of the part is tackled later. Ample, really ample, drying time should be allowed after cementing has taken place, since evaporation of the solvent is very slow in such enclosed areas. A week would not be too long, and a really heavy unit might require as long as a month.

Lamination is suitable for all types of solid structures, but it can be very expensive in terms of the amount of plastic used. For bulky assemblies, therefore, such as ships' hulls or tank turrets, each layer may have its centre removed, having regard of course to the necessary strength and rigidity of the finished model. The amount of material saved can be very considerable, and the surplus may be put to good use for other projects. Laminated blocks may of course be shaped by file and filler, and finished, when the solvent is thoroughly set.

It is also possible to build up certain contoured shapes by preparing a framework of thick plastic card, adding formers, and shaping the exterior surfaces by means of butt-jointed patches of plastic card. Additional bracing can be worked into the structure if necessary as sanding proceeds. This technique has the advantage of being fairly economical on material, but it is suitable only for gentle curves and requires a thick gauge of plastic to allow for the inevitable reductions in thickness caused by sanding. The other major drawback is that the joints, the weak points of any plastic model, are the areas most likely to be abraded, thus decreasing the overall strength even further.

It is quite feasible for the modeller to exploit the potential of polystyrene more fully and produce shapes by moulding them under heat. This process, after all, is the foundation of the plastic kit industry, and there is no reason why he cannot adapt it for his own individual purposes to produce shapes consisting of compound curves. Injection moulding requires specialised and very expensive equipment of course, but various methods of thermo-forming with plastic sheet are open to any modeller with the enthusiasm and ability to tackle them.

In order to form a shape in plastic sheeting, two influences are required: heat and pressure. In addition, a mould, over or into which the softened plastic is shaped, must be prepared. The amount of heat required will vary according to the particular type of thermoplastic being used, and this may originate from a natural flame or from an electrical element. The pressure may be mechanical, or it may be induced by harnessing natural atmospheric forces by either raising or lowering the local air pressure acting upon one side of the heated plastic.

The simplest type of themo-forming can be carried out with very basic home-made equipment and incurs very little financial outlay. The procedure involves pressing a plug into a piece of softened plastic sheet and allowing the moulded shape to cool. The plug may be fabricated from any rigid material and should be furnished with a simple handle so that it can be easily managed. The plastic sheeting is best mounted across a frame, the vacant centre of which should be a little larger in overall dimensions than the plug so as to allow the latter to pass through it with generous clearance all round. Heat is then introduced to the area of plastic that is to be moulded, and when it has made the material soft and pliant, it is removed and the plug immediately pressed on to the plastic and through the frame aperture to the required depth. The plastic will assume the shape of the plug, to the extent of the forward portion as far as its maximum circumference, after withdrawal, and will cool within seconds. All thermo-forming techniques are refinements of this basic process.

From simple beginnings such as these, more sophisticated equipment may be devised and greater finesse developed, and experience will enable the modeller to choose the system best fitted to his requirements. The difficulties and shortcomings of thermo-forming were discussed at some length in Chapter 1, and considerable patience and experimentation are generally needed before success is consistently achieved. Technically, it is but a small step from simple plug moulding to vacuum forming, which allows a more neatly defined shape to be moulded, decreases the risk of webbing and also permits the reproduction of any number of identical forms. Commercial vacuum forming equipment is available at considerable expense, although a hand-pumped machine with rather limited potential is obtainable quite cheaply in the US, but it is possible for the modeller with the necessary skills to make a simple drape vacuum former.

A wooden, open-topped box 2in (5cm) deep is made from ½in (1.25cm) blockboard, and 1in (2.5cm) spacers are fitted to the interior around three of the sides. The fourth side is provided with an opening to accept the flattened nozzle of a household vacuum cleaner. The joints are made completely airtight by using a suitably viscous adhesive, and the unit is firmly clamped and allowed to set. An appropriate fitting is added to the air outlet hole so that the vacuum cleaner nozzle will form an airtight seal yet remain detachable — some sort of flexible grommet is ideal. The size of the box is very much a matter of personal preference, depending as it does on the modelling requirements of the individual, and clearly, forming, say, a 1/76 scale tank turret on a machine tailored to the size of plastic sheet sold in model shops (typically about 13in by 9in — about 33cm by 23cm) would be uneconomical, whilst for moulding the hull of a 1/600 scale ship such a size might be too small.

A wooden clamp frame to hold the plastic sheet should be prepared to the dimensions of the vacuum box and provided with a suitable number of holes so that the sheet can be sandwiched firmly between the two members and screwed or bolted in position. An airtight seal should again be made. A pattern base of ½in blockboard should next be prepared so that it fits tightly into the vacuum box, on top of the spacers provided inside. Foam rubber strip is glued around the top edges of the box and just inside the lip to prevent air passing through the joints between the pattern base and the box, and between the frame and the box, whilst the machine is in operation. The frame is then fitted on to the box by means of hinges on any side except that provided with the air exhaustion hole. A number of vents are drilled through the pattern base with a very fine drill, and the pattern itself may then be prepared, vented, and fixed firmly to it.

In order to operate the machine, the pattern is fitted in position and the vacuum hose connected. The frame carrying the plastic sheet is swung up to

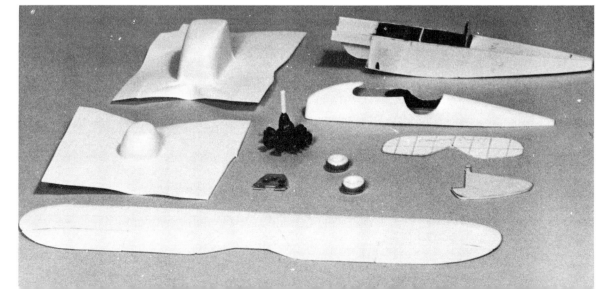

Top: the basic essentials for a simple plug moulded shape are male and female moulds, plastic card, and a heat source. Shown here are the tools for a 1/36 scale front fairing for a DH Gipsy engine, posed with a formed moulding and a trimmed component. The moulds are made from balsa wood, the female acting as little more than a support for the plastic card whilst the male plug is pressed into it.
(Preparations by Tony Woollett)
Centre: an example of a plug moulded component incorporated into a model is shown here with the driver cooling intake on this 1/12 scale Lotus 49C. Parts requiring hollow interiors, such as aircraft cockpit canopies, radomes, ships' boats and scoops and intakes of all descriptions can be convincingly produced by this method. Undercutting is not of course possible, and major components such as drop tanks, engine nacelles, tank turrets, etc have to be moulded in two halves and then joined.
(Model: Dave Patrick)
Bottom: components for a 1/36 scale Comper Swift at various stages in the production sequence. The basic fuselage (top right of picture) is essentially a 'box' of plastic card with (in front of this) the upper section plug moulded and trimmed to shape. The lower contours of the forward fuselage (top left) are also plug moulded and can be seen as initially formed. The wing (foreground) is made by folding plastic card over a balsa core, the latter being fixed on to the half that will become the lower surface of the wing. Prior to folding the card, the wing leading edge is scored with a ballpoint pen 'inside' the curve. The fin and tailplane are here shown as card templates.
(Preparations by Tony Woollett)

the heat source, for which a conventional electrical element such as that found on an electric fire may be utilised. When the plastic has softened, the frame is brought down on to the pattern and held tightly in position, and the air in the box is evacuated by switching on the cleaner.

Success in forming components in this way depends very much upon three factors: the trouble that is taken to make all the joints in the vacuum box airtight, the condition of the heated plastic sheet as it comes into contact with the pattern, and the speed with which the whole operation is accomplished. Other considerations such as draft, depth of draw, and the thickness of the plastic are important, as described in Chapter 1. The chief advantage of positive forming such as outlined above is that relatively little work needs to be done on the pattern. The only requirement is that it should be of the correct basic shape, since moulded detail cannot be reproduced on the exterior surfaces of the finished article and has to be applied by hand afterwards. The use of very thin plastic sheet on a machine of sound design will permit more intricate contours to be moulded, but the component produced will be extremely fragile.

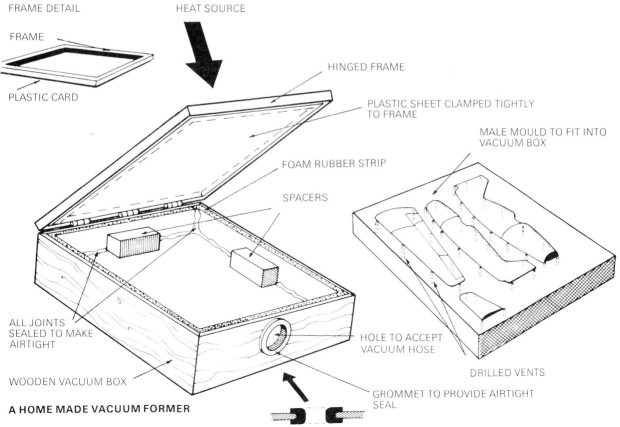

FRAME DETAIL

FRAME

PLASTIC CARD

HEAT SOURCE

HINGED FRAME

PLASTIC SHEET CLAMPED TIGHTLY TO FRAME

MALE MOULD TO FIT INTO VACUUM BOX

FOAM RUBBER STRIP

SPACERS

ALL JOINTS SEALED TO MAKE AIRTIGHT

HOLE TO ACCEPT VACUUM HOSE

WOODEN VACUUM BOX

DRILLED VENTS

GROMMET TO PROVIDE AIRTIGHT SEAL

A HOME MADE VACUUM FORMER

It is possible to form plastic negatively with vacuum equipment, in the same way as some of the leading companies specialising in this kind of kit, by providing a female mould into which the plastic sheet is drawn. For modelling purposes, this would involve making a cast of the pattern in plaster or resin, but the work is so involved and the tolerances so much more difficult to achieve that the time expended on it is hardly worth the effort unless large production runs are anticipated.

Much has been written in the past about the use of non-plastic materials to make some of the larger components for an essentially plastic model, notably wood. Whilst there is undoubtedly merit in using this material to produce parts with compound curves such as nose cones and drop tanks for aircraft models, gun turrets for warships, or even larger units such as complete fuselages and hulls, the problems associated with its use are such that it holds few if any advantages over plastic in the final analysis. One obvious limitation is that it cannot be used for small parts which need to be shown as hollow casings, like engine cowlings and car bodies. Another difficulty is that it possesses grain, and whilst this might be acceptable on large scale models where wooden areas on the prototype are to be represented, the portrayal of smooth finishes requires a great deal of filling, sanding and general preparation, and textured surfaces necessitate the use of very skilful techniques, so much so with a wood like balsa that the material may be regarded merely as providing a framework for a filling compound and therefore has little to offer over any other. The problems of joining non-compatible materials have already been mentioned, and with wood these problems are complicated further by the susceptibility of the material to atmospheric influences. Even if the thermo-forming of shapes in plastic cannot be undertaken, polystyrene sheet can be laminated and then carved and sanded in much the same way as wood.

Two further methods of producing parts for plastic models must also be mentioned. Reference was made above to the casting of a female mould for use on a vacuum former, but of course it is also possible to cast positive components that may be applied directly to the model using a female mould without recourse to such equipment. This method is particularly useful where the production of a quantity of small, simple, and identical parts is desired, for example sets of wheels. A casting tray should be prepared — this may be fabricated from wood or strong cardboard, sealing all the joints, or alternatively a strong plastic carton such as margarine is sold in may be used — and the inner walls well greased. A rubber silicon sealer such as Silastic is

Top: the M103A3 120mm-gun heavy tank illustrated here is based on the 1/32 scale Monogram kit of the M48A2 Patton but incorporates, amongst other items, a completely new turret that has been produced on a 'domestic' vacuum forming machine. Whilst it might be argued that wood could just as effectively be used to achieve the same ends, the time taken in final surface preparation can perhaps more usefully be employed in thermo-forming the shape from it, especially as the pattern can be used to produce any number of components of identical appearance. (Model: Paul Giltz. Photo: Greg Bieszczad)

Bottom: mass production — on the modeller's workbench. The wheels for both the Scammell tank transporter and the Comet tank in this photograph were produced by first making masters from blocks of vulcanised rubber and then making female moulds for each type of wheel half from Silastic, the solution being poured into ordinary tobacco tins and the masters pressed home. After the solution had cured, the female moulds were freed and the required number of parts cast using epoxy resin, the appropriate wheel halves then being joined up. For both the silicon solution and the epoxy resin, household furniture polish was sprayed into the moulds to act as a release agent. The models themselves — whose components are, apart from the tank tracks, completely hand made — were designed principally by scaling up existing 1/76 injection moulded kits to 1/35. (Models and photo: Gary McCrudden)

prepared and poured into the tray to a depth at least half as great again as that of the component to be produced, and any air bubbles present are released by tapping gently at the sides and base. The pattern to be cast is then greased and pressed into the solution, and the tray is set aside for a couple of days so that thorough curing takes place. After this period, the tray can be stripped away and the silicon mould flexed to release the pattern. The casting to be used on the model is made by mixing up an epoxy resin such as Casting Glass or Bondaglass and pouring it into the greased mould, dealing with air bubbles by drawing them out with a needle. After a day or so the casting should be fully hardened off and ready to use.

Parts thus produced have detail only on one side of course, the other being flat, but making a casting in two halves and joining them afterwards with epoxy resin enables complete units to be manufactured. With such components, particular care should be taken that the pattern is pressed into the silicon solution to precisely the correct depth. One way of assisting this is to prepare the master so that it is identical in all respects to the finished casting by cutting it exactly along the parting line. When pressed into the silicon its flattened side must lie flush with the surface of the solution. To make things easier, a piece of flat plastic card can be attached to the back of the pattern, leaving a

generous margin all around it. This ensures that the depression formed in the solution is precisely the required depth.

The cast part may be trimmed with a sharp knife and filed as necessary although care should be exercised since it is extremely fragile, and the silicon mould may be used any number of times. The principal drawbacks are that undercutting is restricted to only a very shallow depth, and that the parting line for components cast in two halves has to lie along a flat plane.

The same limitations do not apply to modelling clay such as Plasticine, which may be fitted to a polystyrene surface provided adequate keying is made. The clay may be moulded with various instruments and sliced with a knife, and a couple of coats of banana oil will seal the surface so that it can accept paint. The disadvantages of this material are that it will not support very much weight and that its constituents are able to penetrate slowly through polystyrene and cause a noticeable darkening of any matt-finished paint on the surface of the model, unless special precautions such as varnishing are taken. However, modelling clay is much used by the figure modeller for representing various forms of clothing, headgear, etc., and it offers a great deal of scope for these purposes.

ADDING DETAIL

So far, it is mainly the basic structural form of a model that has been considered in this chapter, and although it would be wrong to underrate the importance of a well-constructed, accurate overall shape to a model, it is the way in which the smaller details are executed that can really make it convincing.

The addition of detail will take one of two forms. The first is where the surface of a component is too plain to look authentic. This may be due to the fact that the moulding is not provided with detail in the first place, or that what was supplied has been removed either deliberately because of its inaccuracy or incidentally in the sanding of a joint. This form of detailing thus has to be applied directly on to the component since it is an integral part of it,

and may stand proud of its surface or be recessed into it. The second kind of detail is that which serves to embellish a model's fundamental shape rather than form part of it, but which for a variety of reasons, principally moulding limitations, cannot always be incorporated in a kit or, if supplied, may be overscale. These small parts can only very loosely be defined but would include, for example, aerials and antennae on AFVs, rigging and rail on ship models, spoked wheels for motorcycle models, buckles and shoelaces for figures, and undercarriage components, pitot tubes and gun turrets on aircraft. Such items are not normally fitted to a model until the painting of the basic shapes has been completed. The subject of detail will be considered more fully in the specialist chapters to follow, but for the moment a few basic principles can be outlined.

Detailing incorporated into the body of a component may take various forms, depending basically upon how best to represent the material of which the prototype is composed. Thus if a metal object is being portrayed it may be necessary to show detail that is cast into its surface, and if it is made up of a number of plates or panels the seams, weld lines or rivets may have to be shown. Wood textures might need to be simulated on the plastic surface, bolt heads shown or joints depicted. Glazed panels may be required in aircraft, ships or vehicles, together with the necessary framework, and fabrics such as leather, canvas and wool differentiated on a figure model.

Recessed detail may be applied to a model's surface with a variety of tools. A sharp point may be used to scribe fine lines, a razor saw is useful for etching more prominent lines, files can be used to produce a number of different effects including gouged channels, hatching and variously shaped apertures, drills and gouges will produce rounded openings or depressions, and a hot needle or pyrogravure can be used to form furrows, welded seams and a wide range of heavy textures. Random detail of this kind such as may be found on fabrics or areas with rough wooden surfaces is comparatively straightforward in its application, although experimentation on scrap plastic is recommended before any techniques are applied to a model, and there is room for individual interpretation and even error. Representing more regular features — rows of rivets, panel lines of uniform width and depth, and so on — is a much more difficult proposition and one that warrants some further thought.

The scribing of detail is in most instances best done before the parts being worked on are assembled. Since a certain amount of pressure will have to be applied, the component in question should be

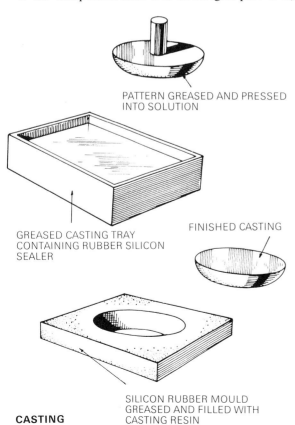

PATTERN GREASED AND PRESSED INTO SOLUTION

GREASED CASTING TRAY CONTAINING RUBBER SILICON SEALER

FINISHED CASTING

SILICON RUBBER MOULD GREASED AND FILLED WITH CASTING RESIN

CASTING

firmly supported in some way. With solid, flat pieces this presents no problem since the part may merely be laid on to the work surface, tacked down with double-sided Sellotape if necessary, but with fragile, hollow or contoured parts this may not be enough. It is often possible to support the part in the hand, but sometimes a jig is necessary — an example of this might be where a thin vacuum-formed aircraft fuselage requires a neat panel line. Small blocks of wood or plastic carefully arranged will usually solve the problem.

The positions of panel lines, rows of rivets, and so forth should be marked out on to the surface of the plastic using a sharp, soft pencil, and wherever possible templates should be prepared to assist geometrical precision and symmetry during the scribing process. These need not be elaborate — strips of 0.01in and 0.02in plastic card are ideal — but should be flexible to a certain degree to take in the major contours of the component being detailed. The templates may be held steady with the forefinger while being used, but for intricate work they may be temporarily attached to the model with double-sided adhesive tape. On some parts, for example where conical forms are present or difficult angles occur, it may not be possible to use templates. In these cases the etching will have to be done freehand, having first pencilled in the positions of the detail.

The effect that the paint to be applied later will have on the surface detail should always be borne in mind. As well as imparting the required colour to the finished model, it will also act as a filling compound, especially if it is gloss in character or relatively thick. Lightly etched lines or those scribed with a sharply pointed instrument such as a needle are likely to disappear under a coat of paint, and so due allowance for this should be made by slightly over-emphasising the features. Care should also be

Below: Plasticine, a modelling clay substitute, can be a very useful material in the construction of plastic models, although it requires special treatment before it is entirely compatible both with polystyrene and with modelling paints. The exhaust manifolds for the Lotus 49C were prepared by rolling out strips of the substance on a flat surface with the base of a saucepan, shaping them, and then placing them in a refrigerator for several hours to harden. After the manifolds were positioned on the model, the Plasticine strips were cut to the required length and their surfaces given several liberal coatings of liquid polystyrene cement to seal them ready for painting.
(Model: Dave Patrick)

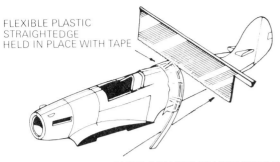

FLEXIBLE PLASTIC
STRAIGHTEDGE
HELD IN PLACE WITH TAPE

RAZOR SAW DRAWN VERY GENTLY
OVER SURFACE

**PRODUCING RECESSED LINE
DETAIL**

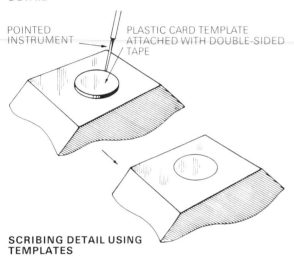

POINTED
INSTRUMENT

PLASTIC CARD TEMPLATE
ATTACHED WITH DOUBLE-SIDED
TAPE

**SCRIBING DETAIL USING
TEMPLATES**

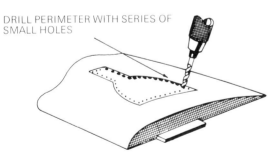

DRILL PERIMETER WITH SERIES OF
SMALL HOLES

SHAPE CURVES WITH ROUNDED
FILE

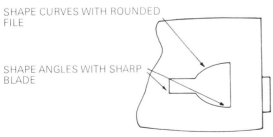

SHAPE ANGLES WITH SHARP
BLADE

OPENING UP APERTURES

taken when providing recessed detail that material is actually removed from the model and not merely pushed away. A razor saw or a file will cut a groove to the accompaniment of debris, and a drill will produce swarf, but material will also be displaced, and friction may produce local melting of the plastic, forming a ridge around the gouge mark. This effect is even more pronounced when a sharp point, or of course a heated instrument, is being used. Scribing should therefore be complemented by gentle sanding, and the whole process should be repeated as often as necessary for each detail feature in order to produce a clean, smooth result.

The opening up of apertures in the surface of a model calls for a number of special techniques. Whatever the shape of the aperture, be it for a rectangular sighting port in a gun turret, a circular scuttle in a ship's hull or an oval glazed panel in an airliner, a drill should be the instrument to produce the initial hole. The position of the drill may first be pricked with a sharp point so that no slippage occurs — for irregularly shaped or large openings it may be necessary to mark several points inside the circumference so that the drilled holes overlap. The general shaping of the aperture may be carried out by cutting with the tip of a sharp blade, or by abrasion with the point of a file or slivers of abrasive paper. Sharp edges and angles are best achieved by using a knife since abrasion, however carefully undertaken, will tend to leave slightly rounded contours; perfect circles may be formed by drilling, rotating a round file — with the cut of the file rather than against it, to avoid splitting the plastic — or by rotating a pointed blade in a scouring action; ovals can be shaped with a round or half-round file, although a drill can be used in the same way as a file, which is very helpful if tiny apertures are being worked; irregularly shaped holes may be prepared by using a combination of these methods. In all cases, the plastic being removed should be done so piecemeal rather than in a single operation, thereby reducing the chances of error.

Surface detail in relief may be provided in one of two ways. In most cases it involves the production of finely executed items which are then affixed to the surface of the model as assembly work proceeds, but where thin plastic is being used for the structure of the model it is possible to give the material an embossed appearance by pressing the interior surfaces with a fine but blunted instrument such as a stencil stylus or even a ball point pen. Ribbing effects for aircraft models to simulate fabric covered wings and representing mushroom-head rivets on tanks are instances where this technique is useful. Once again, the positions of the detail to be incorporated should be marked out on the exterior of the model with a pencil, and the marks can be transferred to the interior surfaces by holding the plastic against a strong light — its translucency should be sufficient for the pencilling to show through.

In many instances, surface features need to be shown in very sharp relief, and these may best be depicted by preparing finely detailed components separately and then adding them to the model. Examples involving this kind of work would include raised panels on aircraft surfaces, fishplates, reinforcing strips and mushroom-head rivets on large scale tanks, chafing plates on ships' cable decks and buckles and buttons for figures. Most of this type of detail can be shown by using one of two materials, thin plastic card or heat-stretched sprue, although there is a host of others that may be suitable, including foil, notepaper, thin card, tissue paper, wire and thread.

The principal difficulty with this aspect of modelling concerns the intricacy of the work of course — preparing, handling and fitting such delicate items calls for considerable dexterity — and the tools employed should naturally be appropriate to the job. Fine pointed tweezers are essential, and the finest possible abrasives and blades are mandatory for shaping the parts. In addition, special equipment such as a stand-mounted lens to reduce eyestrain and a dental descaler for positioning the parts are beneficial. The working surface may also be modified to advantage. A rectangular tray about 1ft (30cm) square, formed from a base of 0.060in plastic card with edges made from the same material about ½in (1cm) high, and all joints sealed, will prevent the loss of tiny parts. A thin sheet of paper laid inside the tray, coloured so as to contrast with the materials being worked on, will greatly assist the location and identification of the details under preparation.

It is perhaps appropriate at thus juncture to discuss the technique of producing heat-stretched sprue, the modelling jargon for fine polystyrene filament originating from the unwanted plastic runners carrying the parts for an injection-moulded kit. Unfortunately, this is a technique that is often taken for granted in the modelling press, and its potential is rarely explored in any depth. In simple terms, producing the filament is achieved by softening a length of sprue over a heat source and then pulling it apart so that the molten material is drawn out into a thread. The heat source need not be elaborate — a candle or pocket lighter flame is entirely adequate — but the way the material is drawn out is important and, like so many tasks in modelling, this will benefit from a simple jig. The requirements for this are a flat, smooth surface as

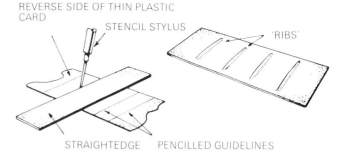

REVERSE SIDE OF THIN PLASTIC CARD   STENCIL STYLUS   'RIBS'

STRAIGHTEDGE   PENCILLED GUIDELINES

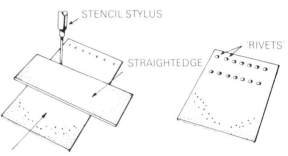

STENCIL STYLUS   'RIVETS'

STRAIGHTEDGE

REVERSE SIDE OF THIN PLASTIC CARD

EMBOSSING DETAIL VIA INTERIOR SURFACES

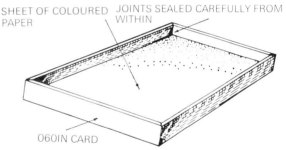

SHEET OF COLOURED PAPER   JOINTS SEALED CAREFULLY FROM WITHIN

060IN CARD

A HOLDING TRAY FROM PLASTIC CARD

long as possible — a splinter-free plank with its edges bound or brushed with several coats of gloss paint is ideal — with a clamping device at one extremity arranged in such a way that the sprue is held a short distance over, and away from, the edge. A small bench vice is excellent for the purpose.

One end of the length of sprue is then fitted into the clamp and, while the other end is held between the fingers, the flame is positioned beneath the centre, with the apex about ¾in (2cm) from the plastic. This distance is somewhat arbitrary, since different thicknesses of sprue have different heating requirements, but the object is to apply the heat slowly, so that the plastic becomes softened right through, not just around the edges, and both bubbling and actual combustion are avoided. The next step is perhaps the most vital. The flame is removed, and a second or two should elapse before the end of the sprue that is held in the hand is drawn away from the clamp, using the edge of the plank on which to rest the hand to ensure a straight, even action. The delay is important because sufficient time should be allowed for the exterior of the molten plastic to cool slightly to prevent premature breakage and because it is a determining factor in the thickness of the filament produced. The speed at which the filament is drawn out also has a bearing on the thickness of the final product: the quicker the rate of stretching, and the shorter the delay before it takes place, the finer the filament produced.

The sprue used should be as smooth as possible and free from junctions and prominent seams. The choice of colour is significant, for not only will a careful selection obviate the need for painting the filament later, but different stretching properties are also encountered. 'Silver' sprue is easily drawn but produces a very frangible filament, whereas coloured sprue, whilst not always readily drawn, will often produce a tough, pliable thread suitable for bending to form angles if required. Clear sprue is also, in general, easily snapped, but it possesses high tensile strength and has the added advantage of appearing thinner than it actually is.

Sprue can be stretched in this way to quite prodigious lengths, several yards being quite easily attainable, and filament of hair thickness can be drawn by heating the sprue until it is virtually liquified. The mass of molten plastic can be increas-ed by pushing together the two ends whilst the sprue is being warmed and compressing the plastic as much as possible, and the greater this mass the greater the length of filament that can be produced. Once the plastic has cooled, a process which takes but a few seconds, it can be cut up into convenient lengths, graded according to thickness, and stored by suspending the lengths from a hook, adding a weight such as a small ball of modelling clay to the other ends to keep them taut.

Round-section sprue will produce filament of a similar character, as will that where the molten plastic has been worked by compression before stretching takes place. However, it is also possible to produce filament of different cross-sectional shapes by preparing the sprue to be heated accordingly. Thus sprue sanded to an oval section will draw to oval filament, and square-section sprue will produce square-section filament, although the edges will be rounded off. The one proviso in these instances is that the plastic is heated only just enough — at no time may any distortion of the original shape be allowed to take place. It follows, therefore, that flat plastic strip may also be drawn in a similar fashion, and even miniature tubes can be produced from tubular plastic. The tapered ends formed by stretching standard sprue will also prove handy and may be stored separately for use later as required. A great deal of practice and experimentation is needed, however, before the modeller becomes familiar with all the techniques and the full potential of stretching sprue, and success, even for

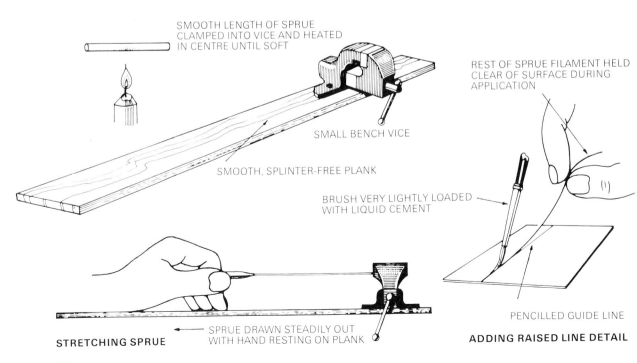

SMOOTH LENGTH OF SPRUE CLAMPED INTO VICE AND HEATED IN CENTRE UNTIL SOFT

REST OF SPRUE FILAMENT HELD CLEAR OF SURFACE DURING APPLICATION

SMALL BENCH VICE

SMOOTH, SPLINTER-FREE PLANK

BRUSH VERY LIGHTLY LOADED WITH LIQUID CEMENT

PENCILLED GUIDE LINE

SPRUE DRAWN STEADILY OUT WITH HAND RESTING ON PLANK

STRETCHING SPRUE

ADDING RAISED LINE DETAIL

those experienced in these processes, is never guaranteed.

The applications of stretched sprue in plastic modelmaking are very considerable in number, but for the moment its use in simulating raised surface detail may be examined in outline. The presence of raised lines to represent panel boundaries is rarely desirable, although the majority of injection-moulded kits adopt this approach because it is easier and more economical to do so. The restoration of these features where they have been scarred or removed through joints being sanded is sometimes called for, and this can be undertaken using polystyrene filament. The location of each length should first be accurately marked with a pencil and the raised line trimmed back so that it finishes sharply. The filament is then attached at one end, using a minimum of liquid cement on a fine brush. The other end should be held above the surface of the model since otherwise capillarity will cause the thread to be joined to the model in the wrong position. The filament is then laid along the pencilled line and cement introduced to the joint at intervals, using a template immediately after application to obtain the correct alignment. The length required may be determined either by measuring it out with a pair of dividers or by trial and error as the thread is applied. Raised continuous lines for other purposes — degaussing cables for warships, moulded trim on car running boards, and so on — may be shown using a similar method, and if a groove can be scored along the pencilled lines before any cementing is undertaken, positioning is made that much easier.

A variety of finely-produced items can be prepared by subjecting stretched sprue to further heat influence. Holding one end of a length of filament towards a flame and rotating it in the hand will cause, with practice, a perfect mushroom head to be formed. Keeping the filament by the flame for longer periods of time and at different angles, and using filaments of varying thicknesses, will enable irregularly-shaped heads of differing sizes to be formed, and these can then be shaped with file or abrasive paper to the required configuration. Detaching the head a short distance along the shank will give a locating stub which can be inserted into a drilled hole on the model. In this way, rivets, nuts, boltheads and other miscellaneous items can be produced. Bringing filament under the influence of a hot needle, pyrogravure or even a burning cigarette end will enable curves and angles to be formed, and, once applied to the model and thoroughly set, the filament may if desired be gently sanded to give a flattened effect, which is useful for showing thin reinforcing strips, frameworks, and so forth.

Above: 'stretched sprue' – the plastic filament produced by heating sections of the runners contained in injection moulded kits – is especially useful to the ship modeller. This model, representing one of the famous US 'four stackers', shows the versatility of the material: liferaft racks, 20mm and 3in gun details, rail, rigging and other small components have been made up from it and patiently applied. The result, as can be seen, is extremely rewarding.
(Model: Paul Giltz. Photo: Donn Buerger)

It should be stressed that such detail should be affixed to a model using a brush that has been merely dampened with thin liquid cement. Excessive use of the fluid will reduce the definition of the detail once the model is painted, and in extreme cases may even melt it completely. The same can be said when relief is depicted over a comparatively large surface, such as with a prominent wing panel on an aircraft model. The use of thin plastic card, particularly that less than 0.005in gauge, presents peculiar problems since the effects of liquid cement can be quite insidious, perhaps only showing themselves some days after the work has been completed — wrinkling, creasing and general decomposition commonly occur if too much cement is used because of the slow evaporation rate. For this reason, many modellers prefer to use an adhesive rather than polystyrene cement, or else make the panels from materials such as foil, paper or card, where adhesion, though sometimes more difficult to achieve satisfactorily, has results that are at least reasonably predictable. Where these more tradiional substances are used, it is best to coat the finished surface a few times with liquid cement so as to prevent any subsequent lifting around the corners and to provide an impermeable base for the paint which will later be applied.

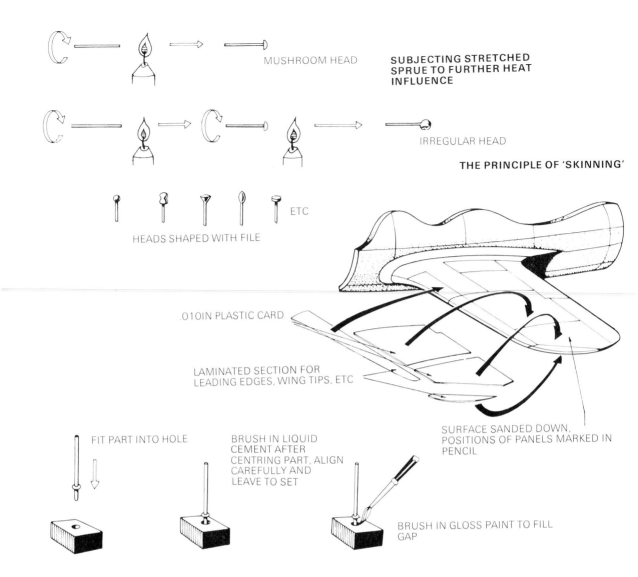

MUSHROOM HEAD

SUBJECTING STRETCHED
SPRUE TO FURTHER HEAT
INFLUENCE

IRREGULAR HEAD

THE PRINCIPLE OF 'SKINNING'

HEADS SHAPED WITH FILE

ETC

.010IN PLASTIC CARD

LAMINATED SECTION FOR
LEADING EDGES, WING TIPS, ETC

SURFACE SANDED DOWN,
POSITIONS OF PANELS MARKED IN
PENCIL

FIT PART INTO HOLE

BRUSH IN LIQUID
CEMENT AFTER
CENTRING PART, ALIGN
CAREFULLY AND
LEAVE TO SET

BRUSH IN GLOSS PAINT TO FILL
GAP

LOOSE-FITTING LOCATION HOLES

A development of the technique of adding panels from plastic card to provide raised detail is a process usually referred to as skinning, whereby a complete unit is covered with panels of this kind, thus in effect producing recessed detail because of the joints between them. As long as thin card is used, there will be no appreciable effect on the scaling of the model, assuming it to be accurate in the first place. This method is especially recommended if an attempt is being made to duplicate the surface structure of a panelled prototype, and may be regarded as an extension of the technique of producing structural shapes of compound curvature referred to earlier, although it involves work of much greater precision since, ideally, the use of filler should be avoided. Careful measuring, fitting and cementing are necessary, and in many cases experience in thermoforming plastic sheet is essential.

For some models, chiefly those with irregularly contoured surfaces such as figures, it is possible to use filler, paint, or a combination of plastic card and filler in much the same way as that described earlier for remodelling kit components. Tiny globules of fairly thick gloss paint can be used to represent coat buttons, for example, and a combination of filler and card might be used to produce pockets, collars, gauntlets, and the like. This kind of detailing calls for a fair degree of skill, since although errors can be rectified the intricacy of the work is such that the techniques involved are best applied only when thoroughly learnt.

One other form of surface detailing, if such it can be called, is a feature beloved of diorama enthusiasts and entails the representation of damage. Machines of war, after all, do come to grief in battle, and accidents do happen in everyday life. Such damage can lend an air of greater reality to a model since it relates it to an event rather than purely to a physical shape. Superficial damage may be shown by gouging, scraping and chipping the surface of the model with file or blade; more serious injuries might be depicted by using a heated awl to open out irregular holes or to facilitate the bending and denting of the components in question. Filler may be carefully applied in conjunction with these techniques to produce the desired result. At all times the appearance of the prototype should be borne in mind, and if necessary careful modelling to show any exposed internal details should be undertaken.

There is little to be said about small details which do not actually form part of the main structure of the model but are nevertheless essential for the sake of reality, since the preparation and assembly of such components differ little from the methods already discussed, except in the degree of intricacy involved. It is best to regard each of these items as a model in itself, and treat it accordingly, to the best of one's ability. Since access with filler or file is likely to be awkward, everything possible should be done to provide a perfect joint before bonding takes place, and so the preparatory test fitting should be carried out even more conscientiously than usual. Particular attention might be paid to location points. Where holes and other apertures are provided for positioning small parts, a deterioration of the moulds frequently means that kits which have been in production some considerable time have very loose-fitting joints, resulting in unsightly gaps when the parts are added. There are two methods of dealing with this. The locating holes may be filled flush with model putty and be re-drilled to the correct size, in which case care should be taken to ensure that the plastic below is reached so that the cement has something to act upon and make a good bond. Alternatively, the gaps may be filled with gloss paint after the details have been added and the cement has set. Where no locators are provided, such as with a vacuum formed kit, with hand-built components, or simply where detail not included in a kit is being added, it is helpful in securing a strong joint if they can be worked into the model, even if only in the form of a hollow in the surface of the plastic. A tiny pool of liquid cement may then be introduced into the hollow, and the detail fitted 'dry' in position. It is sometimes not possible to hold a small part in position whilst cement is being

Above: the portrayal of damage is a technique dear to the hearts of AFV modellers, but there is plenty of scope for such work with other subjects. Here, the careful application of heat has enabled dents and twisted panels to be shown on a stock car racer based on the Airfix 1/32 kit of the Sunbeam Rapier. Such vehicles allow the modeller to exercise considerable imagination with regard to damage and, resplendent in their garish colours, they make for interesting, out-of-the-ordinary models. The battered oildrum in the foreground is made from paper. (Model: George Hale)

applied — the adding of lengths of stretched sprue for rigging, whip aerials, and so forth are cases in point.

Details that are painted before being fitted to the model should have the paint removed by abrasion before the cement is used, since the covering sometimes prevents the solvent from reacting with the plastic. A good forty-eight hours should elapse between the painting of a component and the application of cement — longer if, for example, artists' oils are being used — so as to avoid the possibility of seepage crazing the paint.

The remark was passed earlier that the addition of detail to a model can really make the latter look convincing, but at the same time the importance of keeping everything in scale should be stressed. All that can be represented should be, but the inclusion of finely detailed parts can spoil the appearance of a model if they are out of proportion to the basic structure. If a particular item cannot be produced to the correct size, then it is better omitted — one would hardly expect rail to be added to a 1/1200 scale model of a ship, or eyelashes to be fitted to a 54mm figure. Some things, plainly, are impossible.

Chapter 4
Painting and finishing techniques

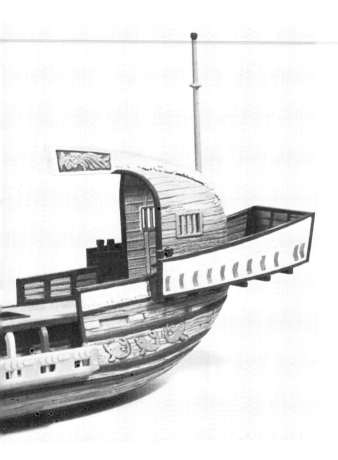

Above: natural substances are amongst the most difficult to simulate successfully by painting, and natural wood is perhaps the most challenging of all. This Greek warship (Imai, about 1/80 scale) is provided with finely textured parts which may be gently emphasised in painting, to good effect. An overall coat of sand coloured paint was applied to the 'wooden' areas of the model, varied from plank to plank by slight shading and tinting, and thinned brown paint was then allowed to run into the recessed detail. 'Shadow shading' has been carried out around the ornamental work using the same method.
(Model: Mick Miller)

The successful construction of a plastic model — indeed, any model — requires a certain level of physical skill allied to an appreciation of the structural shape of its prototype, but painting and finishing a model to a similar standard is rather more demanding. Skilful technique and a knowledge of the prototype are again called for, but these alone will not produce realism. Artistic ability, something more difficult to define, is also needed. This may be an understanding of the effects of light, a sense of colour interpretation, an ability to create illusions — call it what you will; it may be present as an innate talent and therefore practised unconsciously in the mechanical application of colouring matter to a surface, or it may be acquired by study and repeated exercise. In whatever way it is developed, artistic ability is necessary if a neat model is also to be a convincing one. Although there are a number of basic requirements for producing a satisfactory finish on a plastic model, therefore, some thought should perhaps first be given to what the modeller is trying to achieve when he applies colour to his model.

PRELIMINARY CONSIDERATIONS
Before selecting a particular medium to work with, it is advisable for the modeller to contemplate the type of surface he is striving to represent. Whilst the simulation of a painted surface such as may be found on a warship, tank or camouflaged aircraft is relatively straightforward and may in theory be achieved simply by scaling down the procedure adopted for the full sized subject, the imitation of natural hues such as occur in bare wood, natural metal, flesh, and so forth, or materials in which artificial colouring has been diffused, such as dyed wools, cloths or stained wood, is very much more difficult to accomplish convincingly. The major problem is that the colour values presented by such materials are rarely homogeneous. Wood is never

brown, cream or yellow, rather is it an accumulation of many differing hues in close proximity to one another; bare metal is rarely silver — more often is it a bluish, yellowish or greyish silver; human skin colouring is almost infinitely variable, depending as it does upon racial origin, geographical location, time of year, the amount of recent physical exertion, and so on, and even in one subject it is never of a uniform hue; cloths and similar materials are generally to be seen with an intricate pattern of folds and creases, creating subtle shadows and highlights which are extremely difficult to imitate purely by the application of paint that has a colour corresponding to the original, even if the sculpture itself is faithfully executed. The pursuit of realism in portraying surfaces that are devoid of artificial coatings is something that occupies the thoughts of modellers for a great deal of their time and is a problem for which there are no universally accepted remedies.

It is reasonable, however, to submit that the majority of plastic models represent prototypes which are themselves coated — for protection, for decoration or for camouflage — and it is entirely logical that a model should be treated in exactly the same way as the original in order to show this coating, in other words it should be painted. Technology has now been advanced to such a stage that the modelmaker has available a medium that begins to approach the ideal — one that is as much in scale as the model he builds. This has been possible through a reduction in the size of the pigment particles and in the viscosity of the medium but at the same time retaining its hiding and covering power. In addition, other desirable qualities such as rapid drying time and evenness of finish (both partly resulting from decreased viscosity) have been incorporated. The primary objective of this technology has been to reduce the thickness of the coating so that it approximates more to the scale of the model. Clearly, it can never correspond precisely, both because each batch has constant properties which can only be modified to a very minor degree by the modeller and because very small scale thicknesses cannot at present be achieved.

Despite the advances made to enable the thickness of the finished paint coating to be reduced, much less attention has so far been paid to scaling down the textural appearance and colour intensity of paint intended for model surfaces. The main reason for this is that these characteristics are not brought about merely by varying the composition of the coating medium but are also determined according to a number of external influences. These are concerned principally with the effects of light, which are many and varied. Colour, a product of

light, is not a tangible object but an effect realised by the reception by the human eye and transmission to the brain of reflected lightwaves of differing lengths and frequencies. Thus the first variable is the fickleness of the human eye, which receives light in a manner that differs slightly from person to person. In extreme cases, this variability is quite marked, for example a colour that one person interprets as green may appear blue to another. The surface that is responsible for reflecting the light to the eye, in other words the 'colour', is determined by the intensity of the light falling on it, the direction it comes from and its environment, meaning the amount and quality of light it receives in reflected form from the objects surrounding it. The less light there is for a surface to receive, the less will be reflected, an obvious example of this being the fact that colours appear darker at dusk than they do in broad daylight. Travelling as it does in straight lines, light is reflected from a surface at an angle equivalent to that at which it strikes it, and so the light received by the eye is very much dependent not only upon the direction from which it is transmitted, but also the inclination of the surface relative to the viewer. This can be appreciated by considering an object such as a cube — although it may be painted the same colour all over, one of the faces presented appears darker because it is in semi-shadow, that is, source light is not being reflected because the angle of incidence will not permit it to be. The objects surrounding the surface will modify the light reflected by it, and these need not be tangible in the sense that they are physically obstructive — moisture in the atmosphere is quite able to do the job. The light is therefore diffused, absorbed, refracted and reflected according to the nature of the objects it strikes. Perhaps the most significant result of this is what is known as the 'distance effect', whereby atmospheric particles so diffuse the light reflected from a surface that they begin to neutralise it, or more correctly reduce its saturation, the further away the object is the more neutralisation taking place.

The texture of the surface presented to the viewer is affected by light in much the same way as colour since this is also a function of reflection. If no light is being reflected from an object, it will lack not only colour but also lustre. A glossy surface appears so because the light it receives is reflected in its entirety, the surface being so smooth that none is 'lost' by being reflected at angles that do not permit it to reach the eye of the viewer. The further away the surface is, the more likelihood there exists of light being lost in this way, through refraction, reflection, etc., by particles in the atmosphere.

It should follow from this discussion that the

Above: some modellers dispute the authenticity of a flawless, pristine finish for model aircraft, but such an appearance is never more appropriate than to a pre-war US service aircraft, and there is no denying its attractiveness. A model produced to this standard – exemplified here with this Boeing P-12 built from the 1/32 scale Hasegawa kit – is arguably much more of a challenge than a matt finished, well-worn one, since any mistakes that might be made would be very obvious and difficult to disguise.
(Model and photo: Stan Staples)

modeller may need to think very carefully about the paints he chooses before he applies them to his model. Although modelling paints allow him to achieve something approaching the correct scale thickness of coating for his models, he may wish to modify them in an effort to obtain the best compromise in respect of colour and lustre. The smaller the scale of the model, the further away it is, in effect, from the human eye and the more drastic are the modifications required to capture the sensations outlined above. He cannot hope to be completely successful — taking things to the extreme, a model of a 25pdr gun depicted in action during the initial barrage at El Alamein, for example, might in theory be painted black since the actual event took place at night and the weapon would not therefore reflect any light — but he can attempt to convey at least the effect of distance under normal light conditions (however these might be defined) by reducing the intensity of the paints he uses. This can normally be done by tinting the colour that has been decided upon as matching the original, in other words mixing it with white, by neutralising it by adding grey, or by shading it by mixing in black. As a general guide, dark colours should be tinted, pale ones shaded and intermediate ones neutralised, but shading will usually only be necessary for pure white paint since this is the only one which, when applied, is totally reflective. High gloss finishes

should be avoided for similar reasons, and the lustre of each colour carefully regulated. Modelling paints do go some way towards meeting the latter requirement, but of course take no account of the scale of the model on which they are to be used.

It should also be apparent that any paint that is claimed to match precisely the original surface finish it represents should never be used on a model without being reduced in intensity. The intensity should lessen with decreasing scale: for example, a colour exactly matching the Sea Blue Gloss used on American carrier aircraft during the late 1940s and early 1950s would need to be tinted and have its lustre reduced to an optimum level for a 1/32 scale model, still more for a 1/144 scale model, and still more again for the 1/700 scale models that are included with certain kits of US aircraft carriers. The insoluble problem facing the modeller is the fact that the variables are in no way measurable. He has to rely on what appears to his eyes to be realistic — and what seems right to him will quite possibly seem incorrect to others.

There are further reasons why modellers should be extremely wary of using paints that are claimed to duplicate the colour of that used on the full sized original. It is rarely possible to match another colour with absolute precision, and even when it is, chemical or physical decomposition, or at least chemical or physical change, begins as soon as it is exposed to the elements. This reasoning applies to the paint being used on the model, but more particularly to that used on the prototype. Some pigments are affected quite quickly and quite markedly by ultra-violet rays in sunlight, notably crimson lake, magenta, mauve and Vandyke brown, and as a result suffer loss of permanence. Thus it has to be asked at what stage of its life the prototype colour was matched, and what sort of changes the paint applied to the model is likely to undergo. Another aspect of this proposition is the fact that batches of paint prepared both for the prototype and for the modeller to use, though they may be nominally identical, are very seldom so in reality. Anyone who has over a period of time used a number of tinlets of paint from a manufacturer that are supposedly identical in colour will quickly appreciate this. Once again, 'authentic' paints should be regarded only as an approximation of the colour the modeller requires, and whilst this might at first seem perplexing, it does in fact give him quite a considerable latitude of choice, and provided the general impression conveyed seems to conform with reality, it would take a brave man — or a reckless one — to quarrel with that choice.

Painted surfaces may quite adequately be represented by using any of the proprietary modelling paints, but, as mentioned earlier in this section, the portrayal of natural surfaces, and of materials impregnated with colour, is a much more difficult question. These surfaces may be hard or soft in character, and the harder they are, the more capable they are of being abraded to produce a sheen, provided that they are of a sufficient thickness in the first place. Thus materials like balsa wood and wool cannot be polished by friction in their raw state because of their soft and fibrous nature, but most metals can because they are of sufficient hardness and density to allow it. Some natural substances, owing to the fact that they are homogeneous in character and consist of perhaps a single element, have peculiar reflective qualities not found with any other materials, metals again being the most obvious examples of these. Others, such as wood, are composed of many different chemical elements and have a surface which is extremely irregular, which therefore produces many different qualities of light — and thus many different colours — and a complex arrangement of angles at which the light is reflected. Still others may reflect only one colour, but due to their flexibility may receive and reflect light at a number of differing, though not random, angles across their surface. Because paint is composed of particles bound together with a virtually transparent oil, gum or resin, it cannot adequately reproduce the reflective qualities of a metal; since there is no way of controlling the arrangement of its pigment particles, other than ensuring a fairly even distribution, it cannot, through the application of a single colour, represent a substance composed of a number of differing chemical elements or one whose surface features random irregularities.

A number of other media are used by modellers in an attempt to overcome these problems. Artists' oils, by virtue of the fact that they have a slow drying time, thus allowing them to be blended during application, and that their degree of gloss can be very conveniently regulated simply by varying the amounts of binder and solvent as they are mixed, are particularly suited to the representation of highly heterogeneous materials such as wood, or for showing highlights and subtle changes of colour that may be required in painting a number of other natural non-metallic substances. Another advantage in using artists' oils is that they may quite safely be mixed with other media such as ordinary domestic oil paints and modelling enamels, to give a wide range of possible combinations. Water colours as such have little to recommend them in respect of plastic models, but water soluble paints — acrylics, designers' gouache, and so on — are in common use and offer brilliant colours and good covering power. However, in common with artists' oils, they are not particularly suitable for applying large, smooth areas of colour because of the difficulties in eliminating brush marks and in obtaining even coverage.

The search for a medium that will accurately simulate the scale appearance of polished metal has been one of the great sagas in the history of modelling, and one that has received added impetus with the rise in popularity of the plastic kit. It is probably true to say that an entirely satisfactory answer has yet to be found, although several materials which solve specific problems have been developed. Silver paints that are very finely pigmented have been produced, and their tones may be varied by adding small amounts of other colours such as blue, grey or brown to give a good range of effects, but on close inspection the surface applied with this medium will prove to have been obviously painted. Careful techniques will enable convincing effects to be conveyed when a model is viewed at longer range, however, especially if a slightly weathered appearance is required, but generally the finish will lack the polished undertones necessary for realism. At the other extreme, metal foil will impart a flawless sheen to a model so applied, but complex contours are somewhat difficult to negotiate and the general effect can look a little contrived if the type of foil is not carefully selected or if subtle tone changes are not introduced in suitable places. Other preparations such as Rub 'n Buff and Liqu-a-Plate are more versatile than either paint or foil in that they may be polished, thereby allowing the modeller

RECEPTION AND DEFLECTION OF LIGHT – GLOSSY SURFACES

ANGLE OF INCIDENCE   ANGLE OF REFLECTION

RECEPTION AND DEFLECTION OF LIGHT – MATT SURFACES

The realistic simulation of natural metal on a scale plastic model has been a besetting problem for years, and these four photographs illustrate some of the methods in which it may be tackled.

Top left: three methods have been put to use with this model of an F-104DJ Starfighter, built from the 1/72 scale Heller kit. The rear fuselage has two areas of aluminium foil, between which silver paint has been applied by brush; the rest of the model has been airbrushed with dulled silver paint, with the exception of the upper wing surfaces which are white. The variations in texture produced by the three methods are readily apparent. (Model: Mike Bailey)

Top right: another solution is the application of a metallic paste such as Goldfinger or Rub 'n Buff. The paste may be applied by means of a cloth or a sponge, or even the tip of the forefinger, and for difficult angles a paintbrush may be used. Coats should be applied sparingly and then buffed up until the required sheen is achieved. The substance is readily thinned or removed with white spirit and may be mixed successfully with enamels to give a variety of hues. Rub 'n Buff has been applied with a piece of sponge to this 1/72 scale model of a North American Harvard T2B. (Model: Geoff Prentice)

Bottom left: another product used by modellers to simulate natural metal is Liqu-A-Plate, seen here applied to Airfix's 1/72 F-86D Sabre. This preparation is manufactured in the USA and requires the use of an airbrush, but the 'granular' finish of paint is largely eliminated if it is applied correctly and then gently polished up with a soft cloth. However, since as its name suggests it approximates to a thin layer of foil once dry, it is not particularly durable and may begin to flake off if the model is subjected to careless handling. (Model: Bob Patmore)

Bottom right: a variation of the Rub 'n Buff method is illustrated in these 1/1 scale LS revolver models, a Remington .44 Army weapon (top) and a .45 Colt 'Peacemaker'. The paste is applied with a cloth together with small quantities of aluminium, gold and black ink and then polished up until the correct texture is obtained. (Models: Bob Earey)

to control the lustre of the finished surface. More will be said about metal effects in subsequent chapters.

As with every other aspect of modelling, painting and finishing will always be something of a compromise. Even the lighting conditions prevailing at the time the completed model is under scrutiny may influence the way in which the job is tackled, since artificial lighting can throw strange shadows and produce a number of other peculiar effects that can disturb any impression of realism that has been created, especially if painting has been carried out in daylight conditions. Once again, no hard and fast rules can be laid down, only guidance offered, and the modeller, having taken all the circumstances into consideration, must remain the sole arbiter between any conflicting options.

PREPARATION

The segregation of the construction and the painting of a model into two distinct stages will rarely be possible if a realistic scale miniature is to be built, bearing in mind the types of subjects that find most favour with modellers. The majority of models feature relatively inaccessible but nevertheless visible areas which demand that certain painting tasks must be undertaken before assembly is completed. Vehicle interiors, the clutter of superstructure on a ship and the diversity of personal equipment for a figure, for example, will dictate that a number of sub-assemblies be produced, painted and fitted together — in that order — so that a convincing model may be achieved. A sub-assembly may comprise fifty parts or one part, but will consist of a unit made up of as many components that may be assembled together without creating problems of access while it is being painted. It is often the case that one sub-assembly only forms a part of another, and that the sequence of production, painting and fitting has to be repeated several times before a model is finished. It is therefore desirable that the painting of a model is carefully planned, or at least considered, before assembly begins, although modellers specialising in one type of subject will, as their experience grows, find that a cursory glance will tell them all they need to know.

As soon as a sub-assembly is structurally complete and its flaws have been rectified, the surfaces to be painted should be carefully inspected to ensure that they are perfectly clean. Since each part of a plastic model needs some attention from a knife, file or abrasive paper, it will inevitably collect swarf, and because of the electrostatic properties of the material this cannot adequately be removed simply by brushing it off. In addition, normal atmospheric dust will be precipitated, traces of release agent from the moulding process may be present, and if the surface has been handled a certain amount of natural oil from the fingertips will have been transferred to it. All, or as much as possible, of this deposited matter should be removed.

If the surface still shows signs of fine abrasion, minute particles of swarf may be difficult to see, and the area may be polished with toothpaste or a household metal polish such as Duraglit or Brasso to restore the sheen of the plastic. Liquid cement may be brushed on to obtain a similar result, although larger particles may not be entirely dissolved and may become embedded in the surface. Grease and dust may also effectively be removed by applying metal polish, but the polishing process will itself leave particles of fluff which in turn will need to be got rid of. This may be done by washing the sub-assemblies in water, which if grease is still present should be warm and reinforced with a few drops of liquid household detergent. The water should be worked thoroughly into all the affected areas with a large, soft paintbrush, and the parts may be left on a mesh rack in a dust-free container — an oven is ideal — to drain. To speed up this process, large droplets may be soaked up on the corner of a piece of folded tissue or removed with compressed air blown through an airbrush, but the parts should on no account be wiped clean since further fluff may be deposited and the plastic surface electrostatically charged again. Once the

parts have dried completely, they may be stored in an enclosed container until they are to be painted.

The importance of cleanliness cannot be over-emphasised, and it will follow that some form of jig or other device for holding the units to be painted is desirable so that they need not be handled directly, and an additional jig may be required if there is no alternative to physically grasping them so that a free circulation of air is allowed to take place while the paint is drying out. However, it is frequently possible to hold a model with the fingers in such a way that they come into contact only with a part of the surface that will remain unpainted — a large tank turret with a locating ring at its base, or a hull unit for a waterline ship model, for example — and the parts may also be stable enough to be conveniently rested on a flat surface, paint tin or other suitable support while they are allowed to dry. Painting in the hand certainly permits a greater degree of manipulation and control than would be given if a jig were used, but because of stability problems this is often the only satisfactory method, and small parts will in general have to be managed on a jig anyway.

The most versatile type of jig is simply a piece of modelling clay such as Plasticine. This can be moulded with great ease, and in addition has, if fresh, a certain adhesive quality which enables a part to be held quite firmly. Mounting techniques using Plasticine are a study in themselves, and with a little ingenuity the modeller will be able to devise all manner of intricate shapes to hold the parts in the safest possible way, always ensuring, of course, that the material never comes into contact with any surface that is to receive paint since its oil will have a

CLEAN OFF FLUFF WITH BRUSH
AND WATER

POLISH WITH METAL POLISH OR
TOOTHPASTE

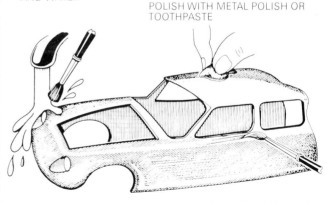

RESTORE SHEEN WITH SINGLE
STROKE OF LIQUID CEMENT

**FINAL PREPARATION OF PARTS
PRIOR TO PAINTING**

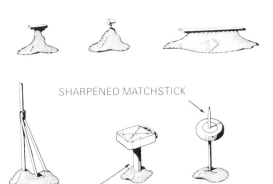

SHARPENED MATCHSTICK

SPRUE CEMENTED TEMPORARILY
TO 'UNSEEN' FACE OF PART

PLASTICINE JIGS

SPINDLE BEARING

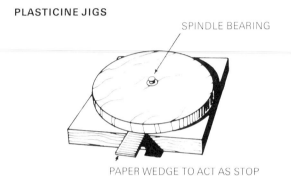

PAPER WEDGE TO ACT AS STOP

TURNTABLE SUPPORT

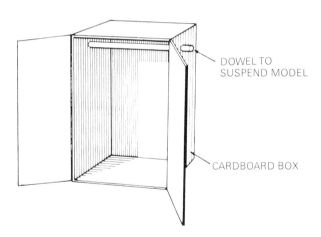

DOWEL TO
SUSPEND MODEL

CARDBOARD BOX

A SIMPLE SPRAYING BOOTH

detrimental effect on the finish. The most useful moulded shape is the basic pyramid or cone, into the apex of which may be pushed the locating pins of small injection moulded parts, or against which may be pressed the contact or otherwise hidden surfaces of structures that lack these pins. The apex may be pinched out so that it may more conveniently support narrow surfaces, or worked into a wedge for long ones. A block of clay may be moulded into

several cones to conform with complex surfaces or to support a number of small parts at the same time. Parts such as wheels, where the location point may be in the form of a hole or a circular recess rather than a pin, can be adequately supported by shaving a piece of kit runner or a matchstick to a point and pressing it into the part, pushing the free end into a piece of clay while the paint dries. In some cases it is possible to drill a tiny hole into a contact surface and press a pin into it to form a handle; on other occasions it is sometimes helpful to attach a piece of dowel or runner with glue to serve the same purpose for larger units. Parts may also be painted by gripping them in a pair of pointed tweezers during application, and then stored to dry by transferring them to a piece of modelling clay.

To guard against difficulties of identification, it is often helpful to use a numbering system for small parts of similar configuration. As each is removed from its runner, shaped and cleaned, it can immediately be mounted on a piece of modelling clay and transferred to a piece of card with the number quoted on the instruction sheet set down by it. Alternatively, individual numbering cards can be pushed into the base of the clay support.

With some types of model, notably aircraft, a painted surface may have to be handled whilst further paint is applied elsewhere, and to protect the finish a flat piece of thin foam rubber may be laid over the area to be touched. Movement of this material is to be avoided so as to remove the possibility of any accidental buffing, and so it may be lightly bound with adhesive tape to keep it in position. If a model or a separate sub-assembly is to be painted overall, it can often be tackled in two stages, mounting it accordingly in two different attitudes, but where this is not possible it will have to be mounted on a rather complicated jig — this is especially important if the paint is to be sprayed rather than brushed. Stout wire may be bent in such a way that it springs against hidden interior surfaces and holds the part securely — openings like exhaust nozzles, intakes and gun muzzles are sometimes available, and external locating holes can be utilised as well, provided care is taken to ensure that no paint is allowed to fill any gaps occurring between jig and model. Each structure will have to be treated on its own merits of course, but the essential requirements are that it is held firmly and remains undamaged whilst being held.

Two larger pieces of equipment for supporting a model, especially for spraying operations, are frequently used by modellers. One is a simple turntable, which might consist of a piece of ½in (1.27cm) blockboard 10in by 10in (25.4cm by 25.4cm) into the centre of which is located some form of metal bearing mechanism, perhaps from a child's constructional toy such as Meccano or adapted from an old record player, over which fits a circular piece of ½in blockboard of an appropriate diameter, say, 10in again. This enables a model to be set down and rotated so that the optimum position relative to the paintbrush or airbrush can be obtained, and ensures that physical handling of the model is kept to an absolute minimum. A number of turntable tops of differing sizes may be prepared so that models of all dimensions are readily accessible. The other piece of equipment, which may be used in conjunction with the first, is simply a large cardboard box turned on end to form a spraying booth. It will be obvious that not all the paint that leaves the nozzle of an aerosol or an airbrush actually lands on the model, and so some form of protection for its surroundings is essential. Further, models or assemblies on a wire jig can be suspended from the roof of the box or otherwise mounted in it to permit spraying from all directions.

BRUSH PAINTING
Paint, the substance most widely used for coating

Below: provided care is taken, quite realistic deception can be achieved merely by painting. The 'sea' around HMS *Campbeltown,* the subject of this 1/600 diorama, was made from plaster, but an impression of depth around the submerged stern has been conveyed by blending the paints used to finish the model and adding a stroke or two of gloss varnish.

plastic models, consists essentially of three ingredients. Its pigment is made up of a large number of fine particles, and not only provides the colour element but also enables the original surface colouration to be obliterated, and may have other less important functions such as modifying sheen and assisting adhesion; its binder enables the pigment particles to be held together and adhere to the surface over which the paint is applied; its liquid may dissolve the binder, or it may merely allow the pigment and binder to be held in suspension, but in either case it is the ingredient which gives the paint its fluidity, and it is usually, if rather loosely, referred to as the solvent. As well as these constituents, a number of different additives may be used, each performing a specific task in modifying certain characteristics of the paint. These are generally concerned with altering viscosity, accelerating the drying process or determining the final surface sheen of the paint, and it will be readily apparent that these substances assume great importance in the manufacture of modelling paints since the qualities they impart are held in high regard by the modeller. The actual amounts used are relatively insignificant in terms of volume, but the effects are far-reaching.

The development of paints involves complex chemical technology in order to cope with their required physical properties. The tolerances needed for paints that are to be used on models are much more stringent than for the average household product, which partly explains their high relative cost. Of particular importance is the nature of the pigmentation. Perhaps the most obvious require-

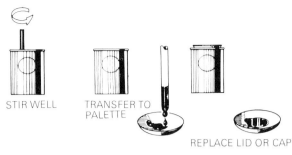

STIR WELL TRANSFER TO PALETTE REPLACE LID OR CAP

PREPARATION OF PAINT – ENAMEL

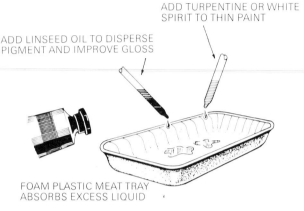

ADD TURPENTINE OR WHITE SPIRIT TO THIN PAINT

ADD LINSEED OIL TO DISPERSE PIGMENT AND IMPROVE GLOSS

FOAM PLASTIC MEAT TRAY ABSORBS EXCESS LIQUID

PREPARATION OF PAINT – ARTISTS' OILS

DIP BRUSH UNTIL ABOUT 1/3 BRISTLES ARE COVERED

DRAW OFF EXCESS PAINT

LOADING THE BRUSH

ment is that it should remain insoluble in its vehicle, that is its binder and liquid, so that the application of a second coat of paint may be accomplished without any bleeding of the first. Lightfastness, dependent basically upon the pigment's resistance to chemical decomposition, is another consideration and one of special relevance to model finishes, where the paint is primarily decorative in function and is not generally subject to periodic renewal. A further factor in the preparation of pigment for scale modelling paints concerns the size and shape of the particles of which it is composed, since this

will to a large extent determine its covering power, its reflective qualities and the volume of vehicle required.

The respective functions of the binder and liquid elements in paint are in some ways inter-related, and many of the substances used for each task in fact perform both and others besides. The actual composition of a binder or a liquid will of course vary according to the type of paint being produced, but the former is generally a natural or synthetic resin or a natural extractive drying oil or gum, whilst the latter is usually a petroleum-based solvent or a natural substance such as turpentine or water, which evaporates after the paint has been applied. Although, as it will be readily appreciated, many of these substances are incompatible, there is considerable latitude available when combining liquids and binders, even to the extent of admixing natural and synthetic materials.

The paint supplied in the tinlet or jar which is purchased by the modeller has thus been very carefully prepared to give the best possible properties, given its retail price. If the best possible results are to be achieved when using it, therefore, it should be treated with respect, and to this end a few simple rules might be observed. First, it is of paramount importance that the ingredients of the paint are mixed thoroughly together before use so that they have the opportunity of being evenly dispersed over the surface of the model when applied to it and so that the ratio of pigment to binder to liquid remains constant throughout the paint's shelf life. Ready-to-use paints such as modelling enamels will quickly have their constituent substances separated according to their respective densities if they are left undisturbed, and not only must the paint be stirred before it is used, it must also be continually agitated during use. The stirring instrument should ideally be metal, since this gives the required strength and is easily cleaned, but lengths of plastic runner may also be used and can be considered as expendable. Stirrers made from other substances such as wood are generally to be avoided since they will readily transfer dust, splinters, and so forth, into the paint. The agitation will need to be kept up for a considerable period of time — perhaps five minutes — and steps should be taken to ensure that all the pigment is intermixed and not left in the corners of the container.

Secondly, it is essential that the unused paint in the container is kept airtight. Contact with the air will quickly cause evaporation of the liquid, and the residue will consequently thicken up. Paint should never be applied directly from its original container since this would require its cap, lid or stopper to be off for a long period of time, and if the brush were continually being dipped into the paint, some would inevitably be transferred to the rim and begin to harden, thereby preventing the airtight seal that is needed once the lid is replaced. The paint that is to be applied to a model should therefore be conveyed to a palette, using either a miniature ladle from a mustard pot or a simple syringe such as an eye-dropper. Any build-up of paint that occurs on container or cap should immediately be removed with a lint-free cloth or tissue and the cap replaced as soon as the required amount of paint has been taken. The type of palette required will depend upon the volume and viscosity of the paint, but for most purposes a shallow foil tray or a porcelain dish will suffice, although disposable containers such as bottle tops or pre-formed trays that are supplied with boxes of sweets will, provided they are properly rinsed out beforehand, be preferred by some.

Paints such as artists' oils should be treated in similar fashion; in fact, because of their composition, they will *have* to be transferred to a palette and carefully mixed before use. It will also be necessary to increase the ratio of vehicle to pigment before they can be smoothly applied by adding more diluent (linseed oil or turpentine) or solvent (turpentine or white spirit). An absorbent palette such as a foam plastic meat tray is favoured by many modellers since excess liquid can be easily dealt with. The thinning of any paint should be carried out in a palette and not in the original container. With artists' oils and other media supplied in a tube this will be imperative anyway, but it applies equally to ready-to-use paints. The reasons are that the thinning agent may have a detrimental effect on the pigment or vehicle by reducing its durability, sheen, covering power or colour intensity if stored with them over a period of time, especially if they are of synthetic, oleoresinous origin, whereas the specific function of thinners is to improve the fluidity of the paint without affecting any of its other properties, and it is rapidly evaporated when the paint is applied to a surface in a thin layer. Caution should also be exercised when colours are mixed together, even if they originate from a common range. Where a particular colour is unobtainable, sufficient paint should be prepared to cover the required area and enable any retouching to be carried out at a later stage — an old tinlet or an airtight jar may be cleaned out to act as a storage container. A record of the colour may be kept on a sample card and its tin marked accordingly for future reference, together with details of how it is prepared, but if such mixes are stored over a long period of time the ingredients may prove to be not entirely compatible and the quality of the paint may suffer.

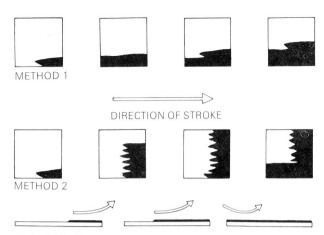

METHOD 1

DIRECTION OF STROKE

METHOD 2

ARC DESCRIBED BY BRUSH

BRUSH STROKES

HAND PAINTED BOUNDARIES

1 DRAW OUT BOUNDARY WITH SOFT PENCIL

2 DRAW BOUNDARY WITH BRUSH

3 FEATHER EDGES AWAY FROM BOUNDARY

4 FILL IN

MASKED BOUNDARIES

1 DRAW IN BOUNDARY LINE WITH LIGHTLY LOADED BRUSH

2 FEATHER EDGES AWAY FROM BOUNDARY

3 FILL IN

4 REMOVE MASKING TAPE BY PEELING BACK ALONG ITSELF

BRUSH PAINTING BOUNDARIES

WHITE SPIRIT

DIRTY ◄──────► CLEAN

DRAW BRISTLES THROUGH CLEAN RAG. RINSE UNDER TAP IF REQUIRED

CLEANING BRUSHES

The decision as to which type of brush needs to be used for a particular painting task is very much a matter of personal choice, but it might be mentioned that it is not so much the size of brush as the manner in which it is wielded that determines whether a paint finish looks neat or not. Fine brushes are available from very small (000) sizes up to large (10) and are pointed; also available is a wide variety of more specialised brushes such as mops, stencil brushes and chisel-head brushes, all of which are useful in their way but could be regarded as being not entirely necessary. The principal requirements for a brush that is to be used on small scale models are that it should be of good quality, possess fine hairs and be tapered so that it can be brought to a fine point. Broad, flat brushes are helpful in covering large, unimpeded surfaces of a model, but they do pose problems when a stroke is being started or finished, and they are not easy to clean thoroughly. Very small brushes tend to lose their effectiveness very quickly and cannot really perform any task that a slightly larger brush brought to a fine point cannot undertake. Good quality, sable haired brushes, which are the best obtainable, are extremely expensive, and therefore many modellers have to be very selective when purchasing them. Sizes 1, 2 and 3, provided the individual specimens are chosen carefully and are used correctly, will meet virtually all the modeller's needs and will last him a long time.

It is possible successfully to paint a model with a single application of the finishing colour, but priming and sealing will normally have to be carried out in certain areas, an undercoat is often desirable, and two or more topcoats are sometimes necessary. To guard against problems that may crop up at a late stage in the painting of a model, all areas of filler should be primed with thinned household primer, or sealed with a thin coat of white or grey paint. The porous nature of many filling compounds can often lead to differential sheen or colour value in these areas if only the topcoat is applied, and sealing or priming has the added attraction of providing yet another opportunity for inspecting the model's surface for flaws and dealing with them if necessary. Priming will also be required for any areas of bare metal that may need to be painted and for providing a base for water-soluble paints, whilst polyethylene surfaces will require a special primer in the form of diluted PVA glue before paints can be applied. Undercoating is sometimes necessary, particularly where a light coloured topcoat is required on a dark plastic surface, where the topcoat is extremely fluid, or where yellow, orange or red surfaces are involved. Experience will enable the modeller to determine whether an undercoat is a

helpful factor in achieving a satisfactory finish, but if any doubt exists it is better to apply one. The number of topcoats required can be ascertained as painting proceeds — generally speaking, the thinner the paint the more likelihood there is of additional coats being necessary. Thin paint will allow rapid coverage and reduce the risk of brushmarks, and it is more workable than thick, permitting awkward angles to be negotiated easily and diminishing the prominence of overlapping coats; on the other hand, the application of several coats will prolong the overall painting task since the increased proportion of thinning agent will usually act as a solvent for any paint over which it is applied, and ample time should therefore be allowed to elapse between each application, forty-eight hours being not too long a period.

Whilst a carefully prepared model surface, carefully prepared paints and good quality brushes are essential considerations, they will be of little consequence if some thought is not given to the actual brushing process. The loading of the brush and the positioning, direction and pressure of the strokes all contribute to successful painting, whilst the size and shape of the area to be covered will influence to some extent the techniques used. The amount of paint loaded on to the brush should be such that even coverage is achieved throughout the length of the stroke. The brush will normally need to be dipped into the paint until approximately one third of the head is covered. It should then be drawn across a clean surface to remove excess paint, thereby ensuring that a pool does not develop at the beginning of the stroke that is applied to the model. The head should never be totally immersed in the paint since this will cause flow problems as the liquid on the outside of the bristles begins to set and also difficulties when the brush is being cleaned — a general guide is that only that part of the brush which may be expected to come into contact with the model should receive paint during loading.

The physical size of the object being painted does not really affect the brushing technique, although it will of course determine the amount of paint that is loaded and, to some extent, the size and shape of the brush employed. The method of brushing is largely controlled by the need to ensure that an even, thin coat is achieved, and the most important consideration here is that the paint from one stroke is not allowed to set before being overlapped by another. The surface being painted should ideally be horizontal so that the paint has no chance to move under the influence of gravity once it is applied; where this is not possible, extra care needs to be taken to give the thinnest possible covering so that the paint sets up quickly before it can begin to flow away. This is another argument for applying an undercoat — the absorbent nature of the first covering promotes rapid drying of the second. Strokes should be applied lightly and evenly throughout their length. They should be begun on a part of the surface not previously covered, the initial stroke being made towards the edge of the surface or towards an area where any build up of paint caused by overlapping a coat that has dried out will not be immediately obvious on the finished model. The second and subsequent strokes may either be made ahead of the first, the brush being lifted gently from the model as it overlaps the previous stroke; where the second and subsequent strokes are made adjacent to the first, a very light stroke with an unloaded brush may be made at the junctions to assist even coverage. The final strokes are in many ways the most important. Unless there is a well defined edge to the shape being painted, the start of each stroke will have to be made in much the same way as it is finished, that is, the brush will have to first meet the surface under virtually no pressure, with only its very tip in contact. As the stroke proceeds, more pressure can be applied, and the stroke is completed in the same way as the previous ones.

However, painting a model is not quite as simple as this, since surface detail, nooks and crannies and complex contours have to be negotiated. Moreover, demarcation lines between contrasting colours have to be accurately represented, and highlighting and shading may be necessary for effect. Fortunately, the specialised modelling paints available have excellent covering power, and so the direction in which each stroke is executed is not as important as for other types of paint. The general rule to be followed in dealing with the nuances of scale models is never to allow paint to accumulate in corners or recesses or against raised detail, and strokes will have to be made in a number of different directions in order to ensure that this is so. The brush should therefore be used for mopping paint as well as applying it, and subtle changes of pressure will enable a covering of reasonably uniform thickness to be achieved, always provided that the paint is sufficiently diluted with thinners to remain workable for long enough. Once the applied paint has begun to lose its wetness, it should not be touched, even if it has not adequately hidden the underlying colour — a second overall coat should be administered when the first has completely hardened off, and gentle sanding with a very fine abrasive paper will level out any irregularities that need attention. It is similarly very risky to attempt to remove paint from a surface once it has been put on, unless the complete application is removed. A rag moistened with white spirit or other suitable solvent may be

Above: it would take a very steady hand to produce a scheme like this without having recourse to masking tape. The red recognition bands on the upper wing surfaces, typical Italian practice during the late 1930s and early 1940s, were masked off prior to painting them by using ordinary clear adhesive tape. The fin striping, a feature often provided in decal form with plastic kits, has also been painted in conjunction with masking tape – decals do not always hold the complex leading and trailing edge contours satisfactorily. The model, representing a Savoia-Marchetti SM81, is built from the Supermodel 1/72 scale kit.

used to remove unwanted paint, but the consequent problems of fluff and the probable effects on any surrounding paintwork will have to be dealt with before recoating can take place.

Boundaries between paints of differing colours can cause a great deal of trouble to modellers, mainly because of the need to ensure that they are precisely positioned. Where each area of contrasting colour is large, such as on a two-tone paint scheme for a vehicle or with a disruptive camouflage pattern for a ship or a tank, it is generally advisable to apply the lightest colour over the complete structure since this will act as an undercoat for subsequent applications and will ensure that only one boundary for each colour change will need to be tackled. Whether it is better to mask off surrounding areas before the second colour is brushed on or merely to paint freehand is an argument that is fairly easily decided for hard, straight boundaries, but one that is not so easy to resolve for irregular ones. Masking will permit an accurately positioned hard boundary to be shown on the model, but the natural capillarity of the paint makes it very difficult to avoid a ridge forming along it when the mask is removed. A compromise is favoured by many modellers — the positions of the boundaries are lightly marked out with a soft pencil and the paint is then applied freehand, and this is perhaps the best general solution.

Masking materials, as outlined in Chapter 2, take two principal forms, the flexible adhesive papers and tapes, and the rubbery solutions that are applied by brush. The tapes will fairly easily conform to simple curves and can usually be stretched to take in compound curves of a gentle nature; adhesive stencil material may be used to assist accuracy in painting broad localised areas such as camouflage bands or sharply defined shapes such as circles, squares and triangles, and again will conform to simple curves; fluid masking materials are essential if small or intricately contoured areas need to be masked, but they can be considered as being of lesser significance when a model is brush painted than when it is airbrushed since they themselves need to be applied with a brush and call for neat and accurately positioned edges too.

To minimise the prominence of the ridge that might be formed when the paint is applied, the masking tape should be as thin as possible, be cleanly cut and be pressed very firmly on to the model. Sellotape or Scotch **transparent** tape cut into thin strips using a steel ruler and craft knife on a sheet of glass is probably the best material to meet these requirements, and provided the plastic surface below has been correctly prepared so that the paint has keyed properly, and sufficient drying time has been allowed for each coat, the tape will have no effect on the model when it is later removed. For curved boundaries, actual masking tape may be preferable because of its semi-elastic qualities, and this can be prepared in similar fashion. It does, however, have the disadvantages of being some-what thicker than Sellotape and can thus leave a more prominent paint ridge when it is removed, and of forming a less satisfactory seal with the model surface, which encourages paint to creep beneath it. The tackiness of any tape used for masking should not be deliberately reduced before it is put on to the model as this may also lead to seepage underneath it.

As with freehand painting, any handling of the model whilst the tape is positioned should be kept to a minimum, and the use of a soft, lint-free glove is to be recommended. Every effort should be made to position the tape correctly at the first attempt, and to assist this, only one end of the tape should initially be positioned. The edge that is to form the boundary may be gently burnished with the tip of a smooth metal spatula once it has been accurately placed, and the remaining length of tape kept taut, away from the surface of the model, until the boundary line has been correctly sighted. It can then be laid gently along the model, its edge burnished as before. Particular care must be taken where the tape crosses areas or surface detail — its stretching qualities will allow most minor irregularities to be taken in successfully, although more prominent detail may have to be masked separately. The tape, in fact any adhesive masking material, can be shaped whilst on the surface of the model by slicing

it with the tip of a sharp blade, although this should be done very delicately so as not to damage the paint surface below. Any unwanted material can be gently lifted at one corner with the blade and then peeled back on itself to be removed.

The painting of an area bounded by masking material may be treated in much the same way as any other area, but paint should not be encouraged to build up against the mask. Strokes should therefore be made parallel to or away from the mask, and the brush should be very lightly loaded. The masking material should be removed at the earliest opportunity after painting has been completed, ideally while the paint is still wet, so that a clean edge is made. If the paint is allowed to dry, it may adhere to the mask and a ragged edge may result when the latter is removed. If a second topcoat is required, the area to be painted may be masked off again when the paint previously applied has completely dried out, but it is often possible to apply the paint freehand, since the ridge that will inevitably be formed along the boundary acts as a barrier and will tend to confine the paint within it.

Where demarcation lines are applied by hand, the sharp paint ridge caused by a masking material will not be formed, but the care required to achieve an accurate boundary line generally means that the paint has to be administered much more slowly, thus giving it a chance to dry, with the consequent problems of overlaps when infilling is tackled. There are two ways of avoiding this. One is to paint the boundary lines section by section an inch (2cm) or so at a time, infilling the remaining area as each part of the boundary is produced. This method is suitable for relatively small areas, since the work still has to be accomplished very rapidly. Alter-natively — and this is the system that will generally have to be adopted for large areas of contrasting colour — the boundaries may be drawn with a fine brush and the paint then feathered away from them towards the area that has to be infilled. Once the paint has thoroughly hardened, the vacant areas may be painted in a more leisurely fashion, the paint again being feathered, this time towards the boundary so that it overlaps the first application. A flawless finish is very difficult to achieve, but with practice quite convincing results can be obtained.

Contrary to popular opinion, it is perfectly feasible to produce a soft boundary line with a paintbrush in order to represent a sprayed finish, although the method is so time consuming that many may not wish to take it up. It is based on the principle of dry brushing, wherein the brush is dipped into the paint in the normal way and then wiped straightaway on a soft rag until all traces of paint have vanished — or appear to have vanished.

Above: whether a model should be finished as a 'factory fresh' product or whether it should be painted in order to demonstrate the wear and tear that some subjects display (especially in wartime) is an argument that has followers on both sides. However, simulating a well worn finish, if undertaken with careful reference to a prototype, can result in a very interesting piece of work. Such is demonstrated here with this photograph of a 1/48 scale Nakajima B5N2 ('Kate') from the Nichimo range.
(Model: Y Aoto. Photo: Susumu Yoshida)

In fact, minute particles will remain on the brush which, when the latter is applied to a surface in a gentle stabbing motion, will be transferred from it. The paint used for this technique must be thinned very considerably and the brush wiped very thoroughly to preclude the risk of fluid paint being applied to the model. It may in fact require several minutes' work in one particular spot before any trace of colour appears on the surface of the model, which can mean an hour or more being expended before a boundary line of any length is produced, and the brushing action involved is likely to spoil the appearance of the instrument before very much work is completed. However, cheap brushes are quite adequate for the purpose, and if a few hairs are shed it is of little importance since the paint will be virtually dry before it touches the model. Some modellers are able to produce soft edges by means of a sponge or a piece of foam rubber instead of a brush, but the boundaries tend to be harsh as well as uneven. This and the dry brushing technique will be referred to again when various other painting effects are considered.

Good quality brushes will need to be looked after if they are to last any length of time, and as well as using them with respect the modeller should pay some attention to the way they are cleaned and stored. Brushes should of course be cleaned immediately after any painting operation, but if they are being used for a long painting job they should also be cleaned periodically to ensure that the paint does

not become set anywhere on the bristles. This can be done by dipping it into a suitable solvent — white spirit is ideal for oil-based paints, water for acrylics and other water-soluble varieties — and then drawing the bristles through a clean, lint-free cloth held between the fingers. When the painting task has been completely finished, this process may be repeated several times to ensure that all traces of paint are removed, with the final rinsing taking place in clean solvent. The bristles may then be carefully washed in warm, mildly soapy water, rinsed in clean water, brought to a point by passing them between the lips, and stored in a dust free container. In order to protect the bristles, a collar made from a section of drinking straw may be slipped over the ferrule — most good quality brushes are supplied with a collar similar to this — but otherwise the brush should be stored vertically with the bristles uppermost or laid across a rack that will keep it away from other brushes and will hold it firmly in position.

AIRBRUSH PAINTING

Of all the trends that have developed over recent years in the field of plastic modelling, there can be little doubt that the use of the airbrush has had the most profound effect. To say that it has completely revolutionised the attitudes to painting of a very large number of modellers is no overstatement. Unfortunately, with revolutions, excesses are committed by some of those caught up in them — painting by brush demands the development of certain techniques, a lot of experience, and an appreciation of the appearance of the prototype the model represents, and the same is true for painting with an airbrush — and it is all too easy to produce a pretty effect which has little connection with realism.

An airbrush equips the modeller with the means

to produce an even covering of paint and a soft edge to a colour boundary with considerable ease. It can do this because the paint it carries is directed on to the surface of a model as an atomised, controllable spray, and the instrument used never actually comes into contact with the object being painted. Being no respecter of sharp demarcations, an airbrush requires that steps be taken at all times to confine the paint to the area which is supposed to receive it. The techniques of masking have therefore much more relevance to airbrushing than to hand painting.

The preparation of the model surface, and of the paint, for airbrush work is broadly similar to that required for hand painting. Particular care should be taken that the paint is of the correct consistency before it is loaded into the reservoir — most will have to be thinned considerably before it can be used since if the paint is too thick it can clog the nozzle of the airbrush. On the other hand, too thin a consistency can also have unfortunate results such as dribbles on the surface being sprayed. Experience will soon enable the modeller to discover the correct consistency required. Priming and undercoating may be useful for the same reasons as for hand painting, although it is perhaps less necessary as, with an airbrush, the required thicknesses of top-coat can be built up without waiting for separate applications to dry completely.

Unlike ordinary brushes, the purchase of air-brushing equipment will rarely depend upon the type of results the modeller requires; because of the high costs involved, it is much more likely to be regulated by the amount of money he has available. It is therefore rather impracticable to recommend that he should acquire the best obtainable. Basic equipment will enable him to project a fine spray of paint on to the surface of his model; a more sophisticated airbrush will merely offer him a greater choice in the width of the spray, the speed at which it is delivered, and its density. It is therefore only possible to discuss airbrushing techniques in fairly general terms, and at the same time emphasise that their application demands a great amount of practice and that experimentation will to a large extent determine the particular approach best suited to the modeller's needs.

One of the major difficulties with airbrushing, like hand painting, is the starting and finishing of a single stroke. The initial and final bursts of paint ejected from the nozzle of the instrument can be unpredictable in character, and if the airbrush is stationary while the moves are executed paint will build up to an excessive thickness. The control button should therefore be both depressed and released with the nozzle directed away from the surface being painted. A stroke should be preceded by a test spray on a piece of clean card or paper to ensure that the delivery is free from problems, and the airbrush can then be moved across the surface of the model in one smooth movement, keeping the instrument in one plane only relative to the surface. The distance from the nozzle to the model will depend upon the width of line and the density of coverage required. Many modellers lightly mist the first coat with the nozzle held several inches away in order to provide a key for succeeding coats, which in turn may then be built up with the nozzle closer to the surface and allowing a few minutes between each pass. The direction of the strokes will normally be determined by the nature of the surface, and if it is very irregular the angle at which the airbrush is held will have to be varied to ensure that all corners and small details are completely coated. For large, unimpeded surfaces, strokes may be made either in one direction only or in opposing directions, but it is generally advisable to apply the spray in a different direction for each coat to ensure even coverage. Edges and areas where access is difficult should be painted first, as with hand brushing, and infilling tackled last.

The relatively indiscriminate application of paint produced by the nozzle of the airbrush, especially if it is some distance from the surface affected, requires that the modeller is conversant with the various methods of masking that are an inseparable aspect of the technique of spray painting. The production of well-defined colour boundaries was referred to in the previous section, and tape may be used in a similar fashion for airbrushing work, although it will usually be necessary to cover all areas of the surface where paint is not required. This may be done by laying the strips of tape in the way described for hand painting, and then using a combination of paper and tape to close off the remaining areas. Optionally, liquid masking fluid may be painted over the required sections of the model — this method is particularly suited to closing off small, intricately contoured areas such as cockpit canopies — or adhesive film may be used, and provided the usual precautions in respect of surface preparation are taken, no harm should be done to the model. With glossy paint schemes, thin, non-adhesive plastic film such as that sold for covering food containers may be positioned over the model surface and gently burnished along the edges. Cavities within the body of a model that cannot adequately be sealed off with tape may be protected by crumpling pieces of damp tissue paper and pushing them gently into place. With every masking operation, it is naturally of the utmost importance that all paint surfaces have thoroughly dried out before any material is laid over them.

Failure to meet this basic requirement can ruin many hours' careful work.

With airbrushing, it is possible to utilise a hand held mask to enable a soft boundary to be drawn without exposing adjacent areas of the model to overspray. The mask may be made from stiff paper or card cut to the shape of the boundary, and held at a distance from the surface being painted that will vary according to the definition required. The closer the card is to the model, the harder the boundary line will be, and the size of the mask will of course be determined by the spread of the paint delivered from the nozzle. The model being sprayed must be very carefully positioned for this technique since both hands are occupied, but with some ingenuity it is possible to construct a jig that will be useful for certain operations, perhaps by adapting a retort stand, which will keep the mask steady and allow greater flexibility of movement for the model itself. With some surfaces, for example those of convex shape, the mask may be lightly taped in position so that its edge is the required distance from the model. Accessibility will often be a problem for the modeller, and a certain amount of touching up can normally be expected in order to cope with this.

When using an airbrush to show soft colour demarcations, it is important to bear in mind the scale of the model being worked on. It is all too easy to betray the fact that a model has been painted with an airbrush by exaggerating the size of the blended area. On a 1/72 scale model, for example, a one inch overspray on the prototype would hardly be detectable, and anything much narrower would appear as a hard line. There is also a tendency amongst modellers to show the effects of erosion and the deposition of foreign matter over their handiwork by indiscriminately projecting a fine spray of paint on to it. More will be said about these topics later.

The cleaning of an airbrush is vital to its successful operation, and unless this is done thoroughly trouble may lie ahead. Clean thinners or white spirit may be sprayed through the nozzle in the same way as paint, and the airbrush may be dismantled and the various parts wiped very gently with a soft cloth slightly dampened with thinners and then dried. It should be reassembled immediately and stored in a dust-free container. If this job is done diligently each time the instrument is used, an expensive investment will be made only once.

APPLICATION OF COLOUR BY OTHER MEANS
Although hand painting and airbrushing are the methods most in use for applying colour to the

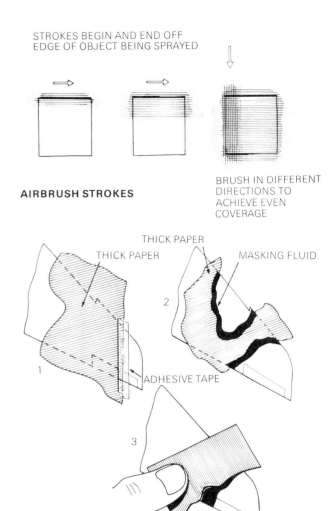

STROKES BEGIN AND END OFF EDGE OF OBJECT BEING SPRAYED

AIRBRUSH STROKES

BRUSH IN DIFFERENT DIRECTIONS TO ACHIEVE EVEN COVERAGE

THICK PAPER

THICK PAPER

MASKING FLUID

2

1

ADHESIVE TAPE

3

HAND HELD CARD MASK

MASKING FOR AIRBRUSH WORK

surface of a model, there are a number of other ways in which a realistic finish may be achieved. Similar in general concept to airbrushing, though much less refined in technique, is the application of paint via an aerosol spray. Cans of paint suitable for model finishes are available in a limited number of colours and may be used with effective results to achieve an even coverage over a large surface. Precautionary measures similar to those required for airbrushing must of course be taken before any work is carried out, and a spraying booth is essential because of the wide angle of paint delivery. This last feature illustrates the principal drawback of aerosol painting, namely, the fact that the delivery system can in no way be controlled by the modeller. The only variable is the distance from nozzle to surface, which means that painting by this method is generally only suitable for single overall colours such as may be required for large scale car body shells. It is possible to use both card and adhesive masks for producing multi-coloured finishes, although a great deal of paint must of necessity be wasted in its application, and it is also possible to use cellulose-based paint provided the distance between the nozzle and the surface being sprayed is sufficient to ensure that the paint is virtually dry before it touches the plastic. Cellulose paints should never otherwise be used for plastic models because of the adverse chemical reaction that takes place when the two substances come into contact. The other main limitation of aerosol painting is the fact that the composition of the paint cannot be controlled by the modeller, and therefore its colour, fluidity, sheen, and so forth, are fixed by its manufacturer.

Paint may also be applied to a model by means of a cloth or sponge in order to produce special effects such as soft edges or patches of mottle. Rather than using just an offcut, it is better to prepare a complete instrument by mounting a small piece of the material on a handle so that it may be easily manipulated. After the sponge or cloth has been dipped into the paint, as much as possible of the latter should be removed on a scrap piece of paper so that the minimum amount is transferred to the surface at each application. This stippling, as it is often called, may thus be compared with the technique of dry brushing, and it needs considerable patience to enable it to work successfully. Small, intricate designs such as stencilling detail, trim lines and insignia may be painted on to a model by using standard draughtman's lining equipment — pens, ink bow compasses, and so forth — although the paint will need to be thinned before it can be used. Inks and water-soluble paints can also be applied provided the receiving surface is non-absorbent. All such work, however, requires a great deal of skill and a very steady hand in order to execute it convincingly, particularly where symmetrical, regular designs are needed, and there is far less risk of spoiling the appearance of the model if prepared decals are used instead, which is the procedure favoured by the majority of modellers. The subject of transferable decals will be discussed in a separate section of this chapter.

The difficulty of achieving a realistic metal effect on a plastic model has already been referred to, and although painting and spraying are techniques that, skilfully applied, can go some way towards meeting the problem, many modellers prefer to use different methods. One of these is the application of metallic paste. Products such as Rub 'n Buff or Rowney's Goldfinger are supplied in tubes, and can be transferred to a surface in a variety of ways and then gently polished. A small amount may be squeezed on to the finger, a soft cloth or a piece of sponge and then spread evenly over the surface with a gentle rubbing motion. The substance should not be permitted to build up to any great thickness, although subsequent applications over a thin, polished coat can safely be made. The paste may be applied by brush in awkward areas, and can readily be thinned with white spirit, mixed with small amounts of oil based paint for subtle tone changes and successfully masked with adhesive tape, although considerable experimentation is advisable before using any of these preparations. Metallic pastes are available in a good range of colours, each of which may be intermixed with the others, and provided they are used judiciously they produce quite excellent results and are arguably the best method of simulating natural metal finishes. However, their adhesive qualities are not good, and so painting by brush over a surface so coated is not recommended, and the handling of a model after their application is generally best avoided. A product known as Liqu-a-Plate represents an attempt to combine the virtues of paint and paste since it is delivered initially by means of an airbrush and when hard may be lightly polished to the required sheen using a soft cloth. However, like a metallic paste, the finished coating is very thin and reflective, and the plastic surface beneath must therefore be completely devoid of any minor irregularities such as scratches or moulding flaws.

The application of thin foil is advocated by many modellers for producing the impression of metal on a model surface. A number of special foils for models have been produced, for example Metalskin and Bare Metal, but ordinary household foil can also be used to good effect. Since it is a solid coating medium, and to all intents and purposes inelastic, its use is chiefly confined to smooth surfaces of simple contours. Small sections that fit against each other with extreme precision may be prepared to take in more complex shapes, but the tell-tale joints will always be visible. Close attention needs to be paid to the adhesion of the foil in order to avoid any possibility of the material lifting after application. Non-adhesive foils may be laid over surfaces tacky with gloss varnish and then gently but firmly burnished in position, and additional protection is given to all foil surfaces if they are coated with clear varnish after they have been applied. As with aerosol sprays, however, the colour and texture of foil finishes cannot fundamentally be altered by the modeller to

Top: although there are dangers in applying cellulose paint to plastic models, there is no doubt that, provided certain precautions are taken, the results achieved can be very pleasing. The plastic card seat 'fishtail' on this Honda Café Racer (Tamiya, 1/12 scale) was first sprayed with a light coating of matt white enamel and, when dry, finished by using an aerosol can of black cellulose paint. Such paint should be applied in a series of light 'mists' so that its particles are virtually dry as they touch the model. If the paint is allowed to 'attack' the plastic there is little else one can do but sand down the parts affected and start again. The seat padding on this model, incidentally, is made from Das modelling clay.
(Model: Peter Hancock)

Bottom: one method of building up a mottled effect without having recourse to an airbrush is to apply the paint, in minute quantities at a time, by means of a piece of sponge or soft cloth mounted on a slim handle for ease of manipulation. This system has the advantage of being cheap in terms of tools, but the amount of control that can be exercised over the thickness and extent of the paintwork is limited. The subject of the photograph is the 1/32 scale Frog/Hasegawa Messerschmitt Bf 109E, finished here in a JG54 scheme used during the Battle of Britain.

suit his personal requirements and, like pastes, they do not accept paint very readily.

DECALS

A large number of plastic models require the application of carefully executed designs such as letters, numerals, badges, and so forth, and although a skilled artist will be able to show these vital embellishments simply by painting them directly on to his model, the precision demanded to achieve the correct scale appearance is beyond the abilities of most modellers. To overcome this problem, kits will usually include the necessary designs ready printed, and these may be transferred to the model after first removing them from their backing paper. Although a few kits have in the past required the modeller to cut insignia, etc, from a sheet of paper and physically glue them on to the model, and though a few even nowadays supply them as self-adhesive prints that have simply to be peeled from their backing sheet and placed in position on the model, the vast majority consist of a layer or layers of ink or lacquer on a transparent film which is carried, through water soluble glue, on a stiff paper sheet.

In common with other aspects of plastic modelling, the manufacture of decals, as these designs are generally called, has seen a number of technological developments over recent years. The goal of the decal manufacturers is to produce a design that will have complete opaqueness yet remain so thin as to appear to be part of the paintwork of the model. In addition, the design should have a certain degree of elasticity to enable it to conform to the sometimes intricate contours of the model, exhibit good adhesive qualities, be mounted on a carrier film that will be as inconspicuous as possible on the finished model, possess sufficient strength to ensure that it will not break up on being transferred to the model, be of an acceptable accuracy in respect of its scale size and colour values, and, if more than one colour is incorporated, be of good register, at the same time maintaining its economic viability. The task is thus formidable indeed, and it must be said that in most plastic kits the majority of these requirements are completely satisfied.

The successful adhesion of a decal depends to a large extent upon the nature of the surface over which it is applied. The rough texture of a matt paint finish prevents a good bond being achieved between decal and model, since total area contact cannot take place and, in addition, tiny pockets of air are trapped below the film. A much more satisfactory result is obtained if the model surface is completely smooth, and it is therefore desirable to coat matt paintwork with gloss varnish before any decals are applied. This is particularly relevant if the decals are, as in the majority of cases, of the waterslide variety, where the water soluble gum backing is extremely thin.

The application of waterslide decals is relatively straightforward and can be successfully accomplished by following a few simple rules. The backing sheet should be cut into sections, each one carrying a

separate design, and each section should be allowed to float for a few seconds only in a dish of tepid water. It is important that the water is not permitted to come into contact with the upper surface of the design since there is a chance that the colours may be adversely affected, and it is even more important that the decal itself does not become separated from its backing sheet whilst still on the water as its adhesive qualities will be impaired. The complete section of sheet is then picked off the water and placed on an absorbent surface such as a piece of blotting paper. After a minute or so the moisture will have penetrated through the decal backing sheet sufficiently to have dissolved the gum — and therefore freed the decal — and any droplets of water will have soaked away. The complete design is then positioned over the model, and the decal is slid carefully off the backing sheet into position with a soft, dry brush. The decal may be pressed firmly into place after a short while from the centre of the design outwards using a soft tissue or other absorbent material to remove any trapped bubbles. A damp cloth should be carefully wiped over both the decal and the surrounding paintwork to remove any traces of gum that, when dry, would be visible on the model.

Top: decal application can be time consuming if a convincing effect is required. The designs for this 1/32 scale Grumman Hellcat (Frog/Hasegawa kit) were closely trimmed and applied over a glossy paint finish. They were then eased into the panel lines by using the blunted point of a pair of compasses, and when dry the model was brushed overall with matt varnish which had been thinned and reinforced with additional matting agent. The result is close to the 'painted on' look and the clear film around the 'No step' warning signs is virtually undetectable. Not all kit decals are thin or elastic enough for this to be achieved, although the Micro System of decal setting aids does help even the most awkward designs.

Centre: commercial decal ranges considerably extend the scope afforded by the plastic kit, such companies as Micro Scale and ESCI producing sheets of designs that cater for aircraft and AFV enthusiasts. A number of specialist decal companies, like some enterprises producing vacuum formed kits, have unfortunately disappeared from the scene, but those still in business issue products of a generally high quality. Modeldecal, a British concern producing decals principally for models of modern combat aircraft from NATO countries, is one of the best-known manufacturers, and an example from the range is shown here applied to a Canberra B(I)8 modelled with parts from the 1/72 scale Frog and Airfix kits.
(Model and photo: Ray Rimell)

Bottom: decals of a much more ambitious nature are illustrated in this photograph of two 1/72 scale Revell Fokker DVIIs. The model at the top does not represent a skilful and laborious painting exercise but the painstaking application of decals — apart from a small area around the forward fuselage and a few small detail components, the entire model is clothed in Micro Scale decal panels. The difficult changes of contour have been very successfully negotiated, a job helped by the use of the Micro System of decal setting aids.
(Models and photo: Ray Rimell)

Small liberties are permissible in this form of decal application, and there are ways of dealing with any mishaps that may occur. If the decal fails to adhere satisfactorily to the surface of a model, diluted PVA glue may be carefully brushed under the affected area, and the basic procedure resumed as outlined above. Obstinate bubbles may be carefully pricked out with the tip of a needle, and a wrongly positioned decal may either be adjusted, or if necessary removed altogether — provided it is done directly after application — by brushing water around its edge and allowing it to float off. What is regarded by many modellers as the complete answer to all decal problems is a system developed by Krasel Industries of the USA whereby decals are encouraged to conform to irregular surfaces by using setting and softening agents. The Micro System, as it is called, requires the application of Micro Set to the model surface before the decal is slid into position, and of Micro Sol to the decal surface immediately afterwards. The decal is not touched after it is placed; as the solutions dry out, it shrinks naturally on to the contours of the model. Any traces of adhesive left afterwards may be carefully washed away with clean water.

Whether to trim the surrounding clear film from a decal design or whether to leave it in place is an argument that will find adherents on both sides. The question is largely academic if a glossy surface is produced for the decal to be applied over, since the main problem associated with clear film — the visibility of trapped air beneath — is easily eliminated. However, if only a few very small and unobtrusive decals need to be applied, as often happens with models of ships or AFVs, gloss varnishing the entire model is rather unnecessary, and the decals may be trimmed closely, applied to the matt surface and when dry sealed with a thin coat of matt varnish which will keep them in position and allow the texture of the rest of the paintwork to be matched. In certain circumstances, it is imperative that the decal is trimmed as closely as possible, for example where the rudder striping or instrument panel of an aircraft model is needed. Groups of small numbers or letters may be difficult to separate into individual characters, and indeed this may not even be desirable, and so any clear film may be painted over to match the colour on the model, either before the decal is applied or afterwards. It is as well to remember, however, that many of the badges, insignia, etc, applied to the full sized prototype may themselves be decals — the clear film on these is frequently in evidence, and the texture of their surface may be more glossy than the surrounding paintwork. Once again, familiarity with his subject is one of the modeller's keys to realism.

The other principal type of decal is that of the 'rub

1 FLOAT DESIGN IN TEPID WATER FOR A FEW SECONDS

2 PLACE DECAL ON ABSORBENT SURFACE TO REMOVE EXCESS WATER

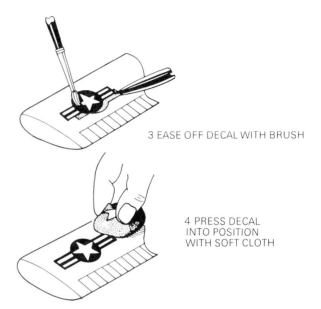

3 EASE OFF DECAL WITH BRUSH

4 PRESS DECAL INTO POSITION WITH SOFT CLOTH

WATERSLIDE DECAL APPLICATION

down' or pressure sensitive variety manufactured by Letraset, where the designs are carried beneath a transparent carrier film and protected on their reverse side by a non-adhesive sheet of wax paper. Once again, each subject should be cut from the film as it is required, leaving a good margin of space all round. The decal itself may be applied in one of two ways: it may either be positioned directly on to the surface of the model and burnished into place by using a ball point pen, rounded stencil stylus or special Letraset burnishing tool; alternatively, it may be pre-released by working the burnishing tool over the carrier film without allowing the decal to come into contact with anything, and then positioned and burnished as before. In neither case is water or any setting agent required.

The application of pressure sensitive decals does have its problems. The burnishing technique needs some experience to master since it is very easy to stretch the carrier film — one reason that designs should be individually cut from the sheet is that the accurate positioning of adjacent designs is otherwise very difficult. To minimize this problem, the burnishing should be carried out lightly and evenly,

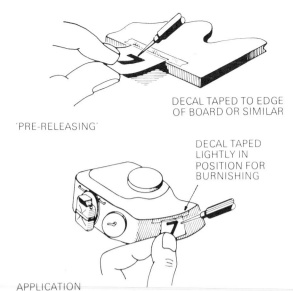

'PRE-RELEASING'

DECAL TAPED TO EDGE
OF BOARD OR SIMILAR

DECAL TAPED
LIGHTLY IN
POSITION FOR
BURNISHING

APPLICATION

PRESSURE SENSITIVE DECAL APPLICATION

starting at one end of the piece of film and proceeding across it in a series of wide strokes back and forth. Any tendency for the decal to break up or wrinkle should also be reduced in this way. Once the position of the decal has been decided, the film may be held in place either by lightly taping it to the model or by applying finger pressure to the centre of the decal, which will give it temporary adhesion. This procedure is not, however, possible if the decal is pre-released, since it will adhere at once fairly rigidly on contact with the model. Burnishing should be confined to the area of the design itself — any strokes that overlap on to the model paintwork may cause scarring that will be difficult to disguise. The successful transfer of decal to model is indicated by the appearance of air between the decal and the carrier film, and once the complete decal is separated the film can be gently peeled away. If on inspection the decal is not entirely smooth, any small irregularities can be ironed out by placing fresh carrier film over it and burnishing again; if it is incorrectly placed, or if it has become in any way damaged, there is no alternative but to remove it completely by applying adhesive tape over it and stripping it off, and then preparing a fresh design.

Pressure sensitive decals are not normally included with plastic kits, but they are obtainable as individually marketed sets, as is a huge selection of waterslide decal packs. These cater for aircraft, AFV and vehicle modellers in the main, and extend considerably the scope offered by the contents of a kit.

The possibilities are further increased by the availability of standard dry-print lettering sheets such as those manufactured by Blick and Letterpress. In addition, the modeller can adapt and alter ready printed designs to suit his requirements, and it is also possible for him to produce his own waterslide decals. By the deft use of the tip of a sharp craft knife or the tip of a fine paintbrush, waterslide decals may be reshaped or retouched whilst still on their backing sheet, and similar work can be carried out with both waterslide and pressure sensitive decals if they are already in position on the model. In this way, poor register may perhaps be corrected, lettering styles modified, or clear film removed. By applying pressure sensitive decals to an area of clear waterslide film, effective transferable designs to fulfil particular requirements may be produced; hand painted designs may be brushed on to clear waterslide film and then cut out and transferred to the model in the usual way; pressure sensitive decals may be used as stencils or masks for painting operations and lifted away from the model by the judicious application of adhesive tape; and many modellers produce their own decals by applying several thin coats of gloss varnish to a sheet of gummed paper, painting the designs they require on to the varnish and treating the result as they would a normal waterslide product.

VARNISHING
The subject of varnishing has already been mentioned in connection with decal application and textural effects, but it is a very important feature of plastic modelling and warrants some further consideration. A varnish is essentially of similar composition to paint, but the pigment particles, and thus the colouring ingredients, are missing. The fluid can therefore be treated in much the same way as paint for cleaning, thinning, brushing and spraying purposes. The advantages of applying varnish to a model are that it will give a homogeneous texture of any desired appearance over all its surfaces, protect the paintwork against penetration by grease and other unwanted matter, give the colours greater permanency, and act as a sealer for decals. There are, however, a number of problems, including the difficulty of achieving an even coverage, the tendency for the varnish to discolour with age, and the fact that it will alter the tonal values of the paint beneath it.

The modeller searching for realism in colour and texture for his handiwork will have to come to terms with the difficulties of applying varnish, and will need to prepare himself adequately against its possible effects. Even coverage may be facilitated first by very thoroughly mixing the varnish so that its various constituents are evenly distributed throughout. This task is not made easier by the fact that pigmentation is absent and progress cannot therefore be evaluated as mixing proceeds. If the varnish is to be applied by aerosol spray, the container should be vigorously shaken for several minutes; if applied by brush or airbrush, it should be stirred for a similar period. This agitation is especially important if the varnish contains any matting additive, whose particles tend to flocculate very readily. Apart from ensuring that it is thoroughly mixed, there is no control that the modeller can exercise over the nature of the varnish as it emerges from an aerosol can, but the production of an even finish is assisted if it is sprayed as three or four very light coats, with ample drying time allowed between each. Applying varnish by brush is altogether a different proposition. There are few problems with gloss varnish, provided it is thinned to a consistency approaching that of water and added to the model in two or three quite separate coats with as broad a brush, and as quickly, as possible. Matt and semi-matt varnish needs to be applied in a similar way but requires more careful preparation, if only because of its somewhat fickle nature. Owing to its tendency to 'blushing' — the appearance of a milky deposit as it dries — it should be applied over a non-absorbent surface, which for most modelling purposes means a glossy one. However, a gloss base will frequently modify the amount of matting that takes place — in other words, depending on the type of varnish used, matt applied over gloss will often produce a semi-matt rather than a matt finish. The matt varnish may be further modified by introducing additional matting agent until the required effect is obtained. One other difficulty in achieving even coverage with matt varnish is the fact that, if wet, it is very difficult to distinguish from gloss varnish, and areas on a model are very easily insufficiently covered during application, or perhaps missed altogether. To overcome this, the varnish should be worked thoroughly over the surface in question, brushing in different directions over each region and then finishing with smooth, light strokes.

Varnish discolouration is difficult to avoid, but can be made less obvious if the fluid is applied only as a very thin coating. The inevitable alteration of tonal values which takes place when varnish is applied over matt surfaces can only be dealt with by compensating for the effect in the preparation of the paint, which generally involves tinting it. If precise colours are required, therefore, a sample card will be a very necessary piece of equipment, and the opportunity can also be taken here for experimenting with different varnish textures so that the desired result can be obtained. Once each mix has been tested, the container, or the sample patch, or both, may be appropriately labelled for future reference.

Top: where no decals are available for a particular scheme there is no alternative but to paint by hand the markings concerned, either on an area of clear decal film, on a varnished sheet of gummed paper (which, with care, can be applied like a normal waterslide decal) or directly on to the model in question. This attractive lady was painted straight on to the nose of Monogram's B-17G after initial experiments on scrap plastic card. The main areas were marked out lightly in pencil on the model before painting proper commenced.
(Model: Geoff Prentice)
Bottom: it is not really practicable to mask off areas carrying complex camouflage schemes and so airbrushing in these instances is hardly applicable. One problem that often arises in the painting of intricate designs is the appearance of brush marks or of slight variations in texture that may become noticeable when different paints are used in close juxtaposition. A neat solution, however, is to apply an overall coat of varnish to the model when the paint and decals are completely dry, a technique that has been used on this Saab AJ37 Viggen based on the Matchbox kit. Note that the radome was painted *after* the varnishing had been completed in order to give it a slightly different sheen. (Model: Bob Patmore)

Below: this interesting photograph, dated 12 March 1942, illustrates a number of 'special effects' that can be incorporated on a model. The aircraft, a Hurricane IIC, displays a great deal of bruised paintwork around the upper wing surfaces and the engine panelling, together with some noticeable exhaust staining below the cockpit. The accumulations of mud around the tyres, the latter bulging out under the aircraft's weight, could also be represented on a model. Note the variations in texture on the paintwork: dull flat surfaces on the wings and fuselage, a semi-gloss sheen around the wing roots and on the spinner, and glossy cannon barrels.
(Photo: Popperfoto)

Opposite top: colouring materials other than paints and decals can often usefully be applied to plastic scale models. The exhaust staining along the fuselage of this By-Planes Polikarpov I-16 (1/48 scale) has been simulated by carefully brushing on graphite powder prepared by sanding down the 'lead' of an ordinary pencil. Powder paints, chalk dust or even natural earth can similarly be applied for particular effects.
(Model: Geoff Prentice)

Opposite bottom: this well worn, 1/35 scale model of an AEC Matador, produced from plastic card by scaling up a 1/76 Airfix kit in conjunction with a first-hand acquaintance with the actual vehicle, has been 'weathered' in a most interesting way. Ladies' eye make-up of a suitable colour was first dry brushed on to the required areas, and the deposits were blended into the surface of the model using white spirit.
(Model: Gary McCrudden)

SPECIAL EFFECTS

Mention has already been made of the necessity for the modeller to consider temporary influences affecting the appearance of his prototype, these being caused mainly by the prevailing light conditions when he sees it, and the advisability of trying to represent these to some degree in his work. A different set of effects — those that are permanent in the sense that they are physically present on the prototype — may also be taken into account, and indeed should be if a model is to be truly convincing. More will be said about these features in the specialist chapters that follow, but some general observations are perhaps appropriate at this juncture. The effects being considered here may take one of two forms: those that result from some kind of physical deterioration of the paintwork, surface or structure of the subject; and those caused by the deposition of foreign matter on to it.

Paint, once applied, will immediately begin to deteriorate because of the natural forces such as heat, light and moisture that act upon it. These influences normally manifest themselves as a reduction in the lustre of the paintwork and as a fading of the colours used. Where one or more of the influences is particularly marked, the deterioration is

in general correspondingly greater unless steps are taken to prevent this, and the result may be the actual removal of a coat or coats of paint. Areas of paintwork subjected to wear by other agents, for example the impact of a tool, the sole of a boot, or bombardment by fine particles of dust or sand, will show similar effects, although these will be more localised in their distribution. Substances other than paint may deteriorate in their own peculiar way: bare wood, for example, may darken in colour, metals may begin to oxidise, leather may take on an additional sheen as it wears, and so forth. When these things are being considered for translation on to a model, the process of deterioration, its agent and its location should all be closely studied in order to get the most accurate representation possible.

Fading can be simulated by careful tinting of the paint used on the model, and a loss of lustre can be shown by preparing a varnish accordingly and applying it over the paintwork. The absence of paint due to wear may ideally be represented by removing the corresponding area of paint from a model, either by gentle abrasion or by easing it off with a sharp blade. The underlying surface will of course have to be appropriately prepared before the paint is applied in the first place, although it is possible to touch in the eroded areas afterwards provided extreme care is exercised. In certain circumstances, it may be possible simply to brush paint representing the exposed surface directly on to that representing the top coat — wear on rivet heads, for example, might be depicted by dry brushing an appropriate paint directly on to the finishing coat of a model — but this entails the very real risk of producing an effect that betrays very obviously the method used to achieve it.

The deterioration of the fabric from which a prototype is composed is more difficult to achieve, since all will depend upon the material itself, the cause of the deterioration, and how far the erosion has been allowed to proceed. Iron and its compounds, for example, will when exposed to moisture corrode to produce ferric oxide (or rust), which forms a deposit on its surface; weathered aluminium, by contrast, will form a less obvious but still noticeable greyish deposit over its surface; certain woods, when exposed to strong and prolonged sunlight, will bleach significantly; wood that has become waterlogged will darken considerably and may even support the growth of fungus, etc. If the deterioration appears merely as a colour change in the material concerned, it can be represented on the model during the painting of the top coat. If it forms a physical deposit, it is best dealt with as a separate procedure.

The portrayal of deposits on models is unfortunately a subject that appears not to have received

much study, since although plenty of modellers show vast accumulations of representative mud, grime, soot, oil and dust over their handiwork, they are often too enthusiastic in the application of such deposits and, more importantly, are too often apparently unaware of their cause and nature. Depicting rust, oil and general dirt by dry brushing appropriate paints over selected parts of the model will more often than not produce a bizarre effect, since such matter tends to collect in joints, crevices and angles over the surface of a machine and not on top of raised detail, as will be shown if this method is followed. Lightly spraying a model with a mist of an appropriate colour is also in general ill advised, since the very areas which should show accumulation are likely to be the last to receive it. Nature's attack on any exposed surface is always a levelling off process — prominent features tend to be worn away and depressions infilled — and a model showing realistic weathering effects can only be produced if this is borne in mind.

Chapter 5
Special considerations ~aircraft

by RAY RIMELL

It is a fact that aircraft are the most popular subjects with kit manufacturers. Hardly a week goes by without a new model released somewhere, and usually it is of a type that has been made available many times before. Just what does motivate the creation of a static miniature aircraft, and why is it so fascinating to so many? This is not an easy question to answer, but whether one's particular interest lies in constructing a Bristol Boxkite of 1910 or the USN's F-14 Tomcat the same attitudes should apply. Aircraft modelling demands many skills, a lot of research and, understandably, a natural feeling for the subject. Perhaps it is the last condition more than any other that is really what it is all about.

The scales of available aircraft kits do vary quite considerably, ranging from 1/20 right down to 1/200 or even smaller. 1/72 remains the most popular scale, although 1/48 has made a welcome comeback in recent years, largely at the expense of 1/24 and 1/32 which are now slowly diminishing in numbers. If the modeller is prepared to amass a

Above: models of vintage aircraft, particularly those representing World War I subjects, are unfortunately often somewhat heavily moulded and frequently contain inaccuracies in configuration, which means that a kit will usually require very considerable refinement if it is to look convincing. This 1/72 scale Albatros DIII, for example, is based on the Revell kit but has had its wings completely reworked to show fine trailing edges and accurate wing taping. The fuselage has also been corrected by deepening it and lengthening the nose with wedges of plastic card. Note the repositioned control surfaces. (Model and photo: Ray Rimell)

large collection of models, whichever theme he chooses, 1/72 is undoubtedly the best scale in terms of sheer available numbers, reasonable size, and of course cost. Whatever kind of collection is intended, be it WWI German two-seaters, naval floatplanes, aircraft produced by a particular manufacturer, or those operated by a particular airline, the approach must basically remain the same: research, improvements and additions, coupled with patience and a modicum of common sense.

PRELIMINARY CONSIDERATIONS

Having decided to construct a particular model aircraft — and a relatively simple kit is suggested for an initial attempt — the modeller needs to apply certain rules before and during the building process in the form of checks on various basic areas, areas that if not attended to will spoil the authenticity of the finished result. The following checklist, which is by no means exhaustive, is one which the writer carries out before any actual construction is begun, and it highlights the most common shortcomings found in plastic aircraft kits:

1 Is there any moulding flash?

2 Are the trailing edges of the flying surfaces thick and unconvincing?

3 Are the control surfaces separated?

4 Are the propeller blades finely shaped?

5 Is enough cockpit detail provided?

6 If the undercarriage simulates a retractable type, are there proper wheel wells?

7 Are the undercarriage legs to scale, and, if the subject has a tricycle undercarriage, does the nose need weighting?

8 Are the moulded panel lines too heavy?

9 Are rivet heads visible?

10 Are the transparencies thin and clear?

11 Are small parts such as engines and wheels detailed enough, and are pitots, struts, and the like to scale?

12 If the model subject represents a vintage aircraft, is a 'fabric weave' effect present?

13 Is the suggested colour scheme accurate?

14 Are the decals satisfactory?

15 Finally, are the outline and dimensional shapes accurate?

The list may seem rather lengthy, and the writer apologises for this, but stresses that it comprises the essential areas that one should look towards when seeking to build a convincing model. If a standard approach such as this is applied to *every* model tackled, an improved result is generally assured, and not only will one's collection be of a consistent high standard, but in time one's skills will obviously be improved. Each point may now be discussed in greater detail.

MODELLING TECHNIQUES

The removal of flash is all important, and was considered in some depth in Chapters 1 and 3. It should be trimmed away carefully with a sharp knife and the parts in question cleaned up with a file or wet-and-dry paper until all evidence of it vanishes. This is a simple and obvious requirement appropriate to all types of injection moulded kit, but it is surprising how many modellers overlook it, and its importance cannot be overemphasised.

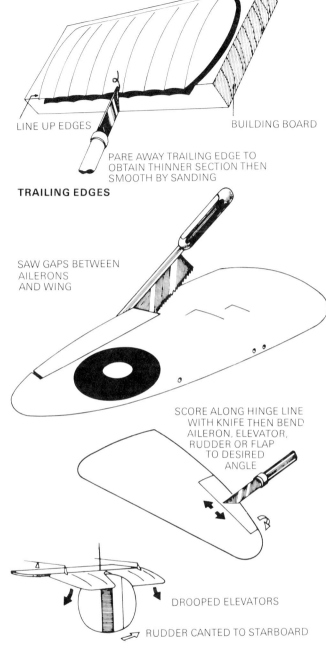

LINE UP EDGES   BUILDING BOARD

PARE AWAY TRAILING EDGE TO OBTAIN THINNER SECTION THEN SMOOTH BY SANDING

TRAILING EDGES

SAW GAPS BETWEEN AILERONS AND WING

SCORE ALONG HINGE LINE WITH KNIFE THEN BEND AILERON, ELEVATOR, RUDDER OR FLAP TO DESIRED ANGLE

DROOPED ELEVATORS

RUDDER CANTED TO STARBOARD

CONTROL SURFACES

In most aircraft kits, the wings are moulded in two halves, and usually these halves will be full chord. The result is that, no matter how thin these parts, edges — particularly trailing edges — will always be overscale. It is vital that all edges of flying surfaces are as fine as possible if the model is to appear at all realistic. A careful study of a full size aircraft will illustrate the point. It is particularly

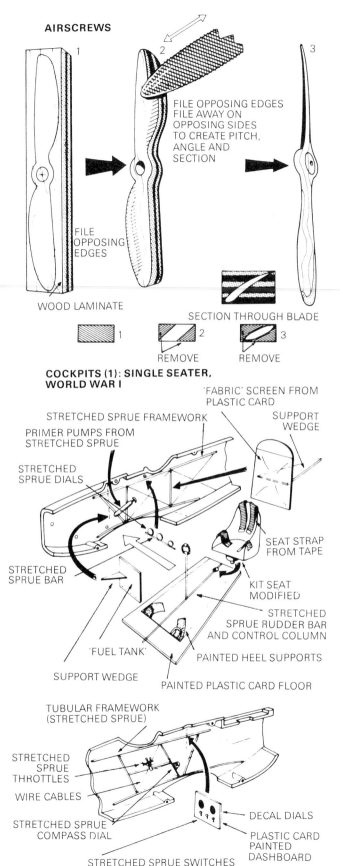

AIRSCREWS

1

2

3

FILE OPPOSING EDGES
FILE AWAY ON
OPPOSING SIDES
TO CREATE PITCH,
ANGLE AND
SECTION

FILE
OPPOSING
EDGES

WOOD LAMINATE

SECTION THROUGH BLADE

1

2

3

REMOVE

REMOVE

COCKPITS (1): SINGLE SEATER, WORLD WAR I

'FABRIC' SCREEN FROM PLASTIC CARD

STRETCHED SPRUE FRAMEWORK

SUPPORT WEDGE

PRIMER PUMPS FROM STRETCHED SPRUE

STRETCHED SPRUE DIALS

SEAT STRAP FROM TAPE

KIT SEAT MODIFIED

STRETCHED SPRUE BAR

STRETCHED SPRUE RUDDER BAR AND CONTROL COLUMN

'FUEL TANK'

PAINTED HEEL SUPPORTS

SUPPORT WEDGE

PAINTED PLASTIC CARD FLOOR

TUBULAR FRAMEWORK (STRETCHED SPRUE)

STRETCHED SPRUE THROTTLES

WIRE CABLES

STRETCHED SPRUE COMPASS DIAL

DECAL DIALS

PLASTIC CARD PAINTED DASHBOARD

STRETCHED SPRUE SWITCHES

significant with vintage aircraft, where trailing edges are not only extremely thin, often merely the thickness of a cable, but when viewed along their edge are anything but straight. With plastic aircraft kits these edges must be refined by paring them with a sharp blade and cleaning them up with wet-and-dry paper. This operation should continue until a knife edge is achieved and is particularly relevant for 1/72 and 1/48 scale models. Recent years have seen attempts by manufacturers to overcome the problem by moulding only about 70% of the lower wing halves, leaving trailing edges moulded in one piece with the upper half, generally along aileron and flap positions. This often results in the correct appearance. Lastly, one should not forget that wing tips, too, will frequently need to be refined and can benefit from careful filing and sanding.

On the larger aircraft models, ailerons, rudders and elevators are usually separated and in certain cases designed to operate. Model aircraft always look better if control surfaces are posed at realistic angles, such as with a rudder cocked to the left, or with drooped elevators. Ailerons, too, can be shown in a different mode, with the port drooped and the starboard *slightly* raised, or vice versa. The gaps between integrally moulded ailerons and wings should always be cut with a razor saw, and the craft knife may be used to score down the hinge point; the surface can then gently be bent to the correct angle.

The one item most often poorly represented in model aircraft kits is the airscrew, or propeller. Common faults are overscale edges, ill-defined hubs, and blades which are incorrectly shaped in section and profile. Remedies involve a close study of references and careful reshaping with a knife and wet-and-dry paper. In extreme cases, completely new parts should be considered, and with regard to vintage aircraft these can be carved either from plastic or wood. Even laminated propellers are possible for 1/48 scale models and larger by using varying grades of fine wood sheet from marquetry kits glued together with PVA adhesive and carved to shape.

The majority of aircraft kits now available are furnished with plenty of cockpit detail, although this is not always accurate and is often simplified. A cockpit is one of the first areas upon which onlookers focus when viewing a model aircraft, but if there is nothing to see, the model is irredeemable, especially so if the aircraft features an open cockpit or a slid back canopy. Obviously, references must be sought in order to acquire enough information to detail such important areas, and photographs and pilots' handbooks (where available) provide the better sources. The writer always adds most of the detail — usually prepainted — *before* assembly, and the additions can be as complex or as simple as one wishes. Much time and effort can be spared by omitting detail that will be invisible on completion, and here a little careful planning can enable some visual 'tricks' to be performed. For example, internal structure need not actually be built up on small models; it is usually sufficient merely to paint the basic colour and then mark in stringers and so forth with a hard pencil. This does of course depend upon the type of aircraft being modelled — more modern aircraft have plenty of side consoles and 'boxes' which can be made up from scraps of plastic if they are not to be found in the kit. Internal fuel tanks or ammunition boxes may be visible in old aircraft, but it is rarely necessary to build a complete item. A simple painted square of plastic card can look very effective when partly visible through an open cockpit. Bulkheads, too, can be simplified, and carefully applied paintwork often saves the task of producing complicated cutouts. At the very least, a 1/72 scale cockpit requires a seat, a floor (if relevant), a control stick, a rudder bar or pedals, side consoles, an instrument panel and seat straps. On the writer's 1/72 scale models representing WWI aircraft, as much fine detail as possible is applied, as this is part of the charm of vintage subjects with open cockpits. A detailed discussion of aircraft interiors is beyond the scope of this volume, but the accompanying sketches show a few suggestions on tackling these areas.

Many kits of aircraft which feature retractable landing gear now provide proper wheel wells complete with detailed 'walls', although on many others an open maw is all one gets. Wheel wells should at least be walled in, and this can be done with thin strips of plastic sheets. Any internal ribbing and piping that may be present on the full size subject can be applied later by using stretched sprue.

One of the most difficult aspects of aircraft modelling is the correct representation of undercarriage units, and this is especially so for non-retractable configurations and those with sprung oleo legs. Too many modellers are oblivious to the fact that undercarriages depress under the weight of a parked aircraft, and most kits represent their subjects with extended legs. Left uncorrected, the model will never appear to 'sit' properly. Drawings and photographs, or better still the real thing, should be studied whenever the opportunities for doing so present themselves. The same considerations apply to the tyres. These bulge out under pressure, and the effect may be simulated on small models by heating a palette knife and pressing down on the contact area of each tyre.

When undercarriage assemblies are being contemplated, it is important always to check the

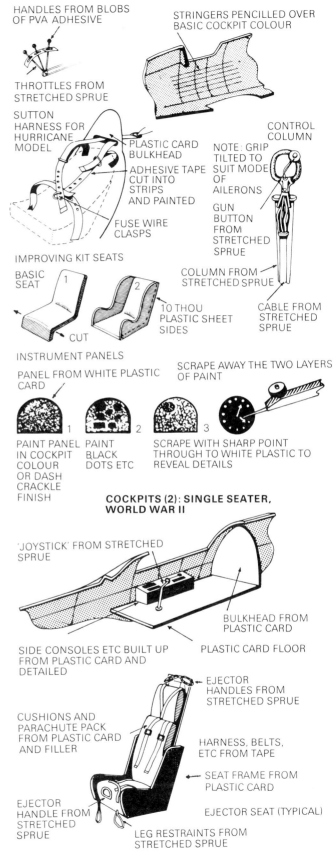

HANDLES FROM BLOBS OF PVA ADHESIVE

STRINGERS PENCILLED OVER BASIC COCKPIT COLOUR

THROTTLES FROM STRETCHED SPRUE

SUTTON HARNESS FOR HURRICANE MODEL

PLASTIC CARD BULKHEAD

ADHESIVE TAPE CUT INTO STRIPS AND PAINTED

FUSE WIRE CLASPS

CONTROL COLUMN

NOTE: GRIP TILTED TO SUIT MODE OF AILERONS

GUN BUTTON FROM STRETCHED SPRUE

COLUMN FROM STRETCHED SPRUE

CABLE FROM STRETCHED SPRUE

IMPROVING KIT SEATS

BASIC SEAT

1

2

CUT

10 THOU PLASTIC SHEET SIDES

INSTRUMENT PANELS

PANEL FROM WHITE PLASTIC CARD

SCRAPE AWAY THE TWO LAYERS OF PAINT

1

2

3

PAINT PANEL IN COCKPIT COLOUR OR DASH CRACKLE FINISH

PAINT BLACK DOTS ETC

SCRAPE WITH SHARP POINT THROUGH TO WHITE PLASTIC TO REVEAL DETAILS

COCKPITS (2): SINGLE SEATER, WORLD WAR II

'JOYSTICK' FROM STRETCHED SPRUE

BULKHEAD FROM PLASTIC CARD

SIDE CONSOLES ETC BUILT UP FROM PLASTIC CARD AND DETAILED

PLASTIC CARD FLOOR

CUSHIONS AND PARACHUTE PACK FROM PLASTIC CARD AND FILLER

EJECTOR HANDLES FROM STRETCHED SPRUE

HARNESS, BELTS, ETC FROM TAPE

SEAT FRAME FROM PLASTIC CARD

EJECTOR SEAT (TYPICAL)

EJECTOR HANDLE FROM STRETCHED SPRUE

LEG RESTRAINTS FROM STRETCHED SPRUE

COCKPITS (3): SINGLE SEATER, POST-WAR

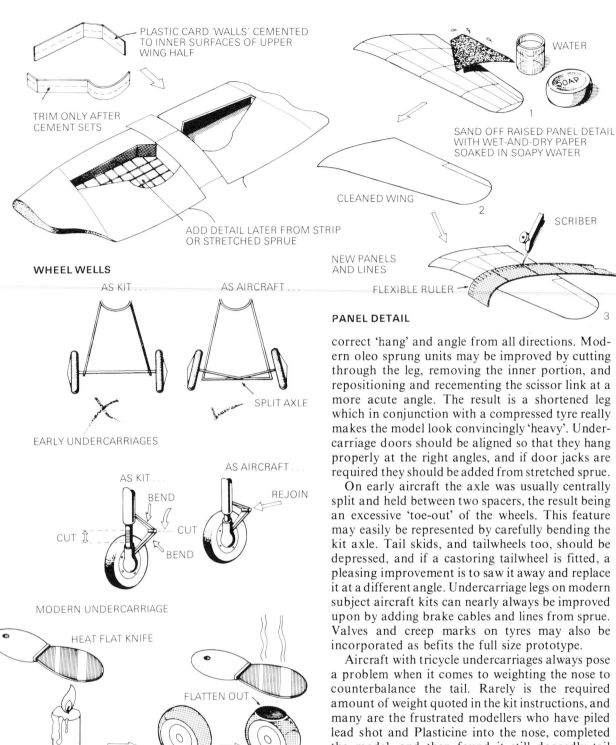

PLASTIC CARD 'WALLS' CEMENTED TO INNER SURFACES OF UPPER WING HALF

TRIM ONLY AFTER CEMENT SETS

ADD DETAIL LATER FROM STRIP OR STRETCHED SPRUE

WHEEL WELLS

WATER

SOAP

1

SAND OFF RAISED PANEL DETAIL WITH WET-AND-DRY PAPER SOAKED IN SOAPY WATER

CLEANED WING

2

NEW PANELS AND LINES

SCRIBER

FLEXIBLE RULER

3

AS KIT . . .   AS AIRCRAFT . . .

SPLIT AXLE

EARLY UNDERCARRIAGES

AS KIT . . .   AS AIRCRAFT . . .

BEND   REJOIN

CUT   CUT

BEND

MODERN UNDERCARRIAGE

HEAT FLAT KNIFE

FLATTEN OUT

UNDERCARRIAGES

PANEL DETAIL

correct 'hang' and angle from all directions. Modern oleo sprung units may be improved by cutting through the leg, removing the inner portion, and repositioning and recementing the scissor link at a more acute angle. The result is a shortened leg which in conjunction with a compressed tyre really makes the model look convincingly 'heavy'. Undercarriage doors should be aligned so that they hang properly at the right angles, and if door jacks are required they should be added from stretched sprue.

On early aircraft the axle was usually centrally split and held between two spacers, the result being an excessive 'toe-out' of the wheels. This feature may easily be represented by carefully bending the kit axle. Tail skids, and tailwheels too, should be depressed, and if a castoring tailwheel is fitted, a pleasing improvement is to saw it away and replace it at a different angle. Undercarriage legs on modern subject aircraft kits can nearly always be improved upon by adding brake cables and lines from sprue. Valves and creep marks on tyres may also be incorporated as befits the full size prototype.

Aircraft with tricycle undercarriages always pose a problem when it comes to weighting the nose to counterbalance the tail. Rarely is the required amount of weight quoted in the kit instructions, and many are the frustrated modellers who have piled lead shot and Plasticine into the nose, completed the model, and then found it still doggedly tail heavy. Weights should always be added to the forward fuselage an/or engine cowlings *before* assembly. In order to check that sufficient weight is being used, the major structure of the model may be held together with adhesive tape, the undercarriage plugged in and Plasticine added to the top of the

nose until the balance is restored. The required weight is then measured and the nose packed with lead shot accordingly before assembly proper begins. Other alternatives to nose weights may be firmly affixed rear access ladders or steps, or even a carefully painted tail prop from wire. Even some full size aircraft need these!

Panel detail on model aircraft kits remains a

Above: these photographs illustrate the scope offered by really large scale kits for adding an almost infinite amount of extra detail: the interpretation shown here considerably enhances an already complex kit, Airfix's 1/24 scale P-51D Mustang, finished as *Jersey Jerk*. Note particularly the repositioned flaps, the additional piping etc around the engine and the seat belts within the cockpit.
(Model: Jim Warnock. Photos: Donn Buerger)

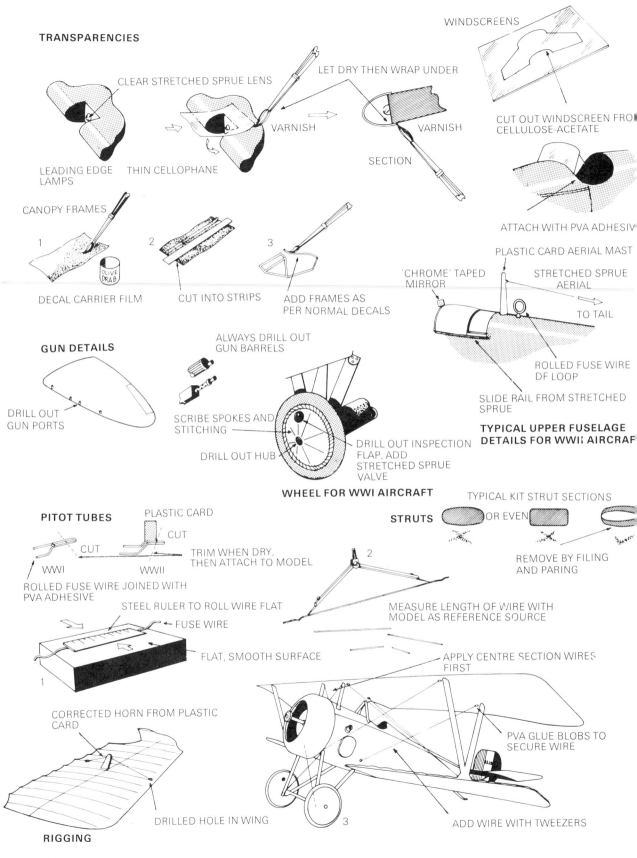

TRANSPARENCIES

WINDSCREENS

CLEAR STRETCHED SPRUE LENS

LET DRY THEN WRAP UNDER

CUT OUT WINDSCREEN FROM CELLULOSE-ACETATE

VARNISH

VARNISH

SECTION

LEADING EDGE LAMPS

THIN CELLOPHANE

ATTACH WITH PVA ADHESIVE

CANOPY FRAMES

1 OLIVE DRAB

2

3

PLASTIC CARD AERIAL MAST

'CHROME' TAPED MIRROR

STRETCHED SPRUE AERIAL

DECAL CARRIER FILM

CUT INTO STRIPS

ADD FRAMES AS PER NORMAL DECALS

TO TAIL

ROLLED FUSE WIRE DF LOOP

GUN DETAILS

ALWAYS DRILL OUT GUN BARRELS

SLIDE RAIL FROM STRETCHED SPRUE

TYPICAL UPPER FUSELAGE DETAILS FOR WWII AIRCRAFT

DRILL OUT GUN PORTS

SCRIBE SPOKES AND STITCHING

DRILL OUT HUB

DRILL OUT INSPECTION FLAP, ADD STRETCHED SPRUE VALVE

WHEEL FOR WWI AIRCRAFT

TYPICAL KIT STRUT SECTIONS

PITOT TUBES

PLASTIC CARD

CUT

STRUTS OR EVEN

REMOVE BY FILING AND PARING

CUT

TRIM WHEN DRY, THEN ATTACH TO MODEL

WWI

WWII

2

ROLLED FUSE WIRE JOINED WITH PVA ADHESIVE

STEEL RULER TO ROLL WIRE FLAT

FUSE WIRE

MEASURE LENGTH OF WIRE WITH MODEL AS REFERENCE SOURCE

FLAT, SMOOTH SURFACE

1

APPLY CENTRE SECTION WIRES FIRST

CORRECTED HORN FROM PLASTIC CARD

PVA GLUE BLOBS TO SECURE WIRE

DRILLED HOLE IN WING

3

ADD WIRE WITH TWEEZERS

RIGGING

110

Top: this 1/36 scale Percival Q6, made from plastic card, has had its cockpit glazing produced in an interesting way. A male mould was prepared for the complete cockpit area and two shapes were plug moulded from it, one in clear cellulose-acetate sheet and the other in plastic card. The latter was trimmed to the shape of the framework and 'roof', painted in an appropriate colour in the inside, and then attached to the model over the trimmed acetate moulding.
(Model: Tony Woollett)

Bottom: the smooth lines of modern high speed combat aircraft belie the complex equipment that is contained within them. This Airfix 1/72 scale SEPECAT Jaguar, however, finished in a scheme for an aircraft of the Sultan of Oman's Air Force, has had some of its panels cut away, 'boxed in' and detailed to show the contents of the nose equipment and electronic bays. Note the substitution of clear plastic for the 'solid' moulding provided in the kit for the laser rangefinder in the nose.
(Model: Mike Bailey)

hotly discussed controversy whenever pundits get together. Some hold that raised lines are more realistic, others that sunken lines are better, and still others that such detail is best removed altogether. A real aircraft should be studied if possible in order to ascertain what the panels *really* look like. Fine indented lines are the most common, and many recently released kits feature these. Many others, though, feature raised lines, and these should generally be removed. Deep, thick 'trenches', which are equally unrealistic, should be filled. New panel lines may be scribed on to the airframe surfaces using a flexible metal straight edge as a guide. The smaller the scale of the model the lighter the scribing should be, for very often such detail is all but invisible on the real aircraft unless one is really close, and so in some circumstances the addition of such detailing is at the modeller's own discretion.

Together with panel details, moulded rivets are another problem area for modellers, and as far as the writer is concerned *all* rivet detail should be removed for 1/32 scale models and smaller. It is usually invisible on the full size subjects as many flush rivetted aircraft had the rivets filled in, and so there is really no excuse for reproducing them in such models — and they rarely look convincing anyway.

The moulding of plastics components is well covered elsewhere in this book, and the writer mentions this now only because many aircraft kits would benefit from new transparencies, which in most cases include lamps, landing light covers, windscreens, turrets and of course canopies. Nearly all need reworking, and many can be produced by plug moulding heated cellulose-acetate sheet. Landing light covers are usually provided as thick wedges of clear plastic and as such are totally unrealistic. The light area should be carefully filed smooth, a circular lamp added from clear sprue, and the 'walls' painted. A small square of very fine cellophane is cut and attached to the upper wing surface with varnish; when dry, the lower portion may be wrapped around beneath the wing and attached with varnish as before. Windscreens are often too thick, and sheets of cellulose-acetate are easily obtainable and may be cut up and applied to the model with PVA adhesive. Turrets and canopies will benefit from being polished with Duraglit or toothpaste, but too much pressure should not be exerted as it is all too easy to crack or craze such parts. Identification and navigation lights are red, green, amber and blue and should always be represented by coloured clear sprue. 'Loud' car kits are generally a good source for such tinted sprues.

The application of canopy and turret framework is often difficult, especially if the frame lines are poorly marked or indistinct. Of course, where kit canopies provide properly moulded framing they can be painted directly, but the writer favours the painting of spare *thin* decal carrier film which can be sliced into strips and applied to the frame area like any other decal. Adhesive tape strips are usually too heavy for small scale models.

The addition of finely scaled details by the modeller — and also the removal of overscaled details present on many kits — is another very important factor when one is aiming for a realistic model. Items such as machine guns, cannon, engines, wheels, struts, pitot tubes, aerial masts, control horns, rigging and so forth are often provided overscale and need refinement. All kinds of guns

Many modellers flinch at the thought of rigging model biplanes – this is perhaps one reason why such aircraft enjoy less popularity as models than monoplanes – but there is no doubt that an unrigged model of a vintage subject does look bare. These photographs illustrate three different approaches to the task.
Top: a 1/72 scale Sopwith Camel F1, built from reworked mouldings from the Revell kit, which utilises 44swg copper wire, as described in the text.
(Model and photo: Ray Rimell)
Centre: a 1/72 Handley Page Heyford, based on the Contrail kit but with rear fuselage and wings from plastic sheet, rigged with clear stretched sprue.
(Model: Jim Charlton)
Bottom: a 1/36 scale DH60G Moth, with its rigging made from rolled out 5amp fuse wire.
(Model: Tony Woollett)
The Camel is also interesting for the fact that foil from a cigarette packet has been used to represent the metal cowling panels; the DH Moth is produced from the modeller's own design.

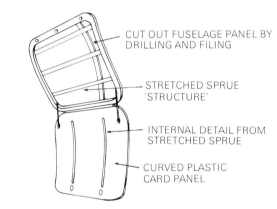

CUT OUT FUSELAGE PANEL BY DRILLING AND FILING

STRETCHED SPRUE 'STRUCTURE'

INTERNAL DETAIL FROM STRETCHED SPRUE

CURVED PLASTIC CARD PANEL

FUSELAGE PANELS

UPPER HALF OF WING

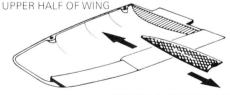

REMOVE MOULDED FLAP AREAS BY FILING AND REDUCE TO THIN SECTION – ONLY INNER SURFACE OF UPPER WING IS LEFT

'RIBS' FROM PLASTIC STRIP OR STRETCHED SPRUE

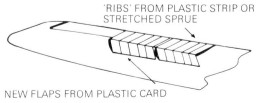

NEW FLAPS FROM PLASTIC CARD
FLAPS

Top: it is important to keep a sense of proportion when one is considering the final surface finish of a small scale model. US Navy aircraft of the late 1940s and early 1950s were painted a glossy dark blue, but if this were translated literally on to a 1/72 model such as the F9F-2 Panther (Hasegawa kit) depicted here the effect would be out of keeping with its scale. Hence a 'toned down' sheen is required, this also preventing details on the model being obscured from view through strong reflection. (Model: K Saito. Photo: Susumu Yoshida)

Bottom: another 1/36 scale model in plastic card, this time a DH Puss Moth. The fuselage has been built up as a 'box' and then 'skinned' with 10 thou plastic card, whilst the wings are constructed by wrapping thin plastic card around balsa cores, as illustrated in Chapter 3. The propeller is carved from laminated wood veneers. The lettering on the wings, just discernible in this photograph, has been applied by painting directly on to the model, first having marked out the shapes with a soft pencil. Note the 'flattened' tyres. (Model: Tony Woollett)

Opposite: a convincing surface finish is never easy to produce and can 'make or break' a model, no matter how expertly the latter has been constructed. The 1/72 scale F-105D Thunderchief illustrated here displays much in the way of subtle variation: the 'soft' edges, produced by using an airbrush over most of the model but by feathering the paint with an ordinary brush on the underwing tanks; some restrained weathering streaks and 'touched up' patches, contrasting with the immaculate finish of the missiles; and just the hint of a sheen to the overall paint scheme. (Model and photo: Mike Bailey)

need to have their muzzles drilled out for extra realism, and drilling should also take place for exhaust pipes, drain holes, ports and so on, not forgetting of course gun positions in wings and fuselages. Engines often need extra detailing, and this is doubly important for a vintage subject where the powerplants are generally readily visible. Piping, tappets, springs, plugs, magnetos, cables, etc, can all be fabricated from sprue and scrap plastic, and rolled 5amp fuse wire is ideal for push rods. We have already dealt with wheels — often poorly represented components — and so next to consider are aerial masts, pitots and struts, all of which should be very delicate in section. The parts in question should be carefully studied and refined or rebuilt as required. Realistic effects can also be achieved by showing the model with flaps depressed and panels open, and for the experienced only, this requires careful surgery on the kit components affected and the production of new flaps and hatches plus any internal detail which may be visible. The sketches provide some suggestions for refining and/or replacing these and other detail items that are so important.

The rigging of biplanes and early monoplanes is essential if the character of these types is to be fully portrayed. For many modellers, stretched sprue is the ideal medium, whilst for others it is 5amp fuse wire or 44swg copper wire, the latter being pre-rolled as shown in the sketch. Whatever the material, the method of application remains exactly the same. The required distance between points is measured off with dividers and then transferred to the wire and cut accordingly. A dab of PVA glue is applied to each attachment point and the wire is installed with tweezers, noting that most flying and landing wires rarely emanate from the struts themselves but from plates adjacent to them. This same basic procedure may be repeated until all the wires are in place, and by the same method one can produce control wires and aerial cables. Control horns themselves, however, are best made up from sprue or plastic sheet as those in kits are invariably overscale and clumsy.

With most biplane kits, and later subjects that had control surfaces covered in fabric, the majority of manufacturers insist on producing a 'fabric weave' texture. This is complete nonsense. Such a texture is well nigh invisible on the full size aircraft, so its appearance on a small model is totally unacceptable. Fabric covered aircraft are doped to tighten the material and fill the pores of the weave, and one shudders to consider the flying performance if one scales up certain kits! Whenever a model that includes such 'detail' is being built, the effects should be removed with vigorous sanding — always.

The painting of aircraft models is an art in itself, and we will be dealing with this a little later on, but first a word or two about kit colour instructions.

Few manufacturers give exacting and complete guides for accurate painting, and here is where a careful study of reliable reference sources stressed in earlier chapters is so important. The painting of a model should never be contemplated until enough information is at hand to complete the job properly. A kit manufacturer's colour guides should never be taken as gospel, and one should never 'refer to the box lid for painting'. Careful checks at each painting stage should always be carried out.

Many aircraft kit transfers (decals) are of inferior quality and often let the modeller down in terms of both quality of adhesion and of accuracy. Happily, there are vast ranges of commercial decals for aircraft modellers, notably those produced by Modeldecal and Micro Scale, the latter also marketing a good selection of associated setting agents, as noted in the previous chapter.

The writer has saved the most important consideration until last: that of outline accuracy. Before even opening the tube or bottle of cement, one should first check the wings, fuselage, tail — everything in fact — against accurate references such as photographs and *reliable* scale drawings. Outline discrepancies are frequently of a minor nature and may be corrected merely by means of some deft filing and sanding, but where serious anomalies occur the modeller may be faced with the prospect of considerable modification using plastic sheet, even to the extent of building new tails or wing tips in order to achieve the desired result. Few kits are faultless, and a common error is a shortfall in span or length. These deviations, however, if not too dramatic, could justifiably be left uncorrected with little fear of them appearing too obvious on the completed model. In extreme cases, a kit may be so inaccurate that totally rebuilding it from more basic plastics materials would be preferable to, indeed

easier than, carrying out corrective work. An indication of the techniques required was given in Chapter 3, and the work, though appearing very involved, is really only a progression from the more straightforward component modification and replacement procedures that are quite frequently necessary with kit construction generally. As the modeller's skills are developed, and provided he is prepared to spend a great deal of time on one model, such techniques come more and more within his understanding and practical ability.

PAINTING TECHNIQUES

As painting has already been considered in some depth in earlier chapters, only specifics as far as aircraft are concerned will be dealt with here. The approaches are quite varied, but first, let us start with early aircraft subjects such as WWI types.

Aside from sprayed patterns on several French and German aircraft subjects, the use of an airbrush is really superfluous for early aircraft types since the scales are usually so small and the structures so delicate that masking would be very difficult if not impossible. Biplanes are far easier to paint prior to final assembly, and complete painting, together with the application of decals, should be carried out *before* assembling the wings and tail units to the fuselage. Small repair patches or 'newly covered' panels in a lighter colour can add great interest to the finished model provided they are carefully and not too liberally executed. In all cases, WWI finishes should be semi-gloss and not highly glossy, for although the latter gives the correct appearance for a newly doped aircraft the finish soon toned down during service, and in any case a high gloss on a small scale model is to be avoided at all costs for reasons of scale effect. The time-honoured advice not to paint tyres black is never more appropriate than where early aircraft are concerned. Most aircraft tyres of the period were very pale grey — almost white in some cases — and this must be borne in mind. The weathering of such model subjects should be carried out with restraint, and a particularly careful study of photographs is strongly recommended. Dark Earth paint can be dry brushed slightly around the tyres, the tailskid and on the undersides of wings in line with the wheels, and even on the lower portions of the rudder. *Slight* exhaust staining along the fuselage sides can be shown by applying thinned dark grey paint and similarly treated dark brown paint may be splattered — carefully! — over engines and adjacent areas.

Silver schemes for inter-war machines are often problematic and, without a doubt, some form of spray unit is essential for a perfect result. If matt white or matt light grey is mixed in with the basic colour first, it is surprising how much more realistic the finish will become.

Moving on to aircraft of WWII, the RAF for example had various camouflage patterns and colours which are quite easy to represent even by handpainting. The most important features are the demarcation lines between the three colours, and both hard and soft edges were to be seen. Whether or not one should attempt to simulate the soft edges on 1/48 scale and smaller models is a matter of personal whim, for the softness is not excessive and when reduced in scale almost vanishes. Nonetheless, the chosen pattern should be marked out first with fine pencil lines. The lightest upper colour may then be applied, followed by the darker, and then both can be masked off and the undersurface coats applied. Once the appropriate markings have been added, weathering effects such as scuffed bare metal areas around engine, gun panels and canopy rails can be considered. These effects can be realistically achieved by using a thinned down silver/mid-grey mix carefully applied. A wash of medium grey paint can also be used to highlight control surfaces and engraved panels. These recessed lines are filled with colour and then the overall surface is quickly wiped over; such effects, however, should always cover adjacent decal markings. Sharp, straight line camouflage such as that used by the Luftwaffe of past and present can be achieved by employing masking tape cut into strips and applied directly. Mottle effects are best produced with an airbrush, although a closely cropped brush used to stipple such effects is a reasonable compromise. The work may be undertaken by first lopping off all but about ¼in of the hairs from an old brush, dipping the latter in the desired colour, wiping it almost dry on a rag and then 'stabbing' it on to the surface of the model. Obviously, such operations, and airbrushing for that matter, really need to be practised thoroughly first, preferably on scrap board or on old kit parts, before they are attempted on a proper model. The aircraft, once the decals are dry, may be varnished — preferably before weathering — to provide a even overall finish. 'Neat' matt or gloss should never be used, rather intermediary sheens, and, again, reference to photographs should be made.

The above techniques can also be applied for most postwar aircraft subjects. Modern schemes on Russian, NATO/European and USAF machines may be painted in much the same way, noting the various matt, gloss or 'eggshell' finishes. However, varnishes tend to darken the basic colours, so prior mixing using a degree of white with the basic camouflage colours may be an advantage.

Finally, we cannot leave the subject of painting without a word or two about metal finishes. Despite brands of so-called 'liquid metal' paint or the use of silver paint or dope through an airbrush, there is only one way to portray realistically a metal finish, and that is with real metal, or foil. Cigarette packets often yield an aluminium liner which can be removed carefully from the backing paper to leave a tacky residue on its inner surfaces. The foil may be cut and applied to the bare untreated plastic — fuselage or wing — and burnished down with a smooth metal spatula such as an old spoon. Really highly polished surfaces can result, and it has no peer for realism. Other foils can be used, but these usually need fixing in place with PVA glue or varnish and this can be a rather messy and laborious process. The foils should only be applied to the really shiny, polished areas of the prototype. Effective it certainly is, achieving as it does the correct 'glint' and reflective quality that paint just cannot do. By varying the amount of burnishing or laying small areas at different angles, a realistic quilt-work of panels can also be made. Once again, the study of reference material is all-important.

SUMMARY

Only the basic guidelines to successful aircraft models have been discussed here, and there is obviously much scope for a more detailed analysis, indeed, enough for a complete book. However, there are a few vital rules if that ultimate goal, the perfect model, is — as it should be — the modeller's aim:

1 A comprehensive set of reliable references should be gathered before any construction is begun and followed carefully at all stages in the building of the model.

2 The outline accuracy of the model should be thoroughly checked and amended if necessary.

3 Detail items should always be replaced if they are in the slightest way unconvincing.

4 The 'stance' and 'sit' of the full size prototype should be duplicated to the best of one's ability.

5 Every detail possible should be added, correctly in scale; internal features will demand a great deal of preliminary work before the basic airframe shape is built up, but diligence here will bring its rewards when the model is finally completed.

If these and our basic list of checks at the beginning of the chapter are remembered, the modeller should be well on the way to becoming one of the next 'experts' to join the swelling ranks of others who have successfully graduated past the stage of simply gluing part B to part A.

Below: in order to produce an accurate model it is often easier (though more expensive) to combine the best features of two kits rather than carry out extensive reworking on one. The 1/72 scale Fairey Swordfish shown here uses the fuselage and tail components from the Frog kit and the horizontal flying surfaces from the Matchbox product. This model also shows an angled tailwheel and some neat lettering on the mainwheel tyres, the latter accomplished by utilising the fine print found at the foot of all standard Letraset sheets.
(Model and photo: Ray Rimell)

Chapter 6
Special considerations ~military equipment

by LEN MANWARING

Before the Second World War, interest in military matters was minimal, and anyone seeking information on military vehicles had to search very hard indeed to find any literature on the subject. The newspapers occasionally carried pictures of vehicles on manoeuvres, and glossy magazines such as the *Illustrated London News* and the *Sphere* sometimes included items on the Forces. The Stationery Office published in 1936 an interesting booklet which carried 12 large, clear photographs of various armoured cars, tanks, tracked tractors and artillery pieces. It sold for 1s 0d but as far as is known has never been repeated in an up to date form. Since the Second World War however, a new breed of enthusiast has sprung up, and whereas previously to have been interested in tanks and army lorries was looked on in a society dominated by sport and apathy as something very way out and not quite nice, it is now an accepted facet of life, with people dressing up as soldiers and riding around in refurbished military vehicles being accepted with good natured tolerance. In order to fulfil the apparently insatiable appetite for information by this new wave of enthusiasts, book publishers are producing what appears to be a never ending flood of literature on the subject of military vehicles and equipment, and whereas not many years ago one sought in vain for a book on tanks, artillery or sub machine guns, now such works share the bookshelves with the classics and excite no comment.

In addition to the incredible number of books on the subject, the manufacturers of plastic kits have also not been slow to meet the needs of enthusiasts, so that now a person who has an interest in this subject can build up for himself (or herself — for many ladies now take an active interest in the hobby) a fairly comprehensive collection of military vehicles of many types used by the main protagonists in the Second World War and in the succeeding years. In addition, of course, kits can often be used to provide the basis for other, perhaps lesser known vehicles which will probably not be marketed due to their rather limited appeal.

Kits for military vehicles are made in varying scales, ranging from 1/76 through 1/72, 1/48, 1/40, 1/35, 1/32 and 1/25 up to the huge 1/16 and 1/9 scales. Kits manufactured in this last scale include the BMW R75 motor cycle combination, the NSU Kettenkraftrad and the Volkswagen Kubelwagen, and models built from these are almost literally replicas in miniature since they include most of the features of the full size vehicles such as engines, transmissions, suspension, movable cowlings, hatches and hoods. Fully detailed weapons are included such as the MG34 machine gun and the MP34/40 machine carbine, as well as tool kits in some cases! The modeller is thus enabled to build a model which with careful assembly and painting can reach the best exhibition standard. These kits are not cheap to buy nor easy to build, but the end result is a large model of which the builder can justifiably be proud.

Kits to 1/76 and 1/72 scales are very popular, especially with younger modellers, as for a pocket money cost the youngster can obtain a kit which, with careful construction and painting will result in a small but (with one or two notorious exceptions) accurate and highly detailed model. Kits manufactured by Matchbox are supplied with a scenic base which allows the model to be placed in a realistic setting and to be easily displayed and stored. The small size of these models makes them attractive subjects if the problem of storage space arises, for a large collection can be displayed in quite a small area, which in these days of restricted living space is a great advantage. Kits for models to 1/40 and 1/48 scales are not as popular now as they once were, but these scales do provide a useful size of model between the small 1/76 and the intermediate 1/35 scales. The amount of detail which can be incorporated in kits of 1/48 scale by such manufacturers as Bandai of Japan is quite incredible, and models built from such kits stand comparison with with those of larger scales. Much internal detail such as engines, transmissions, seats, controls and gun mechanisms is featured in the Bandai kits, but unless the modeller wishes to build a 'cut away' model much of this is lost from view.

Of all the scales mentioned, by far the most popular is 1/35. Pioneered by the Japanese, notably the firm of Tamiya, the acceptance of the scale in the modelling world is rather surprising as it does not fit in with any of the scales used by the international model soldier societies. The nearest is 54mm or 1/32, and although there are several models of popular vehicles to this scale, notably those by Airfix and Monogram, the choice available is not large when compared to kits for models in 1/35 scale. It is

The most comprehensive range of AFV kits is that produced in 1/35 scale, the principal manufacturers being Tamiya, Tomy, Heller, Italaerei and ESCI. Three examples from the Tamiya range are illustrated here.
Top: the eight-wheeled SdKfz 232, the widely-used German armoured radio car of World War II, is built virtually straight from the kit but has modified stowage.
(Model: Len Manwaring)
Centre: the Japanese Type 97 Medium Tank, again with only minor alterations to the kit components.
Bottom: the US M5A1 Light Tank.
(Model: Len Manwaring)

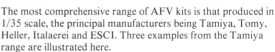

unfortunately not possible to mix vehicles built to these two scales with one another, but the careful intermingling of models of personnel of one scale with another can produce most realistic effects. Of course, not all soldiers were or are of the same height or build, so the placing of 1/32 figures with 1/35 figures can add variety to military dioramas. Kits for models in 1/35 scale are many and varied and include wheeled vehicles, in the shape of the Jeep, Kubelwagen, Dingo Scout Car, Landrover, and various armoured cars and trucks; semi-tracked in the shape of the familiar and famous US half-tracks and the equally famous German vehicles; tracked, with many models of tanks of all the combatant nations being featured; a good selection of artillery pieces; and a plethora of 'accessories' in the shape of weapons, equipment, stowage, etc. All these kits produce models which are, for the most part, both accurate and extremely well detailed.

Kits to 1/25 scale are not very numerous but Tamiya manufacture models of some Second World War and more modern vehicles. The latter include the British Chieftain and Centurion tanks, whilst the World War II models include the famous PzKpfw V Panther and the PzKpfw VI Tiger. All feature working suspensions and tracks which are composed of separate links as in the full size vehicle, and some show full interior detail and are driven by small electric motors and remotely controlled.

A new scale to appear on the military modelling scene is that of 1/16, and two models to this scale are manufactured by Tamiya, the famous US Sherman and the modern German Leopard A4. Both of these models are motorised and are specifically made for radio control, and as they incorporate quite a lot of metal in their construction they are, strictly speaking, outside the scope of this book. The kits are however notable for the huge size of some of their components, which represent supreme examples of plastic moulding.

It will be seen therefore that the military modeller is well served by the kit manufacturer with kits for models of many types and sizes, and a large collection of these fascinating vehicles can easily be built up. However, human nature being what it is, there is no pleasing some people and there are always demands being made for vehicles which are never likely to be manufactured as kits; whilst there is always likely to be a market for a model of a Sherman, an expensive kit for the Vickers Medium or one of a pre-war vehicle is likely to appeal only to a small but enthusiastic minority. Some skilful modellers get over this problem by building their models from basic sheets of plastic card, using plans to construct them from the ground up. Sometimes kit components can be used or modified, which makes the task easier but also more expensive.

The basic assembly of a plastic model of a military vehicle is straightforward and follows the guidelines set out in earlier chapters, to which the reader is referred. There are several aspects of military modelling, however, which relate uniquely to the subject. The vast number of individual vehicles or pieces of equipment that have been built, and the exigencies of wartime operations, allow the modeller a degree of individuality not offered by other subjects; unfortunately, the modeller's response to this opportunity is at times a little over-enthusiastic. A great deal of careful thought needs to be given to what can and cannot be done in the attempt to promote realism, and a discussion of the more pertinent considerations now follows.

WHEELS AND TRACKS

Someone once said that the crowning glory of a car was its wheels, and this probably holds good for military vehicles as well, with of course the analogy stretched to include tracks. This equipment can make or mar the aesthetic appearance of the vehicle and is responsible for much of the 'character' with which the vehicle is endowed, and the same is therefore true for military models. However, the tracks of small scale models present something of a problem as they are somewhat inflexible, and it is thus difficult to represent the track run of a full size vehicle.

The wheels supplied with kits are usually well moulded and their construction is quite straightforward. Wheels and tyres are in the majority of cases moulded in the same type of plastic as the remainder of the kit and are either in two halves, the join appearing around the circumference of the tyre, or have the rear section of the wheel and part of the tyre fitting into a hollow 'outboard' section, the join thus appearing around the tyre wall and being concealed by the bodywork. Some models are now appearing with separate wheels and tyres, the tyre being moulded in soft, black plastic. Some of the larger 1/9 scale kits have their tyres, both solid and hollow, of actual rubber.

Military vehicles are usually equipped with tyres to suit the type of terrain over which they are expected to operate, but owing to the ever present problem of supply and demand, which is exacerbated by the stringencies of war, things do not always work out the way the planners intend. Thus although during World War II there were special balloon tyres with a shallow tread for operations in the desert, many vehicles had to be rushed into action with tyres of the 'Trakgrip' variety which were originally designed for off-road operations in other theatres of war. It was not therefore unusual to see vehicles with a varying mixture of tyres and treads. Each country had its own ideas as to what constituted the best type of tread for cross country operation; the British opted for a bold tread very similar to that in use on farm tractors but with the pattern varying according to the individual manufacturers; the Americans adopted a standard tread pattern of distinctive appearance which was used by all vehicles from the Jeep to the largest trucks and tank transporters.

The early types of pneumatic tyres were made of natural rubber and were thus, when new, white in colour. Although with use they soon became dirty, a study of photographs will show that the tyres were still light in colour with the tread portion much darker. This is a point which should be borne in mind when modelling early vehicles such as the Rolls-Royce armoured car or the famous Crossley tender of the RFC. In later years tyres were seen to be dark in colour because of the dyes which were added to the rubber compound, and many modellers use a dark grey colour to represent this in preference to the rather uncompromising matt black. However, the latter colour, when suitably weathered by the use of appropriate paints to represent sand, mud etc, loses its starkness. A study of actual vehicles will soon provide the modeller with inspiration for suitable colours which can be used on the model. It should also be noted that if the vehicle being modelled is shown as running on a metalled road surface, the tread portion should be of a lighter shade than the remainder of the tyre. Of course, vehicles operating in mud or dust would have these substances liberally distributed over tread and tyre walls, but there could also be a thin ring of basic tyre colour showing between the wheel rim and the mud or dust on the tyre wall.

Kit tyres which are moulded separately from the wheel need careful attention, the shiny black plastic from which they are made being not as easy to paint as hard polystyrene. Often these tyres have a moulding ridge running around the circumference which, due to the nature of the material, is difficult to remove. A very sharp modelling knife is essential for this task. Spare wheels and tyres carried on the sides or rear of a vehicle would of course attract the same amount of road grime and weathering as the surrounding bodywork, but the tyres could appear in a 'new' condition with a sharply defined tread.

Wheel centres are usually finished in the same shade as the rest of the vehicle but are subject to more dust and dirt. Some wheels are of the two-piece variety being held together with a row of nuts. Originally these nuts would be painted red to indicate their importance and if the model is being shown in 'parade state' this finish can be effectively applied. The inner row of nuts securing the wheel to the hub are sometimes picked out in white paint.

Wheels forming the running gear of tanks were (and still are) in the main shod with solid rubber tyres. These are usually supplied in the kit with edges which are too sharply defined. The edges of these 'tyres' become rounded with use and the kit components should have the edges gently rounded. Photographs and the observation of tanks on active service show that the edges of the tyres become chipped due to the action of the tracks rubbing

against them; this 'chipped' effect *can* be applied to a model tank by removing tiny portions of the tyres, but it should be stressed that if this type of effect is to be carried out it must be done in a very restrained manner or the model will end up with its running gear resembling a row of gear wheels!

The tracks supplied with kits are usually in two lengths, moulded in the tread pattern appropriate to the vehicle being modelled and long enough to encircle the running gear with a small amount of overlap to allow for joining. Those supplied with the larger (1/25 and 1/16) scale kits are generally composed of separate links which join together in a manner similar to that of the full size track. The Tamiya model of the Chieftain tank is also supplied with tiny rubber blocks which fit into recesses in the track shoes as in full scale practice. These large scale tracks, being fully flexible, 'sag' over road wheels and top rollers in a most realistic manner. Methods of achieving this 'sag' with the smaller scale, one-piece type of track will be mentioned later.

Tracks may be of several different types. Those used on American WWII half-tracks, for example, were of the endless 'rubber band' variety but tanks and German half-tracks utilised tracks composed of separate links of steel or of the rubber blocked type. These various types of track are completely different in appearance and thus require differing forms of treatment when it comes to painting a model. Rubber tracks should be finished initially in dark grey or matt black colour before the outer surface is 'dirtied up' to suit the terrain over which the vehicle is shown to be operating; the inner track surface would be relatively clean owing to the track running over the road wheels. Steel track should be painted overall 'steel' initially, with dust or mud being applied afterwards, working the paint down be-

Below: a pair of pre-1920 RAF-type Leylands. These models, which are to 1/76 scale, are built primarily from plastic sheet although they incorporate a number of kit components, the wheels for example being adapted from some supplied for a Panther tank. The tilt frames for both vehicles have been made simply by bending lengths of commercially available plastic rod; the tilt on the covered vehicle is from tissue paper. (Models and photo: David Jane)

Top: the problem of realistic looking tracks with small scale AFV models is a perplexing one. Tracks supplied in plastic kits – usually moulded in PVC or EVA (ethyl-vinyl-acetate) – tend to be stiff and on occasions loose-fitting. This Airfix 1/76 scale Mark I (Male), one of the very few kits available for a First World War vehicle, needed several 'plates' removed and the application of epoxy resin around the entire circumference before the tracks 'sat' satisfactorily.

Bottom: one small problem with some models of military vehicles is producing the illusion that the tracks are heavy and not made of soft plastic. A way of solving it is to fix the upper section of each track to its return rollers with epoxy resin adhesive, forcing the track to dip between each by inserting pieces of scrap plastic card before it sets. The finished effect is demonstrated here with this 1/35 scale model from Tamiya of the Russian KV-II.

tween the links. (The portion of the track on which the vehicle rests, and which is hidden from view, need not be painted, thus saving a little work!) Track should have a raised tread and this should be picked out with 'steel' having just a touch of silver added for heightened effect, whilst the edges of the track may be suitably weathered or muddied up and highlighted with 'steel'. The inner surface of the track should be left dulled steel as this is in contact with the running gear, with perhaps just a light coating of dust. Guide horns on the track shoes become worn to a bright finish due to contact with guide rollers and road wheels, and these can be highlighted with a touch of toned down silver paint. The teeth of the drive sprockets also become burnished due to contact with the track and, again, a touch of 'steel' highlighted with silver should be carefully applied to these areas. Rubber blocked track as fitted on some American tanks can be painted overall matt black or dark grey before being treated to suit operational conditions. Track joints should be dealt with in a fashion similar to the steel link variety and highlighted. The inner surface of the track should be left black with guide horns picked out to give the impression of bright metal.

Most WWII tanks carried lengths of spare track, either to replace track when it became worn out, or as additional armour protection. It is unlikely that these spare links would be painted so it would be suitable to finish these with touches of rust. Again, it is impossible to be certain of anything in wartime and some crews may have painted all over the spare track when applying a new finish — this could be translated on to the model and then gently highlighted or touched in with rust.

As mentioned earlier, tracks, being flexible, follow the contours of the running gear and this feature was very noticeable on tanks like the Cruisers and Crusaders which had the Christie type of suspension. Photographs also show some Russian KV-I tanks with very slack tracks draped over the top rollers. The most common method of achieving the effect of the track 'sagging' down on to the running gear is by the use of epoxy resin adhesive or some other form of glue such as Bostik or Uhu (the usual type of plastic cement is not suitable for use with the plastic used in the manufacture of the track). The glue is applied sparingly between the top of the road wheel and the track which is then pressed down. This method is especially suitable for such tanks as the aforementioned Cruisers or the Russian T-34. Another method is the use of cotton or thread which is passed through the track and wound around the road wheel, the track then being pulled down on to the wheel and the thread tied off at the bottom. Yet another method utilises a length of stiff wire passed through the hull of the model just above the track where it curves down — this holds the track in contact with the running gear.

STOWAGE

Stowage is one of the most interesting features of a military vehicle, and can vary from the basic pioneer tools (pick, shovel, crowbar etc) and tow rope to almost anything imaginable. It has to be remembered that a vehicle during wartime becomes a mobile home for its crew who therefore have to carry their possessions with them. This accounts for the blankets, bedding rolls, packs, water bottles, boxes of rations, washing bowls, buckets and the dozens of other items festooning the tank or halftrack which soldiers scrounge, 'liberate' or otherwise take into use to increase their standards of comfort.

Early kits featured the tools and tow ropes moulded on to the surface of the vehicle and, despite careful painting, these items rarely looked as if they were 'separate' or attached to the vehicle. Now kits are supplied with a selection of tools, packs, moulded tarpaulins, helmets, water bottles and even camouflage nets in plastic, and these items can be 'stowed' on the vehicle being modelled. Tow ropes are also moulded separately but are somewhat difficult to install in a realistic manner on a vehicle due to the rather unyielding nature of the plastic. Tamiya however now supply a length of thread or string with loops moulded individually in plastic and which are fitted to the ends of the 'rope' and then secured to towing hooks on the vehicle after being stowed in a suitable position.

During World War II, tools were normally carried in clips attached to the full size vehicle, but sometimes were just thrust into any space available if time did not permit them to be properly stowed; shovels and other tools were often obtained and would be carried in addition to the issue tools. These securing clips and straps can be represented on a model by short lengths of narrow plastic strip or thin plastic card.

A prominent feature of World War II and modern military vehicles is the number of cans used to carry additional fuel, water and lubricating oil. Early British wartime vehicles were equipped with the type of can used in the 1920s and 1930s usually carried in racks of two or three. This type of can is featured in the Tamiya kits of the Daimler Scout Car and the Universal Carrier, and may be improved in appearance by carefully paring away the 'solid' carrying handles and replacing them with items made from plastic strip. In the early days of World War II, British vehicles were re-supplied with fuel which was carried in extremely flimsy tin

Above: many tank kits offer tremendous scope for modification, enabling the modeller to build a wide range of variants from a basic vehicle if he so chooses. The Airfix 1/76 scale Churchill represents the Mk VII, but some extensive reworking of the kit mouldings, the substitution of a 'Petard' spigot mortar (from a drinking straw) for the kit's 6pdr gun, and the addition of a fascine from twigs and its associated tackle from cotton, stretched sprue and scrap plastic, has produced an eye-catching Churchill AVRE.
(Model: Dave Williams)

cans, resulting in huge losses of precious petrol, and thus became coveted another item which featured prominently on military vehicles on both sides of the conflict and which has earned itself a place in history — the jerrycan. The jerrycan was designed originally by the Germans — hence 'jerry' — and was subsequently copied by the British and the Americans. Originally the British utilised captured German cans but soon introduced a home produced version which was almost identical even down to the cam-operated filler cap. The United States produced a modified version with a flat bottom and a screw filler cap. Despite the fact that the jerrycan is so well known, practically no kit manufacturer has managed to produce an accurate replica of this simple item of equipment. Tamiya's version is slightly too small and narrow and has only two carrying handles — all jerrycans had three — whilst some models have a solid piece of plastic to represent the handles. The Historex company, famous for its plastic figure kits, produces accurate versions of the British (which can double as German) and US cans. Armtec also manufacture replicas of jerrycans in addition to other items of 'stowage'. The Tamiya cans may however be modified by carefully thinning down the existing two carrying handles and fitting a third, central handle made from plastic rod or stretched sprue.

Jerrycans were carried in racks, some of which were fitted in standard positions, but many vehicles, especially German, had improvised racks constructed from strip metal, placed in easily accessible non-standard positions on the vehicle. Tanks of the Afrika Korps often had a row of cans across the turret or across the engine decking. The non-standard racking can be represented in model form by lengths of plastic strip, and a study of wartime photographs will provide much inspiration for the modeller in fitting jerrycans to the model. The racks fitted to American vehicles held one can and were more elaborate, with the can being secured by a webbing strap. If the kit can is to be replaced, new racks will be needed and these can be simply made from thin plastic card moulded around the actual can (Historex or Armtec) with the strap represented by a length of plastic strip. Buckles can be fabricated from fuse wire or thinly stretched sprue. American vehicles such as the Scout Car M2 or the many versions of the half-track carried their jerrycans prominently mounted on the scuttle, whilst other vehicles such as the Dodge Command Re-connaissance Car carried the racks on the running boards, and the Jeep had the rack mounted on the rear body panel next to the spare wheel.

Colours of jerrycans varied. German versions could be either grey or sand coloured, and if used for carrying water they had a prominent white cross painted on them, whilst the US versions were the standard olive drab. Jerrycans carried on British vehicles would be the same basic colour as the vehicle.

Perhaps the most important point to be remembered when 'stowing' a vehicle with items of equipment is to ensure that they can be fitted in the chosen spot on the model. It is easy for a modeller to attach a tarpaulin or a pack with a spot of cement, but it has to be asked whether the stowage position would be possible on the full-size vehicle. Again, a study of photographs will give a good indication of where equipment can be placed, and where it is not likely to fall off. Thus all kit stowed on vehicles should be placed where it can be wedged safely or secured by straps or ropes. American half-tracks (especially the personnel carrier versions) provide excellent examples of maximum stowage. Straps on a model can be fabricated from thin strips of plastic card and ropes represented by suitable thicknesses of thread. It is also very important to remember that stowage should not impede the traverse of a tank or armoured car turret or obscure the driver's vision slits.

Much stowage consists of rolls — tarpaulins or bedding rolls — and in many kits these are represented, often very cleverly, in hard plastic. However, despite careful and skilful painting these still look solid, and because they do not vary from one example of a model to another, this impression is reinforced. These items can be replaced and represented by tissue or an old piece of fine linen either rolled up on itself or wrapped around a core of modelling clay or wood. Thin thread or plastic strip will serve as the securing rope or strap.

It has been mentioned that some kits, especially in 1/35 scale, feature stowed camouflage nets moulded in plastic. These items should be discarded as no amount of attention with a paintbrush will disguise the fact that they are plastic. Netting can be represented on a larger scale model by the use of net curtaining or bandage, and in smaller scales by portions of ladies' nylon tights. Sometimes camouflage netting was carried rolled or 'draped' on the vehicle and these effects should be aimed at on a model. Camouflage netting was adorned with 'scrim' which was strips of hessian threaded through in disruptive patterns; this is difficult to represent in a small scale, but tiny pieces of tissue stuck to the 'netting' can present a realistic effect. Some vehicles,

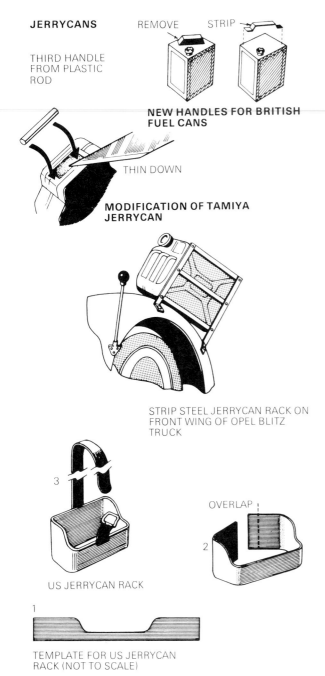

JERRYCANS

THIRD HANDLE FROM PLASTIC ROD

REMOVE   STRIP

NEW HANDLES FOR BRITISH FUEL CANS

THIN DOWN

MODIFICATION OF TAMIYA JERRYCAN

STRIP STEEL JERRYCAN RACK ON FRONT WING OF OPEL BLITZ TRUCK

3

OVERLAP

2

US JERRYCAN RACK

1

TEMPLATE FOR US JERRYCAN RACK (NOT TO SCALE)

notably Russian and World War I tanks, carried unditching equipment in the shape of logs, tree-trunks or sawn wooden beams and these can be represented in miniature form by suitable lengths of twig or carefully prepared sections of wood. The beams were often carried along the side of the vehicle or lashed to the track guard. Photographs frequently show steel helmets hung on the outside of the turret or hull of an armoured vehicle, the main reason being a lack of stowage space inside. These items are often supplied with a kit and can be secured quite easily with a blob of cement — but it should be remembered that they would be secured to or hung from something (a hook or shackle) by something (a strap). The helmet chin-strap can be represented by a narrow length of plastic strip. Packs containing items of personal kit might be festooned about a vehicle, and these too are supp-

Below: a well 'muddied' M16 Multiple Gun Motor Carriage, one of several versions of the basic US half-track available in the 1/35 scale Tamiya range. Much of the stowage fitted on the model is not provided with the kit, including the tow chain around the winch and the roll of netting over the windscreen. The netting is prepared from net curtaining, suitably painted and fitted with securing straps. Note the jerrycan in the US-type rack, the kit component having been altered to show three carrying handles.
(Model: Len Manwaring)

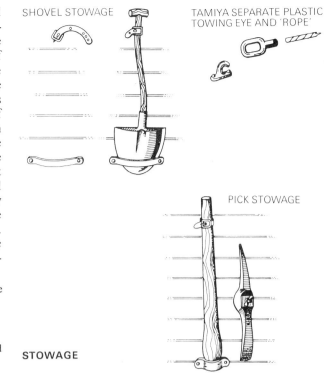

SHOVEL STOWAGE

TAMIYA SEPARATE PLASTIC TOWING EYE AND 'ROPE'

PICK STOWAGE

STOWAGE

lied in model form. Again, these items were usually secured by straps which were fastened to suitable attachment points on a vehicle.

Whilst perhaps not strictly coming under the heading of 'stowage', odd track shoes or lengths of track featured prominently on World War II tanks. Some of these were spare shoes carried to replace worn or damaged components, but others were attached to vulnerable portions of the hull or turret to reinforce the armour plating. Often the shoes were worn out items or were taken from wrecked vehicles. They were sometimes of a different type and often welded in position. Kit manufacturers frequently supply separate shoes or short lengths of track which enable the modeller to duplicate the added protection provided on full size vehicles. Again, care should be exercised on positioning spare tracks on a model — track shoes, like many other items of military equipment, are very heavy and thus cannot be attached to a part of a vehicle which will not bear their weight. This should also be borne in mind when constructing a diorama where perhaps odd lengths of track are laying around or draped over something: someone had to put them there in the first place. Other items such as sandbags, timber and even cement were used in World War II by the crews of armoured vehicles (notably the Sherman) to provide additional protection. Some kits include plastic 'sandbags', but these lack realism as they do not have the 'sagging' effect of the real thing. If the modeller wishes to equip his model with sandbag protection, the question of securing must be considered, and if rope is to be represented then it should be remembered that sandbags are not solid and that the rope would cut into and crease the bag.

Some modellers secure entrenching tools to the external surfaces of hulls and turrets, which would seem to be a questionable practice as these are items of equipment issued to the infantry and thus would be out of place on an armoured car or tank, although possibly not on a half-track. Others choose to leave that item of equipment known as 'Bren magazine pouch' laying around in their vehicles, which whilst giving the impression of 'stowage' is not strictly accurate and highly unlikely. The British soldier's webbing equipment, which included his belt, bayonet, water bottle, pouches and shoulder braces, all came off as one item, and pouches were seldom if ever detached singly — they were too much trouble to put on! One of course cannot be dogmatic about things that took place in wartime, but a little thought and a careful study of photographs will enable the modeller to decide how he may stow his vehicle realistically.

Personal weapons in the form of rifles, carbines, sub machine guns and pistols were carried on both soft-skinned and armoured vehicles. Most vehicles were fitted with racks to accommodate these weapons but often the racks were ignored and the

weapons carried where they would come easily to hand in an emergency. Most kits contain miniature weapons, thus enabling the modeller to place them where he wishes. However, it is unlikely that weapons would be left laying around on turrets or on the decking of armoured vehicles where they could easily fall off, because even in wartime and with the ease that these things could be obtained or scrounged, weapons were still items to be looked after carefully.

The main points to be observed when considering stowage on a model, therefore, are to ensure that the equipment being carried does not impede vision slits or hatches and most importantly does not impede the traverse of a gun turret. Also it should be ensured that the items of stowage can be placed in the desired position by being wedged, tied or lashed. Finally, a study of photographs will indicate what types of items were carried as stowage.

BATTLE DAMAGE

Because of the use or misuse to which they are put, it is inevitable that virtually all military vehicles, wheeled or tracked, armoured or soft-skinned, will suffer some form of external damage. This can be caused by any number of reasons. In the case of a truck, it might be a scrape or a collision with a hard object, due perhaps to the inexperience of wartime-trained drivers; in the case of an AFV it might be battle damage due to an air strike or involvement in some engagement or other. Tanks and other armoured vehicles are more likely to suffer from 'battle damage' — a term which is self-explanatory and which can be caused by a myriad reasons. Such damage can range from a crumpled track guard to shattered or missing bazooka plates and scarred hulls and turrets where armour piercing shot has struck a glancing blow. Such 'damage' when applied sensibly and in a restrained fashion can lend an air of realism to a model. It must be stressed however, that any such application of 'damage' should be

understated rather than too blatant.

Battered and dented mudguards can be featured on a model, but to achieve the desired effect the plastic must first be softened. This is done by the gentle application of heat — a soldering iron is ideal for the job — which then enables the mudguard to be moulded into the desired shape. Heat, and not too much of it, should only be applied to a localised area, taking care not to bring the heat source into actual contact with the component which is being 'damaged'. It is advisable to practice on scrap plastic before attempting to carry out the work on the model. If the total use of plastic is not too important, parts of the mudguards on model armoured fighting vehicles can be carefully removed and replaced with sections of thick foil such as is found around the necks of wine bottles or can be cut from toothpaste tubes. These metal portions are shaped to a likeness of the discarded plastic portions and secured in place with epoxy resin adhesive, and they can then be 'battered' most realistically.

A study of wartime photographs is of course a necessity, and these will often provide inspiration for many differing forms of battle 'damage'. One very effective form of 'damage' is the representation of a hit which has perforated, and this is usually seen on the *schurtzen* or bazooka plates which were hung along the sides of some World War II German armoured vehicles or the sandguards on some British tanks. The object of the *schurtzen* was to

Left: another example of a reworked kit, this is a 1/76 scale Sherman Crab, with its mine-clearing flails depicted by using lengths of Armtec tow chain. The model is essentially an Airfix Sherman kit, but there is extensive use of plastic card for the flail support structure and the lane-marking chalk boxes. The mantlet cover has been modelled from a tissue handkerchief stiffened with liquid cement. Note the 'wear' on the tracks, simulated by picking out the shoes with metallic paint. (Model: Dave Williams)

Right: a straightforward adaptation of an available kit, this 1/76 AEC Matador has been completed as an RAF Gantry Crane of World War II. The sides of the flatbed and the crane structure have been built from sliced plastic card, with the 'ropes' from cotton thread. (Model and photo: David Jane)

explode the hollow charge warheads of the American bazooka or the British PIAT before the tracks and running gear were reached. The plates could often be ripped off altogether or sometimes they were holed. The latter effect can be achieved in miniature form by gently forcing a point such as found on a pair of school compasses through the plate, working it around to enlarge the hole to the desired size. This should give the impression of metal being pierced from one side with the force of impact causing the surface to bow slightly inwards. Smaller holes can be made with a drill to simulate the effect of small calibre hits or splinters. Some careful painting using a metallic colour (*not* silver) around the holes, if they are recent hits, or the judicious use of 'rust' to represent an old scar and the surrounding surface with some paint knocked off, will create a most realistic effect. Modellers will almost certainly have their own pet methods of making 'holes', and it should also be remembered that not all punctures are round, some hits causing elongated holes. The damage caused by hits which have glanced off hull, turret or gun mantlet can be represented by the careful use of heat and by filing. Caution is the watchword, as in all cases where heat and plastic are concerned, since components can be easily ruined by the application of too much heat. If however, the modeller does not wish to risk his model by some of the more drastic forms of 'damage', then the crumpled wing or track guard, or missing *schurtzen* plate, together with a 'well used' look obtained by careful painting, will be sufficient. Indeed, some of the most realistic models seen at exhibitions bear no signs of damage at all.

A small point of detail which will enhance the realism of a Sturmgeschutz or other German AFV fitted with bazooka plates is that these plates were usually numbered from front to rear, left and right, viz R1, R2, R3 and so on, or L1, L2 etc. The lettering was usually applied in small characters and can be reproduced on the model by careful use of a mapping pen and Indian ink. Another feature of some vehicles was that they sometimes had odd plates retrieved from an abandoned or destroyed vehicle to replace those lost, perhaps in battle. These 'new' plates could possibly be in an entirely different camouflage scheme to the vehicle on which they were being used. This can be reproduced on the model, and looks most effective.

A soft-skinned vehicle which has been involved in a fierce fight may bear evidence of this in the form of bullet holes, which can appear in the bodywork or through the windscreen. A very small drill mounted in a pin chuck will enable these holes to be made, and moving the drill slightly as it is being turned enables the hole to be elongated, as some actual hits

were if made from an oblique angle. Windscreens should be painted to represent the 'starred' effect around holes, but again, restraint should be the watchword. Paint around the holes in metal surfaces would probably be chipped off revealing the bare metal beneath. 'Steel' paint should be applied to these surfaces *before* the main vehicle colour is put on and a narrow band of steel left surrounding the hole. Careful painting can in fact suggest superficial damage without actually marring the surface of the model.

The illustrations contained in the many excellent publications on the market today will provide the military vehicle modeller with endless examples of battle damage which can be incorporated to a greater or lesser degree in the model. Experience and practice will indicate the best way in which the desired effect is to be obtained and once again it should be emphasised that great care should be exercised when scale 'damage' is being applied as otherwise the model may, unwittingly, be irreparably harmed.

WEATHERING

Weathering is a subject about which countless thousands of words have been written and spoken by both expert and novice alike. Most articles and reviews of military vehicle kits seem to contain at least a paragraph or two on this subject. Basically the term 'weathering' can be taken to mean painting a model in such a way as to depict a worn, used look which a vehicle would acquire after hard treatment under extreme conditions. All military vehicles, whether wheeled or tracked, start life clean and freshly-painted, but during the course of their service lives at various times get dirty and often extremely muddy. However, even in wartime, crews take a pride in their vehicles and often do their best to keep them as clean as possible. Peacetime vehicles are, except for times of manoeuvres, kept in a shiny 'bulled up' condition with few concessions made to camouflage and with all bright work kept shiny, although recent years have seen the introduction of more sombre finishes.

Weathering, then, depicts the effects of the elements and hard usage on the finish of a vehicle, and when carefully and judiciously applied to a model its simulation can enormously enhance the appearance and produce an air of realism. Before any weathering is carried out, however, the theatre of war in which the vehicle would be operating must be decided upon, for obviously a vehicle used on the Western Front during the First World War or in the desert or during the depths of the Russian winter in the Second World War will all require differing treatment.

Every country has its own conception of what constitutes the best colour for a military vehicle, with several variations of dark or olive green predominating. In wartime, however, countries frequently adopt various forms of camouflage, and this in turn varies according to the theatre of operations — desert situations call for a sand colour whilst in temperate climates a darker camouflage finish might be worn with perhaps a white coating applied over the basic finish during winter.

Many modellers choose to paint their models in a basic colour or camouflage scheme initially and then proceed with the weathering process. Another approach is to paint the model in the basic colours but a shade or two lighter, thus giving the impression of faded paintwork. Once the model has been completely painted, it can then be 'dirtied up' if it is to be finished as a vehicle operating in the European or Russian theatre of war. A study of photographs, and the close observation of vehicles generally, will indicate how mud and dust collects when thrown up from the road, and this information can be utilised when painting the model. Dark Earth paint used with the 'dry brush' technique is an excellent colour for representing dust, but of course not all dust is of a brownish shade — some can be almost milky white — so the modeller must decide. An overall dusty appearance is difficult to obtain using a brush, but it can be done, and many models are completely brush painted although appearing to have been finished with an airbrush. If the modeller is fortunate enough to possess an airbrush, then a light spray with well-thinned colours can produce a realistic 'dusty' appearance, although there is a danger that the paint will highlight raised detail — exactly where vast accumulations of dust would *not* collect. If 'mud' is to be applied then care should be exercised not to over-emphasise the effect. Often a tin of paint with almost dry dregs will provide the necessary 'mud' which can be applied with a brush; such substances as household filler can also be used, the consistency of this being a matter of taste and judgement. Of course, real mud may be used, but this will have to be 'fixed' by means of matt varnish to the parts of the vehicle to which it has been applied. Whichever method is used, it must be remembered that unless the vehicle is being depicted up to its hubs in the mire the application of 'mud' should be very sparing indeed.

Models of vehicles shown as operating in the desert are ideal subjects for the faded paintwork technique, for as is well known, the effects of prolonged sunlight are very significant in this respect; moreover, desert sand has a terribly abrasive effect and, in WWII, vehicles which were subjected to the vicious sandstorms soon showed

GLANCING STRIKES ON ARMOUR PLATE

DIRECT HIT ON *SCHURTZEN*

BULLET STRIKE ON WINDSCREEN

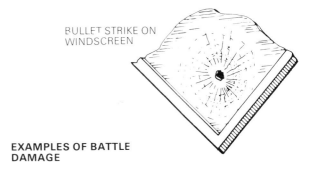

EXAMPLES OF BATTLE DAMAGE

signs of the punishment in the form of faded paintwork and in some cases paint which had been stripped off with bare metal showing through. This last effect can be realistically achieved by the careful use of 'steel' paint which should be applied to the edges of bodywork or armour where the effects of the sand would be felt. Just a touch of this paint, gently applied with the little finger or a dry brush can enhance a model most dramatically.

Although military vehicles were, during wartime,

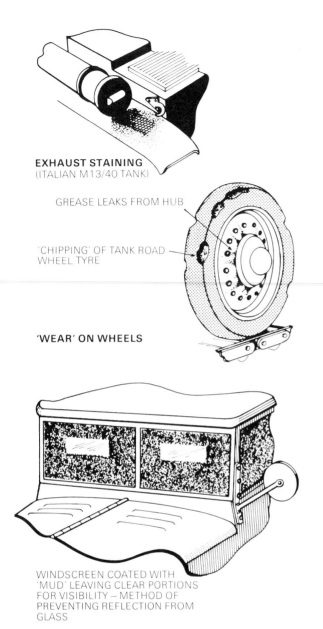

EXHAUST STAINING
(ITALIAN M13/40 TANK)

GREASE LEAKS FROM HUB

'CHIPPING' OF TANK ROAD
WHEEL TYRE

'WEAR' ON WHEELS

WINDSCREEN COATED WITH
'MUD' LEAVING CLEAR PORTIONS
FOR VISIBILITY – METHOD OF
PREVENTING REFLECTION FROM
GLASS

WINDSCREEN 'CAMOUFLAGE'

plates and transmission housings or indeed any other place where bodies and boots were in almost continuous contact with metal. Again, the judicious use of 'steel' enamel, carefully dry brushed or otherwise gently applied to well-defined edges and rounded interior surfaces with the little finger, can produce a most realistic effect. Silver paint used by itself provides far too harsh an appearance, but just a touch of this paint added to the steel can heighten the effect. Metal floorplates often had a raised 'non-slip' pattern on them and these may first be painted in the basic colour, 'muddied' as desired and then dry brushed with 'steel' to give the effect of the paint having been worn off the pattern. Seat covers in vehicles which were driven for long periods in the open configuration, especially in the desert or in the Far East, would soon fade and present a 'washed out' appearance; these may be painted accordingly using lighter shades.

Exhaust gases can stain the paintwork of a vehicle where the outlet pipe is in proximity to the body or armour plate. An example of this is the Italian M13/40 tank where the exhaust silencers and outlets are mounted just above the rear dust-guards. Careful and restrained use of matt black or very dark grey paint on these dustguards, just behind the silencers, will enhance the 'used' appearance of the vehicle. The edges of the exhaust staining will need to be well 'feathered' as the gases became dispersed when they emerged. A study of photographs of the German 8-wheeled SdKfz 232 armoured car will reveal that the exhaust silencers mounted on the rear wings had a protective cover of wire mesh. Heat radiated from the silencers soon discoloured these grilles, and this effect can add a touch of realism to a model of this vehicle.

Petrol and oil also stain the paintwork of a vehicle, especially in the vicinity of the fuel tank filler caps. The Sherman and M3 and M5 light tanks are examples of models which can benefit from the careful application of 'spillage'. Oil and petrol tend to discolour paintwork and observations of full size vehicles will provide inspiration for the reproduction of this effect on a model — the use of thinned glossy black enamel, for example, can provide a realistic finish. Experiments should be carried out on scrap plastic in the first instance to obtain the correct result.

Whilst on the subject of staining by oil, the question of lubrication of wheel bearings should be mentioned. The lubrication of these components is by means of thick grease which under the stress of heat becomes thinned down and sometimes seeps out from the hub cap. This can be represented by fine lines radiating out from the edge of the cap on to the wheel itself. Again, restraint must be exer-

painted in a matt finish, continuous use tended to produce a sheen on certain parts — rounded surfaces such as wings and petrol tanks of motor cycles are two cases in point. Gentle rubbing with the finger on a matt finished surface can produce the slightly shiny look, but as with every other painting process, this should be restrained. Signs of wear soon appeared on WWII vehicles as, for obvious reasons, the amount of paint applied was kept to a minimum. Wear became most apparent in localised areas such as the top edges of doors, door sills and engine hatches, and inside the bodies over wheel arches, brake, clutch and accelerator pedals, floor cised in the application of this type of discolouration.

Another aspect of weathering which receives a lot of attention from modellers is rust. Unpainted steel and iron soon tends to rust when exposed to the elements; moisture collects around projections such as rivet heads, brackets and hinges, and should any of these be of unpainted metal then streaks of rust tend to occur. This effect can be represented on a model by tiny, downward pointing streaks of brownish-orange or 'rust' paint. This should not be overdone however, as no self-respecting crew would allow their tank or armoured car to degenerate into a mass of corroded metal!

One area of a vehicle which by the very nature of its function attracts a great deal of dust and dirt is the windscreen. Early lorries had no windscreens at all; instead a tarpaulin was rigged from the scuttle which covered the driving compartment and ended level with the driver's face. Some early World War

II 15cwt trucks had twin 'aero' screens as used on racing cars of the day, but later vehicles had full-width screens some of which, like that on the Jeep, could be folded forward over the bonnet. Canadian Ford and Chevrolet lorries had the top of the windscreen canted forward of the lower edges to obviate the danger of reflections from the glass. Another method of preventing the tell-tale reflections from a windscreen which was used widely by the Germans, as well as by the Allies, was the covering of the windscreen with paint — usually of the same colour as the vehicle — or mud, with just a slit or small aperture left for the driver's vision. This can easily be represented on a model. Windscreens were often dirty, with dust collecting around the edges with a fairly clean central area. Again, a model truck, US scout car or half-track can be given this treatment by painting over the entire windscreen with the chosen 'dust' colour, slightly thinned down. Then the central part of the screen (or screens if it is of the divided type) is carefully rubbed with a brush or a tiny piece of rag dipped in white spirit. Another treatment of a windscreen is to represent dirty glass with clean portions as though swept by wiper blades. This is achieved by cutting arcs from clear adhesive tape, the straight edge being approximately twice the length of the wiper arm (usually represented on the windscreen component by a raised moulding). An arc is drawn using compasses and the segment cut out — if two wipers are fitted, obviously two arcs will be required. The tape

Below: some of the most impressive plastic models of wartime vehicles show 'wear' in a very restricted manner. Gentle rubbing with a cloth and careful highlighting with metallic paint around areas which would come into contact with the rider's feet have produced a very convincing effect on this 1/9 scale Harley-Davidson WLA-45, built from the ESCI kit. Note also the realistic surface textures on the saddle and pannier bags – the latter have been remodelled with soft paper and treated with semi-gloss paint to simulate the material used on the prototype. (Model and photo: Jacques D'Heur)

segments are stuck on to the windscreen to cover the area swept by the wiper blades, and the whole screen is then painted over and left to dry thoroughly. The arcs of adhesive tape can be peeled off leaving clear areas of 'glass', and the finished effect is most striking in appearance.

Additional touches to an AFV model can be incorporated by darkening slightly the area around the muzzles of the main armament; continuous firing would probably blister the paint on the barrel so that it would tend to flake off. A carefully applied touch of steel around the muzzles of guns not fitted with muzzle brakes adds a further note of realism. Weapons which are fitted with muzzle brakes, however, should have the interior of the brake blackened, and a 'sooty' finish applied to the exterior of the brake itself. Muzzles of small-calibre and machine guns can be drilled out for added realism; this task may be carried out with a fine drill held in a pin chuck. Drilling can also be applied to other items of equipment and components such as exhaust pipes and horns. Care is needed when hollowing out pipes and gun muzzles, but the additional realism achieved is well worth the effort involved.

SUMMARY

Much emphasis has been placed in the foregoing paragraphs on the importance of studying reliable references before a truly representative model can be produced. Photographs can be regarded as the primary source of information, but plans — accurate plans — also have their place. Many modellers working from basic plastic materials will draw their own plans using photographs as a guide — this transference of information from photographs to diagram is really interpretation, and, if accurate plans are to be the result, considerable skill is required. Not all modellers possess the necessary talent, however, and there are on the market some excellent and well-detailed plans of armoured vehicles used in both World Wars. These plans provide all the necessary information which will enable a modeller working with plastic card to produce a really worthwhile model in terms of its structural shape. Modelling publications also feature plans of military vehicles, but many of these should be treated with extreme caution for they are often produced by individuals with little or no real skill and are in many instances wildly inaccurate. Indeed, one such set of plans was drawn using one photograph and some memories — not really a sufficient basis for accuracy. Before one attempts any modification to a kit or starts to build a model from plastic card, therefore, it is essential that as much information on the subject be accumulated as is possible — and ideally this applies to 'straight' kit models too.

A well-researched model does not necessarily guarantee that the end product will be accurate, or resemble the chosen subject, however, for many people have considerable constructional skill but do not have what is called 'an eye for line'. Thus although the model produced may be dimensionally accurate its appearance is incorrect; it does not have the 'feel' of the real vehicle or 'sit' in the correct manner. The slightly tail-down attitude of the Universal Carrier or the squat appearance of the Morris Commercial CS8 15cwt truck, for example, are aspects which are all part of the overall appearance of these vehicles but are very difficult to achieve in miniature. For although a model may have the correct structural shape of its full size counterpart, the 'atmosphere' may be lacking. This is not necessarily restricted to hand built models — kit models frequently suffer from this fault!

The actual methods of construction using basic materials have been dealt with in Chapter 3 of this book, and here it is merely emphasised that careful research and the use of accurate plans, together with as many photographs as possible for reference, are vital ingredients for successful military modelling. Time spent on research is never wasted, for in addition to ensuring that the end result is realistic the modeller's personal knowledge is considerably broadened.

Below: a 1/35 scale Ford 3-ton GS truck, utilising the bonnet and mudguards from Tamiya's Quad kit. The chassis has been extended from Quad components, but the body, tilt and cab have been built from plastic card and rod, the cab roof having been plug moulded. A 'used' look has been achieved by dry brushing several variations of khaki drab paint.
(Model and photo: David Jane)

Chapter 7
Special considerations ~figures

by ALAN EDWARDS

The plastic figure first made its appearance in the late 1950s and early 1960s as a solid polyethylene moulding in a fixed pose and mounted on an integral base. Far more actual moulded detail was incorporated than had hitherto been seen on metal mouldings, but the figures were nevertheless regarded as toys. The world famous Britains company was the pioneer manufacturer of these figures, and most types are still in production. Several overseas manufacturers such as Elastolin (W Germany) and Starlux (France) are now in competition, and whereas some of the painting on the British figures left much to be desired, these two continental firms have achieved quite a high standard of presentation. Not until Airfix (UK) and Historex (France) started producing a variety of models in component parts was the plastic figure to be taken as a serious collector's item.

Although those plastics figures most developed by modellers are produced to 54mm (1/30–1/32) scale, there are many types available in OO (1/76), 1/35 and the large 1/12 scales, and some in 1/24 and 1/9, and most of these are issued specifically to match military vehicle kits or railway layouts. In addition, of course, figures are frequently included as components of aircraft, vehicle or ship kits and are scaled accordingly. Broadly speaking, however, the same modelling and painting techniques apply to all scales, and where special attention is required in any one, this will be outlined in the ensuing paragraphs.

The creation of a figure model has of recent years become an art form in its own right, and there are very many fine examples to be seen at the various competitions and exhibitions held around the world. Looking at other people's work can enable a figure modeller — indeed any modeller — to evaluate and compare various styles and gives an indication of the techniques that may be adapted to achieve a certain result. Membership of an appropriate club or society can give an instant feedback of information. How

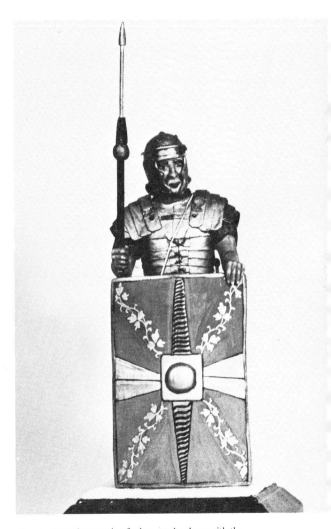

Above: a good example of what can be done with the inexpensive 1/12 scale Airfix figures, this Roman Legionary has had all the armour rebuilt using plastic card, with the rivets and fastenings all faithfully reproduced following a great deal of careful research. The shield and javelin are made from metal and plastic. (Model: John Spinks)

Above: a trio of polyethylene US Cavalry figures from the 1/32 Airfix set, unaltered, primed, painted and incorporated into a small diorama. The arrows in the log are made from stretched sprue and their flights from 5 thou plastic card. The log itself is shown as found in the garden. A purist would alter the officer's pistol and certain items of wear.
(Model: Alan Edwards)

this information is used is another matter altogether, but the development of one's own style should be a matter of paramount importance — the slavish copying of a well-known successful modeller's style will not, in the long run, bring satisfaction.

However, what should be kept in mind is that any hobby or pastime is pursued for enjoyment, and if any competition is won with a particular figure this should be treated as a bonus, a recognition of one's craftsmanship. If competitions become the sole reason for modelling, again, eventual dissatisfaction will probably result. Enjoyment and relaxation — an escape from the pressures of everyday life — this is what any hobby should be about. Whilst the writer does not wish to sermonise, it is hoped that these few gentle words of advice may assist both the novice and the expert — an hors d'oeuvre before the more matter-of-fact aspects to be discussed. One should never press on struggling to complete a model just because one feels that it *should* be completed. When this mental point is reached it is time to sit back, take a deep breath, tidy up the working area and finish the modelling session.

POLYETHYLENE FIGURES

OO scale figures are the smallest on the market in the UK, although a German firm, Preiser, make some in HO (1/87) scale. As the vast majority of these smaller figures are moulded in polyethylene, even the most simple corrections can prove problematic, due

entirely to the fact that the material is most difficult to bond satisfactorily. This is also true of the larger sized 1/32 scale polyethylene figures, and similar techniques apply when alterations are being attempted. Airfix and Matchbox are the major manufacturers of these smaller figures, the former offering the wider choice, from Ancient Britons and Romans to all arms of modern services, plus some civilian subjects.

Simple re-animation of heads and limbs can be effected by cutting clean through the limb to be changed and substituting the required item, inserting a small length of metal pin into the body and pushing the new limb into place. The problems of securely gluing polyethylene remain, however, even with the recent introduction of cyanoacrylate 'super glues'. The most satisfactory results are achieved by pinning the limbs and then coating the entire figure with a white liquid glue such as Unibond which, when dry, shrinks on to the figure, forming a skin which makes an ideal base for painting.

The removal of mould lines and flash (which are

especially prevalent on polyethylene figures) should be done with a sharp blade, in a gentle cutting motion, rather than by scraping. Scraping does not remove flash satisfactorily and feathers up the surface of the plastic into unsightly ridges.

A change in clothing styles can be achieved for polyethylene figures by the use of transparent adhesive tape cut into the required pattern and simply stuck to the figure before it is treated with Unibond. Clear adhesive tape can also be used for belts and strapping, and the use of the double-sided variety is ideal when there is equipment to be affixed to the belts.

The same techniques apply in general for 54mm or 1/32 scale polyethylene figures as for 00 scale, but being larger the former afford the modeller much wider scope in detailing potential. 54mm scale, incidentally, is also known to an older generation of figure modellers as the Standard Scale, as practically all figures were at one time produced to it. However, figures that are bought and sold ostensibly as 54mm scale often prove not in fact to be so, but this will be explained in the following section on 'hard' plastics.

With polyethylene figures, certain areas, for example between arms and body, show a wedge of plastic, but whereas on a tiny model this can be disguised by using a paintbrush it needs to be physically removed on a larger figure. The wedge usually occurs where the mouldings are not, or cannot be, sufficiently undercut to eliminate the surplus material. As with the cleaning away of flash, a sharp blade should be used to carve away any such solid mass, in order to produce a more realistic shape. This can be done to excellent effect on back packs, pouches, etc. Alternatively, such features may be cut off altogether and either replaced by spare items or built up from more basic materials. Again, adhesive tape can be used to attach these parts. One should never be afraid to substitute the moulded items with others that appear to enhance the figure, even if such replacements are polystyrene mouldings or metal castings. It is the end result which counts, and one's own eye should be the greatest critic.

Polyethylene figures are ideal for the younger or less experienced modeller, or those with a tight budget, as a box containing a couple of dozen is very reasonably priced. One need not therefore feel reluctant to experiment with various techniques for fear of ruining an expensive investment. Much excellent detail is apparent on these figures, which seem to improve as time goes on, and such detail can be further enhanced by careful painting.

MODELLING AND ANIMATING POLYSTYRENE FIGURES

There are a very large number of polystyrene figures on the market at present, consisting of ranges of all types which are constantly being revised and added to, so that there is no period in history which, provided the modeller is prepared to alter the kit mouldings, cannot be represented. This is due as much to the foresight and planning of the manufacturer as to the ease with which the material can be worked, and of course the vast array of spare parts and accessories available give the modeller a quite extraordinary choice of subject matter.

As previously mentioned, there is a slight difference in scale between the products of the two 'giants' of the plastic kit figure industry, Historex and Airfix. This is because Historex have measured their 54mm kits to the level of the standing figure's eyeballs, whereas Airfix have gauged theirs to the top of the head, resulting in a 2 or 3mm difference in height. Some modellers like to use Airfix heads on Historex bodies as the heads appear, in some cases, to have more character than the somewhat bland countenances favoured by the French firm. Unfortunately, most Airfix heads are correspondingly too small for use, but matching them on a trial and error basis will soon give some idea of what is possible. Airfix 'Multipose' figures offer a greater variety of heads turned at different angles, and these, together with the types offered by the Japanese (Aoshima, Tamiya), Italian (Italaerei, ESCI) and French (Heller) firms — although these are 1/35 scale and may not always match 1/32 figures — give the modeller a wide range of possibilities for portraying twentieth century soldiers of all nationalities.

Before discussing modelling techniques in more detail, mention should be made of one piece of equipment that is very important to the figure modeller. This is the pyrogravure, which is no more than a small type of soldering iron with a fine, sharp point, which heats up just sufficiently to melt

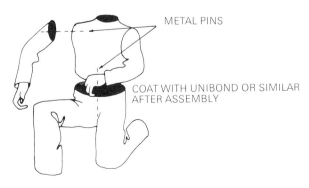

METAL PINS

COAT WITH UNIBOND OR SIMILAR AFTER ASSEMBLY

ANIMATING POLYETHYLENE FIGURES

plastic. Using this, hair, eyebrows, moustaches and beards can be textured to excellent effect.

A realistically animated face is often the highlight of a figure model, and individuality can be presented by following a few simple techniques. To open a mouth, for example, the pyrogravure tip may be pushed between the figure's lips, preserving the top lip if possible, and working the tip downwards until the required extent of open mouth is reached. The depth should not be too great as this could present painting problems later on. Usually, a grotesque funnel-mouth results from this operation, with a subsequent loss of depth or length to the chin. However, if the plastic is allowed to cool, the mouth cavity can be carved with a sharp scalpel to the required shape. It can be made to depict shouting, laughing or screaming, simply by the addition and subtraction of various areas of plastic. Creases assist the facial characteristics, and this is where liquid plastic of various thicknesses becomes

invaluable. 'Liquid sprue' can be made up by chopping lengths of sprue and placing them in a bottle of partially emptied liquid polystyrene cement or, better still, Winsol, a paint solvent for artists made by Winsor and Newton. Various viscosities can be prepared by altering the amount of sprue added, and the mixture can be applied with a brush. Brushing the liquid straight from the bottle smooths over the surfaces worked on, whilst a thin solution makes an excellent coating for those areas filled with body putty prior to painting. A slightly thicker solution can be used to good effect for building up facial areas: noses can be made rounded and swollen, eyebrows and moustaches can be added where none is moulded, and racial types can be indicated by making cheekbones more pronounced, for example, or by slightly narrowing the upper eyelids for Eastern Asiatics. A thick solution works well as a filler where minor surgery has taken place on a model, and it can be pushed into creases as the outer skin dries. Experimentation will soon give the modeller the knowledge needed to achieve a particular effect.

Any head and facial hair can be worked up realistically with the hot pyrogravure tip, but this is usually best done after the headgear has been fitted. An American Civil War kepi, for example, sits fairly tightly on the crown of the head, and so the hair should appear to emphasise this. Similarly, chinstraps should be fitted by first filing or engrav-

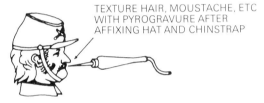

TEXTURE HAIR, MOUSTACHE, ETC WITH PYROGRAVURE AFTER AFFIXING HAT AND CHINSTRAP

DETAILING HEADS

FRENCH DRAGOONS 18th. CENT.

Opposite: these figures, eighteenth century French Dragoons, are from the 54mm SEGOM range, and the horse furniture has been made up from basic materials; the heads are from the Historex range, with remodelled headwear. Note the leggings with the numerous buckles, achieved by using Historex spares. The horse has been widened at chest and rump.
(Model: John Spinks)

Right: the Hun raider shown in this photograph has been built from 54mm Airfix components, much altered with the use of plastic card and filler and textured with the pyrogravure. The unfortunate maiden is a reworked Historex Lady Godiva kit; her hair has been produced by applying nylon string to the head with epoxy resin, teasing it out, blending it to the model with a pyrogravure and painting it with a gold wash.
(Model: Reg Hale)

ing a shallow groove down the sides of the face and under the chin. This need not be overdone, but just enough to show that the chinstrap bites slightly into the flesh. Sideburns and other whiskers can then be gently feathered over this, and the effect can be very pleasing.

Referring again to the mouth, the teeth can be worked in either with liquid sprue or with small pieces of thin plastic sheet. Again, moderation should be exercised or the end result may look grotesque. A tip for examining one's handiwork as it progresses is to hold it up in front of a mirror; this gives the impression of seeing the figure for the first time, and errors can be corrected and a proper 'balance' produced.

The torso sections of most polystyrene figures have a certain amount of detail engraved into them that must be taken into account when one attempts to change the attitude of the body or adds straps and equipment. Generally, it is better to nick off buttons that will underlie straps, to allow the latter to sit into rather than on to the tunic or jacket. Similarly, belts, etc, should look as though they are 'pulling' the cloth, and this can be shown by first filing a groove around the waist, then fitting the belt, and finally lightly building up the cloth above and below the belt with liquid sprue, adding creases as it dries. Crossbelts, with the weight they support, dig into the tops of the shoulders and, again, a shallow groove achieves this effect. Any untidiness can be concealed by the shoulder straps or epaulettes, and these usually need to be rubbed down a little on the undersides as they are often too thick in section. Fringed epaulettes can be worked with the pyrogravure or hot needle.

Where the head is to be turned to one side, the moulded collar will need to be cut away and a new one made from thin plastic sheet. It is usually sufficient to do this by cutting two small triangles of card and affixing them according to the position of the neck and chin. Thus the standing collar can be

shown to be slightly crumpled, under pressure from the chin. This method can be followed to show a tunic open at the top two or three buttons, in which case the moulded buttons should be cut away, an elongated triangle of plastic card placed into position, the buttonholes marked in and replacement buttons added in their new positions. These more delicate operations are better undertaken using light washes of liquid cement rather than the tube variety, and indeed this solvent is necessary for practically all fine work.

Although World War II figures might not need

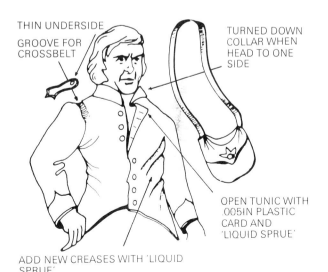

THIN UNDERSIDE GROOVE FOR CROSSBELT

TURNED DOWN COLLAR WHEN HEAD TO ONE SIDE

OPEN TUNIC WITH .005IN PLASTIC CARD AND 'LIQUID SPRUE'

ADD NEW CREASES WITH 'LIQUID SPRUE'

MODIFYING TUNICS AND JACKETS

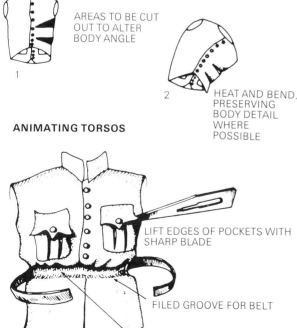

AREAS TO BE CUT
OUT TO ALTER
BODY ANGLE

HEAT AND BEND,
PRESERVING
BODY DETAIL
WHERE
POSSIBLE

ANIMATING TORSOS

LIFT EDGES OF POCKETS WITH
SHARP BLADE

FILED GROOVE FOR BELT

CREASES AND BULGES BUILT UP
WITH 'LIQUID SPRUE'

MODIFYING POCKETS AND BELTS

Above: Zastrow Cuirassiers (Saxon, 1812) in 54mm scale, a trumpeter lending a helping hand to a trooper. Note on the riding figure how the belt 'bites' into the tunic, the body of the model having been built up with 'liquid sprue' as described in the text. The gabions (artillery shields) to the left of the picture are made from straw. Both the figures and the horse are reworked Historex kits.
(Model: Alan Edwards)

Opposite: The American GI depicted here is a 1/35 scale kit figure from the Tamiya range, constructed 'straight from the box'. Note the realistically moulded facial expression and the convincing 'action' pose. The simple addition of a battered oil drum and jerrycan, together with scattered ejected shellcases, helps to relay an authentic atmosphere.
(Model: Alan Edwards)

such drastic treatment to the collar area, mainly because many mouldings show these features anyway, the pocket and tunic detail can be further enhanced by using a sharp scalpel or engraving tool to lift lapels or pocket flaps, etc, at the corners, thereby giving the impression of constant use. This takes off some of the 'parade ground' image and 'humanises' the figure.

As most body mouldings are meant to be constructed in the straight-backed, standing or riding position, they can appear to be too stiff and doll-like in certain situations. For instance, a person sitting

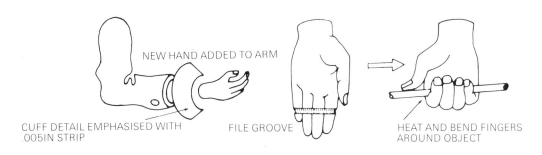

NEW HAND ADDED TO ARM

CUFF DETAIL EMPHASISED WITH
.005IN STRIP

FILE GROOVE

HEAT AND BEND FINGERS
AROUND OBJECT

HANDS AND CUFFS

in a vehicle, or on a wall or a chair, usually arches the spine slightly, and on models this has to be compensated for by a slight bulging of clothing in the waist area. This is admirably shown on some of the figures produced by Tamiya, and these can be used as a guide to anatomical alterations on figures from other ranges. Reducing certain areas of plastic before final assembly gives a new angle entirely to the head or limb to be affixed, and the opposite side to the cut usually needs to be built up to balance the loss. Where no commercially available or usable part is appropriate, the torso can be shown to be slumped or arched in various positions, but this is not achieved without some difficulty, nor of course the necessary confidence to carry it through. The diagrams and sketches show how this can best be achieved by cutting almost through the body section but preserving as much integral detail as possible, and the technique is especially appropriate to Historex components as all the different styles are moulded in the 'straight back' position. In the Airfix Collector's Series, the 10th Hussar's body offers a good example. Used as shown in the instructions, the body is slightly arched forwards, with the right arm raised or more or less straight ahead, but if all the detail is trimmed off and the body reversed, it now gives a body arched backwards with the *left* arm raised — ideal for use in many action poses. With Airfix figures, there are now many variations in arm leg and body positions in the 'Multipose' range that obviate the need for major surgery in many cases. The careful selection of parts, and marrying these with components from the many other manufacturers' ranges whose scales are compatible, can result in a really unique figure. These kits, of course, cater for those modellers specialising in First and Second World War figures and dioramas, but the Napoleonics enthusiast can turn to the excellent Historex range and the intermittent releases in the Collector's Series from Airfix. The latter company has not concentrated entirely on the Napoleonic era, and French légionnaires, Bengal lancers and figures from the English Civil War (a much neglected period) are all repre-

sented. However, with a little ingenuity, the finely moulded Historex figures can be remodelled to represent any desired period; indeed, the company has issued two nude figures, male and female, with a template for cutting suitable clothing included in the instruction sheet.

Choosing the appropriate arms and legs must obviously be done with the necessary end result firmly established in the mind, and any alterations must be carried out with a full appreciation of anatomical limitations. Most kits offer a choice of arm positions, but many hand mouldings leave much to be desired. This is true of many Historex hands, although the Musicians' arms have some interesting hands with separated fingers in a variety of positions. Airfix, however, mould some finely detailed hands that are easily separated from the arms and incorporated into other makes of kit. If this is to be done, the modeller can take the opportunity to add some cuff detail by applying thin plastic sheet around the wrist after the hand has been fixed in position, giving the impression of depth to the sleeve with the hand extending from it.

Hands can be made to grasp an object firmly by gently heating the fingers and easing them around the article to be held. A shallow saw cut on the inside of the hand will create a groove that will make this job more readily accomplished.

Joining the arms to the body will usually necessitate filling and slightly building up the tops of the shoulders and the underarm areas. Nothing looks worse on any model than an obvious joint line, but this can be avoided by dry-fitting the parts first and noting where any building up will need to be done. Again, liquid sprue or body putty can be used to good effect, working in the continuity of the creases as the filler dries. Notwithstanding the fact that in earlier periods clothing was much tighter in cut and fit, some building up of arms that are raised above shoulder level is going to be required for a realistic presentation of physical action, especially where shoulder straps or epaulettes are evident.

The foregoing comments also apply to any change in leg positions, bearing in mind the figure's situation, the pull of the cloth against the leg, and the sort of legwear to be shown. For instance, there would not be as much creasing evident in a tight pair of cavalry breeches as in loose working overalls or campaign trousers. Changing a standing figure to one crouching or seated is not merely a matter of bends at the appropriate joints, as many anatomical changes take place. The hips must be widened and the buttocks shown to be in evidence, and these can

Right: on this 54mm model, a French Line Chasseur, the face has been 'aged' by the addition of heavy brows and a rubicund expression and the figure given a casual appearance by the selection of an appropriate body part. The hips were widened using the 'At Ease' position legs to show the figure off balance. The horse position was achieved by using four different horse quarters. The open tunic is a list Historex spare part, ideal for this sort of casual pose. Note the accessories slung about the saddle – the forage bag is ordinary open weave bandage around some sisal string cut to represent hay.
(Model: Alan Edwards)

Below: the 54mm 'Wild West' figure illustrated here typifies the sort of possibilities that exist with these kinds of kits for bringing together parts from a number of different sources. The torso, arms and legs are from different Historex kits; the legs originate from a mounted figure, but they have been brought together slightly by removing a wedge of plastic from the crutch, and the chaps have been built up with filler. The head is a polyethylene Britains item, fixed to the rest of the model with Dunlop clear impact adhesive. The revolver is from a 1/35 scale Tamiya model of a British WWII soldier.
(Model: Mick Miller)

be built up with wedges of sprue or filler. Bending the leg at the knee requires the removal of a wedge of material from the back of the joint and consequent building up in the kneecap area. The creases should be shown, and these may need a total alteration from those moulded on the figure. A full length mirror can assist the modeller if he himself adopts his figure's required position in front of it, noting where the attitude changes, the fall of the creases and the angles of the limbs. Whatever position is adopted can be translated to the figure, and this helps to eliminate an unnatural attitude on the model.

EQUIPMENT

A figure's equipment should present few problems if a logical sequence of assembly is first thought out. Some belts and straps can be added before the figure is painted, but it should be remembered that the brush cannot always reach where the eye can plainly see, and so it may be advisable to add only those belts that will not be totally obscured by other details.

Whilst plastic card is generally good for representing static straps, belts and webbing, a more flexible material is needed for such things as sword slings and belts that are to be shown hanging loosely. Such a material is thin lead alloy sheet stripped from wine bottle tops. This alloy is very pliable and some excellent natural effects can be obtained from its use. It takes cyanoacrylate glue very well but needs to be primed before it is painted. A good quality writing paper can also be used, slightly dampened, to give a similar result. A liquid cement such as Plastic Weld holds the buckles, etc, to the paper and, again, a coat of matt enamel is usually a good idea before the final coat of paint is

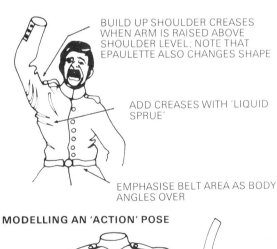

BUILD UP SHOULDER CREASES WHEN ARM IS RAISED ABOVE SHOULDER LEVEL; NOTE THAT EPAULETTE ALSO CHANGES SHAPE

ADD CREASES WITH 'LIQUID SPRUE'

EMPHASISE BELT AREA AS BODY ANGLES OVER

MODELLING AN 'ACTION' POSE

TEMPLATE FOR SHOULDER BELTS

USE BUCKLE TO COVER JOIN

CROSSBELTS

added. Some modellers use various types of gift-wrapping ribbon, which can be torn lengthways to the desired width, eliminating the necessity of a straightedge and scalpel. Each individual modeller will eventually settle on one type or another, and experimentation will show which is most suitable for each effect. When laying the strap or belt on the figure, any joined ends should be encouraged to lie under an appropriate buckle, as the latter will become the 'double security' part when the glue has dried. This also makes for a neater, crisper appearance.

Pouches, haversacks and knapsacks may need to be reduced somewhat at the point at which they come into contact with the figure. This can be done by carving away the plastic so that the article falls naturally against the figure's back or hip. Nothing can detract from good paintwork more than a cartridge pouch or knapsack that looks as though it has no contact with the figure.

Where a figure is portrayed running or falling, the equipment can be shown to be flapping, giving the impression of movement. This technique should be applied with care, however, as it is so easy to make the effect too theatrical, especially with mounted figures shown in full gallop. The weight of the article – a scabbard, for instance — should be taken into account.

Most weaponry supplied with kits is very good, requiring little work for a pleasing result. Barrels of firearms invariably need their muzzles drilled out slightly to give the impression of hollowness, and swords and bayonets are often too thick in section and can be scraped or sanded down to give a truer scale likeness. Sword slings or carrying straps may be added to weapons prior to painting them, as this is often quite fiddly work and attaching such items is near impossible with ready painted surfaces.

At this point, it is appropriate to mention the many accessories available for figures, as there is a tendency amongst modellers to overdress their subjects with impediments with which a real life marching or fighting man just could not be bothered. A carefully chosen miniature wine bottle, water flask and cooking pan, plus a dead bird hung from his rifle may be all that is required to give the right atmosphere to a period character; for more modern military figures, careful reference to contemporary photographs will reveal what is suitable in the way of equipment. Where two or three figures are to be shown together, in a camp scene for example, then various accessories can be positioned to good effect, but care should be taken not to detract from the central theme. Of course, experience will arm the modeller with various 'dos and don'ts' — just because a certain accessory looks attractive, common sense will govern whether it is appropriate for a given situation.

Whilst headwear has already been briefly mentioned, it has not been dealt with in any depth, simply because of the wide variety of types which could each qualify for a paragraph. However, the decorations that adorn early period headgear such

OPEN UP WITH FINE TWIST DRILL

MUZZLES OF FIREARMS

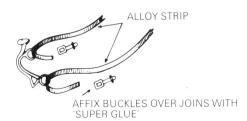

ALLOY STRIP

AFFIX BUCKLES OVER JOINS WITH 'SUPER GLUE'

REINS

as plumes, crests and the like can benefit in appearance from a technique developed by the well-known Historex modeller Max Longhurst. The caterpillar crest of a carabinier's or line lancer's helmet can be given depth or texture by washing thin liquid sprue over it, sticking small pieces of plastic sheet all over this, and using the pyrogravure to push into the crest and pull out long strands of hardening plastic. Covering the entire area of the crest is a lengthy operation, but it results in a mass of long wisps of plastic which can then be trimmed with a small pair of scissors to produce a feathered effect. The end result can be startlingly realistic, and can be adapted for plumes and so on. Painting the treated crest now becomes a trifle difficult, but if the paint is used dark at first and floated on in thin washes this can be left to dry and highlighted later. It is such experiments in techniques that keep a constant flow of interest and enable those new to the hobby, or those less skilled, to achieve a higher standard of workmanship than they may otherwise enjoy.

HORSES AND THEIR EQUIPMENT

The same principles apply for the construction and animation of horses as for their human counterparts. Before altering the pose of a horse it is advisable to become well acquainted with the real animal's anatomy and natural movement, and there are several excellent books available on the subject. Those that have plenty of line drawings and photographs will be most useful as they frequently show the sequence of limb movements essential to the creation of a lifelike model.

Airfix and Historex market a wide selection of mounts, although Historex' are the more versatile as heads and body halves are moulded separately. However, their mounts are fine, thoroughbred types, ideal for light cavalry officers, and need to be thickened at chest and rump for heavy cavalry mounts. Airfix horses, on the other hand, are all of the heavier, muscular type, and with a little ingenuity on the part of the modeller can be animated into any pose. This will involve cutting away all or part of a limb and repositioning it, subsequently filling any gaps. Constant reference to a work on horse anatomy is therefore essential.

Heads can, in general, be gently heated in the region of the neck and bent around to a new position, but cutting away a wedge and repositioning the part is sometimes more satisfactory. The mane, forelock and tail can all be textured with the pyrogravure for a hairy effect. Many modellers dispense with the kit mane altogether, preferring to brush on thick layers of liquid sprue, which is then teased out with the pyrogravure to give the desired effect. Others use teased out nylon cord, or doll's hair and the like, for manes and tails. This method requires much practice to perfect, but it can give satisfactory results when done expertly.

Hooves, if shown raised off the ground, can be hollowed out and have a V-shaped frog cut into them, in the farrier's fashion, for added authenticity. Horseshoes are available as spares, or they can be cut from plastic card with a leather punch. Saddles should be constructed and altered, if necessary, to fit the horse's back without unsightly gaps appearing. They are best built after the horse has been completely assembled and animated. Most of the girths, cruppers, etc, can be affixed prior to painting, but it is probably easier to leave off the bit and reins until the paintwork is dry. Stirrups, too, should be left or if the figure is to be mounted affixed to the soles of the boots with the leathers bonded to the upper insides of the knees. Sheepskin saddles can be worked up with the pyrogravure (as can animal skin shabraques like leopard and tiger), though only lightly, so that essential markings are not obliterated.

Where a mounted figure is to be modelled, it is usually best to construct horse, saddle and rider in that order, constantly fitting saddle to horse and legs to saddle in order to eliminate gaps. A snug fit is facilitated if the insides of the rider's legs are pared away and that part of the saddle in contact with the rider is trimmed down. The reins and bridle straps that hang loose can be made from the pliable alloy mentioned previously and may be fitted whilst the bits are still attached to the kit sprue. The reins may be looped through the rings and the buckles attached over the join for strength. The reins can be painted before they are fitted to the horse, or left until later, as conditions dictate — ease of accessibility is essential for painting. A drop of 'super glue' to each side of the horse's mouth will secure the reins, and these can then be given a realistic droop by easing them into shape with the end of a needle file or paintbrush. The essentials of realistic-looking harnessing are good references, followed by their meticulous reproduction by the modeller. Valises, saddlebags, etc, can be added to the saddle after any necessary painting, any blank areas being retouched afterwards.

PAINTING TECHNIQUES
Nothing causes controversy in the modelling world more than the 'dos and don'ts' of painting techniques. Much has been written on the subject, and it is not proposed here to add fuel to fire any arguments. Suffice to say that there are no clear cut techniques, simply alternatives, and as with other aspects of modelling the individual must find the

Above: the effects that can be achieved on a plastic model by the influence of heat are well demonstrated on this 54mm scale Salm-Kirburg Hussar. Apart from the texturing produced by the pyrogravure, this tool, together with some hot water, has been used to shape the fall of the pelisse (jacket) by locally softening various areas. The model is from the Historex range. A point to be borne in mind with all these 54mm and 1/32 scale models is that the figures themselves are only some 2in high. (Model: Alan Edwards)

style which suits him best. However, the following paragraphs will concentrate on the application of colour by using artists' oil paints, as there can be little doubt that, competently handled, they give an excellent finish to any figure.

Where any surgery has been carried out, or where the colour of the plastic is other than white, it is advisable to undercoat the model with a light wash of matt white enamel to provide a base for the oils. Two light undercoats are better than one heavy coat that may obscure vital detail. The size of brush is largely immaterial provided one is able to draw the bristles to a fine point and to feather them slightly for blending and shading. Good quality brushes are essential for good quality work, and, properly looked after, they will give lengthy service.

Starting with the face and other exposed areas of flesh is to be recommended since it gives one the feel of the character of the figure at an early stage. Where oil paint is being used, only small amounts need to be squeezed on to the palette. A suitable 'flesh' palette might consist of Burnt Umber or Burnt Sienna, flesh tint or Naples yellow and yellow

ochre, white, Alizarin Crimson or a lighter red, black, and a dark blue. There are, of course, many combinations of flesh tints, and a suitable guide from an art shop will offer some variations. Painting a figure's face, and flesh in general, is like making up an actor's face and body, emphasis being on various amounts of highlight and shadow.

It may be helpful to paint in the eye colour first and allow it to dry before continuing with the rest of the face, so that the upper and lower eyelids can be painted without fear of smudging the eyes themselves. The iris may be carefully painted dark blue or brown, ensuring that the paint covers all but the extreme corners of the whites and that the iris reaches both the upper and the lower lid. A small amount of pure white can then be taken on the tip of the brush and carefully worked into the dark colour, trying to leave a dark ring around the pale blue centre. When dry, a black dot for the pupil can be added, and the result is very effective. A 'staring' appearance should be avoided; if this is the result, the iris area should be enlarged. A wide-eyed effect is acceptable for a face registering fear or surprise, but it looks alien when the figure is, for example, in a relaxed pose. Once the eyes have dried thoroughly, a coating of gloss varnish gives an authentic wet

Above: this detail photograph of a 54mm scale 12th Chasseur Trumpeter coaxing his horse illustrates some of the effects that can be achieved by attending to small details. The animal's reins and loose bridle straps have been fashioned from strips of lead alloy such as is found around the necks of wine bottles, whilst the moulded bridle detail has been brought to life by some clever painting. Note the realistic eye, which has been finished with a spot of clear varnish.
(Model: Alan Edwards)

Opposite: this fifteenth century English Man-at-Arms is based on 54mm scale Historex parts, utilising the Nude Man's legs and an odd uniform body and pair of arms. All other items have been built up from plastic sheet and 'liquid sprue', although the mail is from a discarded pair of ladies' tights. These were carefully cut into sections, affixed to the figure with liquid cement, painted first dark grey and then highlighted gradually with gunmetal and silver.
(Model: Alan Edwards)

look to them, and they will catch the light naturally.

The frame of the face may next be lined — the nostrils, neckline, ears and around the hairlines — with the darkest flesh colour (Burnt Umber is ideal). This colour can be used around the eye sockets and to line the upper and lower lids. The rest of the face may be painted with the chosen basic flesh colour which, however, should *not* be blended in with the darker shade at this point. A light touch of crimson is added to the lower cheek area and beneath the

146

1 LINE IN SHADOW COLOUR

2 ADD FLESH TINT AND COLOUR TO CHEEKS

3 PAINT LIPS AND LINES. BLEND COLOURS

4 ADD HIGHLIGHT AND LINE IN AREAS OF EMPHASIS

junction at neck and chin if visible. The brush is wiped clean and the bristles gently feathered between thumb and forefinger into a chisel shape, and the junctions between the flesh colours are lightly brushed, blending them together. Pure white can be added to the tops of the eyebrows, the bridge of the nose, the swell at each side of the nostrils, the tips of the ears and chin and the tops of the cheekbones, together with a light touch on each eyelid. The colours should be blended so that no harsh demarcation lines exist. The lips can be a darker flesh tint, highlighted with white, with a dark line to separate them or, if the mouth is open, a dark bluish crimson inside with white teeth and a pale colour for the lips will give emphasis to the expression. The other bare flesh areas of the body should be treated the same way, bearing in mind any racial characteristics. Dark blue in the Burnt Umber or Burnt Sienna, highlighted with Naples yellow and white, will provide a basis for the very dark skinned types, and other races can be depicted by the variation of reddish-browns and ochre.

Whilst the above techniques should be satisfactory on 1/32 scale and larger figures, the OO/HO sizes require more definition of light and shade, the eyes in these cases being a dark dot. There is some remarkable engraving detail on these miniatures which can be shown up to good effect if lightly handled. The use of some type of magnifying glass will be of great assistance in ensuring the accuracy of the modeller's workmanship.

The paintbrush should never be overloaded during painting, and this applies to models of all scales and situations. It is easy to add more to a surface, but difficult to take it off without spoiling other details. If the painting attempt is a total disaster, it can be cleaned off with turpentine or white spirit or, if the paint is dry, a solution of soap crystals worked in with an old toothbrush will restore the finish for repainting. Needless to say, the surface should be completely dry before painting is commenced.

The uniform details can be handled in much the same way as the flesh areas, with blended patterns of light and shade, and the aim should be to work towards a harmonious balance of colour rather than harsh contrasts. Most modellers agree that the dark shade areas should be laid on first, either over the basic uniform colour or else prior to this, leaving highlighting as the last exercise. A dark shade of the basic colour can be used to edge those areas that require definition, such as where two colours or items meet, the edges of stripes, belts, buttons and so on. The basic colour should always be blended up to the darker shade, as this gives more control of depth over the colour. These principles apply to all areas of the uniforms and weapons and equipment.

ENGLISH MAN-AT-ARMS XVth. CENT.

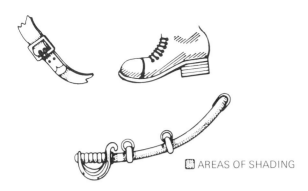

□ AREAS OF SHADING

SHADING EFFECTS

Metallic colours—brass and steel—can be shaded and highlighted also by intermixing a compatible shade of oil paint. Whichever type is used, Humbrol or the powder metallics, Burnt Sienna is suitable for shading brass, and a touch of blue and black will give various steel effects. It is wise to undercoat metallic areas of figures to provide a key for the metallic compounds: orange or yellow matt enamel for brass and gold lace and grey or blue matt for steel and silver lace. The degree of highlighting will usually be governed by the figure's situation — parade dress or on campaign — but one must not be too dogmatic on this point. Artistic licence has its part to play in presentation, as discussed at the beginning of Chapter 4, and, again, it is 'balance' that is required.

Cloth shabraques can be dealt with in the same way as uniforms, but sheepskin saddles need emphasis to their woolly, shaggy texture. A thin wash of Burnt Umber, allowed to dry, over the whole surface will immediately show up the highlights (and any faults!). When this is almost dry to the touch, white can be lightly brushed across the sheepskin. The same technique can be applied to a black sheepskin, but it may be prudent to wipe almost all the white off the brush and go *very* lightly over the surface.

The painting of horses is not as complex as might first appear, although many modellers feel daunted by all that apparent acreage of flesh. There are very many types of colouring for the coats, the browns perhaps being the least difficult to reproduce. A pure black and a pure white are notoriously difficult, but some noted modellers have achieved remarkable results. Reference to that volume on horses will be of inestimable assistance, enabling one to see exactly where colour tones change and to show the positions of markings that look convincing. Supposing the chosen colour to be a

chestnut, the palette might consist of Burnt Umber, Burnt Sienna, black, white and a yellow. In recent years, a method of horse painting has been developed that takes much of the toil away from brushing on paint, and it can be outlined as follows.

The horse is liberally coated with paint, ensuring that all depressions, nooks and crannies are covered, but the legs below the knees are left free. It does not matter at this stage whether paint gets on to the bridle or any other fixed harnessing as this will be painted over later anyway. Using a piece of fine cellular sponge foam, the paint is then wiped with a 'grooming' motion. This removes the paint from the areas of natural highlight and the muscle detail, leaving the darker colour in the hollows. The excess paint is wiped from the sponge and then the painted surfaces are evenly wiped in a firm, on-off stippling motion, ensuring that no heavy areas of paint remain. The results, after a little practice, can be extremely effective, and further detailing, shading and highlighting can be continued once the legs and head are painted. Manes and tails can be painted in thinner washes of the base colour, suitably highlighted with ochre or white administered lightly.

For painting the bridles, harnessing, etc, Humbrol Railway Colour enamels are excellent. These have a semi-gloss finish which gives the right impression for well-used and well-oiled equipment. The reins, already fitted to the bits, can be painted before finally fixing them to the horse, and any necessary retouching can be done afterwards. The horse's eyes can be finished following the method described for the figure's, remembering that very little white should be apparent unless the horse is to be shown in action. A touch of pink in the corners of the eyes and inside the nostrils will give an alert, snorting appearance. When dry, a touch of clear varnish is effective, as for the figure.

Whilst the foregoing is especially applicable to 54mm scale models, the larger scales can be tackled in much the same way and, being larger, give the modeller far more scope for additional detailing. Generally speaking, the larger the figure the more subtle should be the paintwork, avoiding any harsh contrasts that may be necessary on smaller models to show detail.

SUMMARY
In summarising, it may be as well to set out the suggested stages of working in a logical sequence. Following such a sequence should enable the modeller to ensure that no essential component is omitted at a critical stage, such as when painting is about to be commenced.

1 All the parts provided in the kit are laid out and a note is made as to where each is to be fitted.

2 All mould lines and flash are cleaned off, and arms, legs and head are tested for fit. If necessary, alteration of arms, etc, to one's personal requirements can be undertaken before final construction, doing 'dry run' assemblies continuously.

3 The figure is assembled, plus the horse, saddle, etc (if present), ensuring all joint lines are clean, sanded down or blended into creases. The assemblies should be left to dry thoroughly, preferably for 24 hours.

4 Starting with the horse, frogs may be cut in to the hooves, the horseshoes fitted and the mane, tail, girth strap, crupper and chest harness added. The mane and tail can be textured, having regard to the circumstances in which the finished model is to be depicted, ie windy, wet, standing, galloping, etc.

5 The hair, moustache, etc, on the figure may be textured after fitting the headwear. As much detail work as possible should be carried out without creating problems for painting.

6 The same applies to the saddle. At the same time, the fit of rider to saddle and saddle to horse can be checked. Building up the horse beneath the saddle might be considered if the fit is poor and the task of trimming hazardous.

7 The horse is painted in the manner preferred and left to dry thoroughly before any further work is done on it.

8 The figure is painted, starting with the face. The eyes are painted first, and then when these are dry the rest of the flesh areas, followed by thin washes for the hair.

9 The saddle, equipment and weapons are painted.

10 The base is prepared, noting the position of the model and any scenic detail that is to be incorporated. If necessary, the position on the base where the model is to be finally affixed may be marked.

11 The final parts of the horse bridle and reins are assembled, added to the model and painted.

12 The rider is attached to the saddle (or saddle to horse, and then rider to saddle — whichever is more convenient), and any areas that may have been marked or chipped in assembly are touched in.

13 The reins are threaded into the rider's hand(s), ensuring that they look neither too slack nor too tight. Any necessary retouching is carried out.

14 The complete model is affixed to the base and the basework painted as required. These final exercises should not be rushed — this is the point where a relaxed, calm attitude is essential.

15 When all is set and dry to one's satisfaction, the model may be held up in front of a mirror and the work honestly criticised. Inevitably, some tiny area that has missed the brush will be noted. Alternatively, the model may be shown to someone who has not seen much of the stages of construction. Fresh eyes may notice an important omission or anatomical error.

16 The base may be polished, a suitable title label applied, and thoughts turned towards the next model — with a determination to improve.

Right: for this 54mm Roman Auxiliary, the mail was again made from ladies' tights, although the basic figure was completed using ordinary Historex uniform parts. The spear is adapted from an Airfix spontoon, but all other items are from basic materials, the shield decorations for example being made from plastic strip and punched-out plastic sheet. (Model: Alan Edwards)

Chapter 8

Special considerations ~ships

The approach to ship modelling differs in several fundamental respects from that relating to other forms of modelling, and this is especially true with regard to plastic kits. Ships and boats have a special environment all of their own, which endows them with features not found with any other type of man made artefact and, being creatures of the sea little understood, or indeed seen, by the majority of people, they possess a very definite mystical fascination. Seafaring is an ancient pursuit steeped in tradition, and because of the isolation of those intimately involved with it there have evolved, through the centuries, a vast array of terms, customs and other idiosyncrasies with which the ship modeller at least needs to have a passing acquaintance before he can produce a thoroughly convincing model. A knowledge of rigging methods, flag signalling, stowage of seaboats and the many and varied drills, for example, which were and still are to a large extent practised according to a strict discipline on board ship, will enable him to infuse life into an otherwise languid model, and an appreciation of the way a vessel behaves in a seaway, whilst riding at anchor, and so forth, will enable him to capture realism in scenic presentation.

It is an unfortunate aspect of ship modelling that most people — manufacturers included — appear to regard ships as being of two distinctly separate types: those made of wood and fitted with sails, and those made of metal and fitted with funnels. Although it might be argued that the late nineteenth century saw a radical change in the materials used in the construction of ships and in their means of propulsion, and that the principal areas of interest lie before and after this period and not within it, the view has wider implications for the plastic modeller since, unlike aircraft, AFVs, cars and figures, a representative collection of models made from plastic kits tracing the historical development of the

appearance of its subject matter cannot be built up. Thus kits of galleys, vessels of Ancient Greece and Ancient Rome, Viking longships, galleons, clippers and fully-rigged men-of-war abound, as do those of the carriers, battleships, cruisers and destroyers of World War II and their present-day successors, but both the transitional period and merchant ships generally are very poorly represented.

The rather piecemeal approach to the subject of plastic ships kits has had a number of other unfortunate effects, the most frustrating one so far as the collector is concerned being the absence of an internationally recognised scale. There have been attempts to overcome this problem, the most concerted being that of a consortium of the four Japanese companies Aoshima, Fujimi, Hasegawa and Tamiya who, during the period 1969-1977 produced no fewer than eighty-six kits of ships representing the Imperial Japanese Navy in World War II plus twenty-seven of the more famous British, German and American vessels, all to 1/700 scale, a size which has subsequently been taken up and is still being developed by the British firm of Matchbox. There exist a number of smaller ranges to varying scales, but any compatibility tends to be coincidental rather than predetermined: the 1/400 range of Italian warships by Modelcraft matches the larger range of French and other warships produced by Heller and the few produced by Otaki; Airfix's 1/600 range of British, German and American warships is the same scale as a number of other kits, notably some from Aurora; Tamiya's new 1/350 range of warships matches the scale adopted by Imai for their series of famous sailing vessels; the extensive range of 1/500 Japanese warships produced by Nichimo tallies with the smaller range of British vessels manufactured by the now-defunct Frog company; 1/72 subjects are produced by Airfix, Matchbox and Tamiya and of course conform with one of the internationally recognised scales for model aircraft kits; and a number of the larger kits for sailing ships from various manufacturers agree in respect of scale. One problem of course is that famous vessels tend to be very large ones, which demands that the scale is relatively small if a kit of outsize proportions is to be avoided, and if smaller vessels such as submarines, torpedo craft or longships were produced to similar scales they would appear diminutive and poorly detailed by comparison. Whilst this argument has validity, it would seem unenterprising to regard it as being incapable of resolution.

The individuality of ships is another problem for manufacturer and modeller alike. No two ships are ever identical twins, although some of the smaller mass-produced craft are often virtually indistinguishable from one another, and, during their periods of service, repairs, refits, repainting and a host of minor additions and alterations reflecting technological development or expediency result in their varying slightly or greatly in detail from year to year, perhaps from month to month. This characteristic is not found to anything like the same extent with other forms of prototype such as aircraft or vehicles, and partly accounts for the frequent

Below: Plastic kits representing merchant ships are few and far between, and if one's interest lies in this type of model there is not much alternative to designing one's own. SS *Kyle Rhea* depicted here is constructed almost totally from plastic card, plastic rod and stretched sprue, the only exceptions being the counter, which is built up from filling compound, and the ventilators, which originated from a kit of an ocean liner. The model is scaled at 1/600.
(Model: Reg Hale)

inaccuracies contained in ship kits, particularly those representing twentieth century warships. It means that, in order to build a truly accurate model, the modelmaker has to spend an enormous amount of time in research and, frequently, in correcting the interpretation offered in the kit.

Nowhere so much as in ship kits are the technical limitations of injection moulding in plastic apparent. Although quite outstanding feats of scale reproduction have been performed, notably with some of the Tamiya 1/700 products and Heller period ships, the fact that their subject matter consists for the most part of vastly complex designs — and because of the necessarily small scales to which they are produced extremely intricate ones — means that kit manufacturers can only give a general indication of the main features of a ship plus some rather simplified detailing. The modeller must therefore be prepared to scale down the thickness of many of the items supplied in a plastic kit and also work in a certain amount of additional detail of his own if he wishes to produce a convincing representation of his chosen vessel. Delicate features such as masts, yards, small calibre weaponry, rail, rigging and lattice work are usually either overscale or absent altogether, and so great reliance needs to be placed by the modeller in commercially produced or home made plastic accessories such as thin sheet, extruded rod and stretched sprue. Painting demands very careful application, too, since scale colour effects, assuming as they do greater importance with diminishing relative dimensions, may need considerably more study than might those for other types of model.

APPROACH AND GENERAL TECHNIQUE

The complexity of most types of ship and the dictates of their relatively small scale in model form demand a rather different approach from that required, for example, with miniature aircraft or military vehicles. It is very rarely possible for the basic structure of a model to be completed without having recourse at a number of different stages to the paintbrush; it is rarely desirable for tube cement to be used in its construction; it is not often necessary to consider the internal features of the subject being represented; there is rather less scope for showing damage and other effects of violent activity; and it is only infrequently advantageous to use an airbrush in the finishing of the model or necessary to arrange for the application of decals. In addition, complex structural curves are generally confined to hulls, and so the refining of moulded kit components or their substitution by hand made parts is in most cases fairly straightforward.

The construction of a model ship should follow closely the order adopted in the building of the full sized subjects, in other words it is best to start with the hull, progress through to the weather decks, move on to the superstructure if it is present and finish with the fittings. Each sub-assembly — and there are likely to be very many of these — needs to be painted before it is joined to any other, and, because of the difficulty of filling and smoothing joints once it is in place, each needs to be carefully tested for fit and if necessary modified before it can be regarded as complete. The painting of a ship will usually require a number of hard, straight boundaries between contrasting colours, for example between decks and fittings and between decks and superstructure components, which are difficult to

Right: with ship kits it is frequently possible just to introduce small modifications either to represent the kit subject in a different state or to show a sister ship. With very little effort, for example, models of all five battleships of the *King George V* class may be produced from the Tamiya 1/700 scale *King George V* and *Prince of Wales* kits, and each individual vessel can be shown in any one of a number of states and colour schemes, giving a potential of over twenty different models. Here, the *Prince of Wales* kit has been used to show *King George V* as she appeared in early 1941: amongst other alterations, a degaussing cable has been produced from plastic rod and strip and added to the hull, and UP rocket launchers have been installed.

Below: a Revell PT Boat under construction – or rather reconstruction, as the amount of plastic card present shows. Stretched sprue and wire have also been used extensively, chiefly for the radar array and on the guns and gun mountings. Kits for ships and boats, by virtue of the fact that they invariably contain errors of configuration and also because the prototypes are so complex, are always suitable candidates for remodelling work, however minor this may be.
(Model: Greg Faunce. Photo: Donn Buerger)

achieve if the assemblies are too cluttered. For reasons of neatness and accessibility, techniques in the use of liquid cement should be developed as much as possible by the modeller. Very many butt joints are used in the construction of a ship model and many parts have to be very precisely aligned from a variety of angles, and these considerations together with the remarks previously made all militate against the use of any other form of bonding agent.

Because of their small size, model ship kits rarely incorporate any semblance of internal detail, and even where it is possible to include this the need to keep hatches, scuttles and other openings as small as possible, if not completely closed, to maintain a ship's strength and seaworthiness renders such a feature relatively unimportant since it is difficult to

see. In much the same vein, it is only rarely possible to show the effects of extensive damage on ship models. The individuality of ships means that careful research needs to be undertaken to show the effects of collision, battle scars and so forth in order to justify their presence, and if a ship is really badly damaged it will normally have vanished from sight beneath the waves. Moreover, many modellers and other interested parties contend that a full hull model of a ship mounted on a stand or on trestles should always appear in pristine condition and that a scarred or well weathered vessel similarly presented looks faintly comic. The fact is, of course, that a ship model in full hull configuration can never pretend to be anything other than a model unless it is incorporated into a diorama showing a dry dock scene, a pre-launching scene or other similar event, since only the upper hull is visible in normal operating circumstances.

Because a ship model generally consists of a large number of parts of individually small surface area, it is debatable whether the use of an airbrush is desirable for painting it. Natural effects like those required for bare wood are in general more realistically achieved by using a paintbrush; natural metal finishes, which might more easily be applied by using an airbrush, are rarely applicable to ships except in very small detail parts; and since decals are hardly ever used, varnishing, which is more predictably accomplished by spraying, is largely unnecessary. However, for large scale models requiring a finish simulating freshly applied paint, the airbrush and aerosol spray do have their uses, especially for components such as hulls. The intricacy of superstructures and the absence of large uninterrupted surfaces on fittings and so forth make masking a very hazardous if not impossible task, and effects such as feathered edges are rarely

called for — further arguments in favour of the paintbrush.

The building of a model ship may in some respects be likened to the building of a diorama. It can in a way be regarded as the creation of a base upon which many other models are positioned, each one often having distinct characteristics with perhaps the only common feature being that they are for the most part made of similar materials or covered with the same colour paint. The size of the prototype should at all times be borne in mind — it is very easy to lose sight of this. A really large vessel might be ten times the length of a large aircraft; it might be a thousand times the weight of a tank; or it might be the home for one or two thousand men. Its complexity in such instances is therefore quite unique amongst modelling subjects.

HULLS AND WEATHER DECKS
One of the first decisions to be made before tackling the construction of a model ship is whether it is to be shown as a complete structure or whether its apparent configuration when in water is to be imitated. Some plastic kits, popularly described as 'waterline', offer no choice about the matter, many provide the full hull shape, whilst a few give the option of either by being moulded in a particular way. Most people seem to prefer to see sailing ships on stands or trestles, and therefore with a complete hull, but are more open minded with regard to other types of vessel. Whether this is because they are conditioned to the practice generally followed in good quality museum models, whether it is because the top hamper of a fully rigged sailing ship makes the underhull almost unnoticeable, or whether it is purely a question of personal association or memory is not clear, but both modeller and manufacturer tend to sympathise with the view. A

Bottom: reducing a ship kit's hull to 'waterline' configuration is an immediate and obvious step in the quest for realism, as this photograph shows. The model, which is based on Revell's 1/244 scale kit of HMS *Campbeltown,* has been drastically reworked to give another US-built 'flush-decker', USS *Cole.* Amongst the modifications are the removal of the hull side scuttles, a new gun platform amidships made from plastic card and stretched sprue, the deletion of the fourth funnel, the substitution of 3in main armament for the 4in provided and the addition of 20mm guns. An enormous amount of fine detail work has also been incorporated, the overall effect of which is made more convincing by virtue of the fact that every detail is in scale – that which cannot be produced small enough is simply omitted. (Model: Paul Giltz. Photo: Donn Buerger)

Top: in sailing ship kits, as in all others, manufacturers make mistakes. An examination of the contemporary draughts of HMS *Bounty* reveals that all the deck fittings on the Revell kit, which was first produced in 1956 and is scaled at 1/110, are somewhat crude and inaccurate and that some of the prototype's most prominent features (for example the water closet on the quarterdeck) are omitted altogether. The fittings on this model were made up from pieces of plastic card, wood and metal, the gun barrels for example being turned from brass using a Unimat lathe. Only the crew figures and the hull of the launch came with the kit.
(Model and photo: John Tilley)

waterline model may only be turned into a full hull model with some difficulty, perhaps by moulding a plastic card shape, by carving an underhull from wood or by building it up from scrap materials and filler, but reducing a full hull to waterline configuration is less involved. Most kits have a raised line indicating the position of the boot topping, and some include a tooled channel within the hull mouldings to act as a guide for detaching the unwanted portion. Where these are absent, as with many kits representing galleons and other types of sailing ship, a line must be provided by the modeller before he attempts any cutting work. This may be done by first assembling the hull, ensuring that it is watertight, and then floating it in a basin of water. The hull is trimmed accurately by placing weights of modelling clay or any other suitable material within it, and the whole structure is then transferred to another basin of water to which a suitable floating medium such as oil paint or chalk dust has previously been added. If the hull is left for a time and the floating matter very gently agitated, a mark indicating the waterline will appear on the hull, and the latter can then be very gingerly removed and set aside to drain and dry off.

Once the cutting line has been determined, a thin strip of adhesive tape may be applied with its lower edge adjacent to it — this will provide a more permanent indication of the line to be followed and help protect the upper hull against possible damage whilst cutting is in progress. The lower hull may be detached by using a knife or a saw, although for speed a heated blade may be used instead. Careful attention should be paid to ensure that the instrument is always kept at right angles to the vertical axis of the model — this is very difficult to achieve in areas of compound curvature, for example

around the stern, but once the initial groove has been formed the task is eased. Any small deviations from accuracy can generally be dealt with by filling and sanding afterwards.

The removal of the lower hull from a ship model will usually result in a loss of structural strength, and steps should be taken to restore this. A complete base from thick plastic card might be contemplated, but alternatively bulkheads and stiffeners from the same material may be employed. The modification of a hull as described above may be undertaken with the two halves joined together or separated, but any reinforcement is better introduced with the hull complete. The weather decks may be taped or cemented in place beforehand to ensure that the correct hull contours are preserved.

Other, more subtle modifications may need to be applied to hulls. Two which are pertinent to kits of wooden sailing ships are commonly required and concern gun ports and bulwarks. Although the option of open or closed gun ports is a normal feature of most models of sailing ships with lower gun decks, the provision of the decks themselves is a comparatively rare feature, and the guns are normally plugged into simple recesses in the ship's hull. Greater realism can therefore be achieved by cutting out the ports, making decks from plastic card and fitting them within the hull. Two- and three-deckers will of course require this modification to be tackled in two or three separate stages, the lowest deck being produced, fitted and painted before the next is added, and so on. With large scale models, there is considerable scope here for the addition of detail such as framing, hatches, tackle and even lower masts, and of course it will be desirable to produce the requisite number of guns complete with carriages, which could be a formidable and time-consuming task. The usual problem with bulwarks is that they are moulded as part of the hull and frequently lack detail on their inner surfaces. The mouldings can often be modified to show this detail, but it is sometimes easier to strip them off completely and rebuild anew using plastic card.

Scuttles and portholes in all but the largest scales are generally represented in kits by means of raised or recessed detail, and windows in the ornamental sterns of galleons and so on are often similarly depicted. Unless the scale is very large and the number of openings small, it is not really practicable to introduce clear glazing for these features such as is provided for 1/72 scale torpedo boats and the like. The required effects are best achieved by means of careful painting, and in the case of circular scuttles this may be facilitated by opening them out with a few twists of a suitably sized drill. The hawsepipes of modern vessels may be treated in

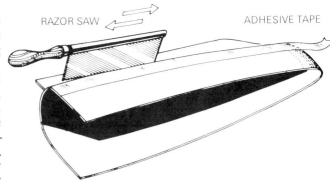

REMOVAL OF LOWER HULL

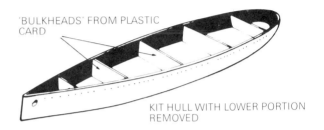

STRENGTHENING THE HULL

similar fashion — and quite frequently the hawsers themselves are moulded directly on to the hull and so realism is greatly enhanced if they are removed, produced individually and then attached appropriately.

The weather decks in ship kits are normally supplied as individually moulded items, although with the 1/700 Waterline Series from Japan they are combined with the hull in a single, complex unit, with perhaps only the forward part of the forecastle deck separate, this due to the problems of producing thick sections of plastic around the bows without undue shrinkage. The fit of the weather deck, particularly with a flush decked vessel, often leaves something to be desired, and a poor joint here will be very obvious and spoil the whole appearance of the model. Technical problems with the production of thin wall mouldings can also contribute to the toy-like appearance of many ship models in this respect, especially with those representing modern vessels where guard rails and spurnwaters are the general rule instead of solid bulwarks, since the thickness of the hull moulding which is necessary for strength often results in an overscale deck edge. It is not always possible completely to rectify this shortcoming, although the top edges of the hull may be chamfered or, in extreme cases, the entire deck may be replaced with a fresh one produced from plastic card, but it is a fairly straightforward job to disguise it. First of all, the actual joint should be as neat as possible. To this end, the weather deck may be precisely positioned within the hull and drawn tightly in place with tape. Careful application of liquid cement, if possible reinforced with strips of plastic card within the hull, will result in a joint that is virtually invisible. Any slight gaps that remain can be filled with gloss enamel paint and wiped flush, a procedure that may be repeated until all traces of the gap have disappeared. A spurnwater made from stretched sprue may then be fitted in the correct position along the top edge of the hull and faired into the deck using liquid cement or, again, gloss paint.

A further common shortcoming with weather decks as supplied in plastic kits is the rather heavy detail inscribed on to the mould which results in planking, non-slip textures and so forth, appearing as raised lines. Although these are often tastefully executed and can look realistic enough when painting is completed and the model is viewed from a distance, the manufacturers tend to strive for

effect rather than accuracy, and the removal of such detail by sanding it away is sometimes desirable. This is seldom a major problem with kits of sailing ships since their scale is generally larger, the detail frequently recessed and their decks relatively uncluttered, but with small scale kits representing more modern vessels a deft technique and a patient approach are the essential ingredients for success. Re-scribing deck planking using a needle and a steel ruler is a task that may be made easier if all moulded detail, including vents, hatches, skylights, bollards, fairleads, windlasses and breakwaters is removed and if the job is done before the deck is attached to the hull.

There may be other reasons for removing all the features moulded directly on to a deck, and these concern draft angles, which even if only of the order of 1° or 2° are very obvious and of course do not permit any undercutting for anchor cables, vents, hatches and capstans, and distributive accuracy, which is frequently awry. Hand made substitutes

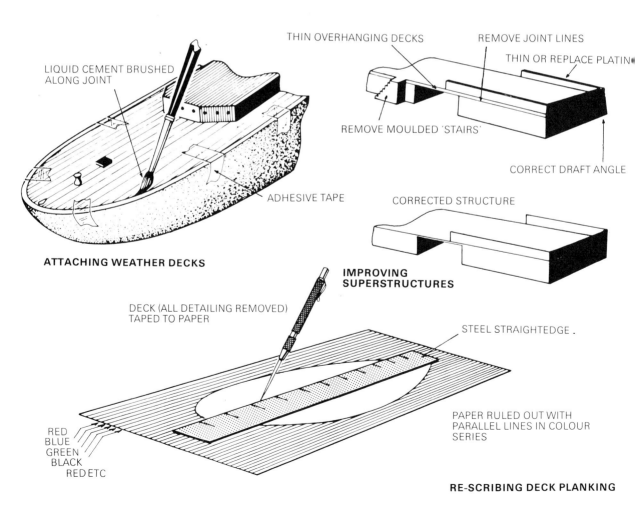

ATTACHING WEATHER DECKS

LIQUID CEMENT BRUSHED ALONG JOINT

ADHESIVE TAPE

THIN OVERHANGING DECKS

REMOVE JOINT LINES

THIN OR REPLACE PLATING

REMOVE MOULDED 'STAIRS'

CORRECT DRAFT ANGLE

CORRECTED STRUCTURE

IMPROVING SUPERSTRUCTURES

DECK (ALL DETAILING REMOVED) TAPED TO PAPER

STEEL STRAIGHTEDGE .

RED
BLUE
GREEN
BLACK
RED ETC

PAPER RULED OUT WITH PARALLEL LINES IN COLOUR SERIES

RE-SCRIBING DECK PLANKING

may quite easily be fashioned for permanent fittings using stretched sprue and thin plastic strip, following the principles outlined in Chapter 3. Anchor cables may be represented by using fine jeweller's chain or Armtec 1/76 tow chain gently stretched to elongate the links, and fine twisted fuse wire can look quite effective and certainly better than the moulded links supplied with some plastic kits.

SUPERSTRUCTURES

Apart from the differences in propulsion systems and constructional materials, the obvious feature distinguishing sailing ships from more modern mechanically propelled vessels is their absence of superstructure. The need to ship engines, fuel tanks, and so forth, means that these have to be placed as low as possible within the structure of a ship in order to preserve stability, and much of the accommodation area which in the days of sail occupied the hull now has to be placed above deck. In addition, the ever-growing requirements of communications equipment and the evolution, in warships, of complex fire control and surveillance systems have meant that the superstructure is in most instances now the dominant feature of a ship's profile.

The basis of a ship's superstructure, therefore, is an arrangement of decks and platforms above the level of the hull. These decks and platforms may be open to the weather, but more usually they are enclosed by means of screens in order to afford protection from the elements or, where appropriate, from the effects of enemy action, in which case they may be armoured, provision being made for access and the requirements of ventilation and perhaps natural lighting. Funnels and other permanent fixtures above upper deck level are also usually regarded as being part of the superstructure.

The principal shortcomings in the way these features are represented in a plastic kit concern scale thicknesses, the oversimplification of detail and, once again, draft angles. Although kit manufacturers have improved their technology quite dramatically over recent years, the limitations of moulding processes and the need to keep the cost of the finished product within reasonable bounds mean that a model built from a plastic kit without any modification cannot hope to be convincing. Typical of the problems with regard to superstructures are deck to screen joints which result in one of the two mouldings involved advertising its thickness, protective plating which is too thick and tapers in section, and the inaccuracy, or absence, of detail in the form of access points, scuttles, and so forth, in screens. The modeller is therefore pre-

Above: another example of remodelling a kit on a major scale, this detail photograph of a 1/600 HMS *Hood* model has its bridgework made up from plastic card, plastic rod and stretched sprue. Although work of this nature is intricate and time consuming it is relatively straightforward in that very many of the parts required are flat and jointed at right angles.

sented with a long list of tasks if he is to do justice to his chosen prototype.

There is no short cut to success. The work required will depend of course upon the configuration and quality of the components in the kit, but the first objective should be the elimination of all join lines, particularly where two parts meet to form a flush surface. This will frequently result in a loss of moulded detail which, however, is often better replaced anyway, so that the parts or sub-assemblies forming the superstructure are reduced to a series of basic blocks. Overscale features such as overhanging deck edges or thick plating may be thinned by careful use of a file, sanding board or modelling knife, but in some instances it will be necessary to replace these parts completely, or the offending areas, with articles made from plastic card. Draft angles might be disguised by careful filing and sanding, but, again, if the problem is serious, complete substitution is normally the only answer. The addition or replacement of detail can follow, using prepared items from stretched sprue and thin plastic sheet, and one or two features here warrant special consideration.

One form of detail that has to be represented on a superstructure screen is that concerning ports and port lights. Circular scuttles, as already noted, pose few problems, but rectangular openings such as bridge glazing and skylights are generally much more difficult a proposition, especially as they usually occur in rows. One method is to make up a screen in two parts, one being castellated and the other consisting of a flat section butting on to it. A strip of card can be positioned behind the apertures so formed to give a recessed effect and to facilitate painting. Those with a steady hand might be able to paint a strip of suitable colour along the line formed by the glazing or vision slits and touch in the framing afterwards, or else apply pressure sensitive decals in the form of black dots or rectangles, and these methods are eminently suitable for models of very small scale. Large scale models can have the appropriate screen fashioned from transparent plastic card and the paintwork carefully applied by brush, leaving the glazed areas clear. Raised detail such as hatches or watertight doors, or rigols above side scuttles if the scale justifies them, may be prepared from card or stretched sprue of appropriate gauge, and the production of a large number of these features, where constant size is essential, may be helped forward by taping a number of lengths of the material side by side on a grid of plastic card or stiff board and slicing them up using a sharp blade and a steel ruler.

Funnels as supplied in plastic kits can always be worked on to give a more authentic appearance. The vents themselves, for example, are often completely featureless; where guards are furnished, these are either grossly thick or incorporated into a solid cap. If a solid cap is supplied, it may be removed by drilling or gouging it out, and the joints visible along the interior surfaces of the funnel filled and smoothed out. The rim may be thinned if necessary and a scale guard fabricated from stretched sprue and added. Steam pipes, frequently moulded integrally with the funnel, are usually best replaced with items made from plastic rod, drilled out at the tops if possible.

MASTS AND RIGGING
Just as the dominant feature of a modern, powered ship tends to be its superstructure, so the obvious characteristic of a sailing vessel is its top hamper of masts, yards and rigging. Although plastic kits generally provide accurate and reasonably well detailed woodwork, their recommended methods of rigging are capable of considerable refinement. Firstly, the rigging pattern indicated by the kit instruction sheet is invariably simplified — a typical kit makes provision for most of the standing rigging but little running rigging. Secondly, the materials provided or recommended do not necessarily produce the best scale impression.

It will be apparent that before any rigging is added to a model sailing ship, it is necessary for the modeller to plan precisely what is required and organise his construction work accordingly. With small scale ships in particular, it is not always

advisable to complete the assembly of the model before any thought is given to attaching the rigging since access is likely to become a problem. Experience will indicate the sort of pattern needed and the order in which it should be tackled, and the novice is well advised to acquaint himself thoroughly with the function and operating methods of rigging in a real situation before he attempts to translate its appearance into model form.

The materials suggested on kit instruction sheets are usually cotton and thread, and shrouds and ratlines, in order to speed completion of the model and make it look neat if not necessarily accurate, are generally supplied as pre-formed 'nets' of plastic coated thread. Although traditional cotton or thread, or their more modern Terylene and nylon counterparts, are used successfully by many modellers to represent all forms of rigging, difficulties are often encountered in obtaining the thicknesses and colours needed and in securing the materials effect-

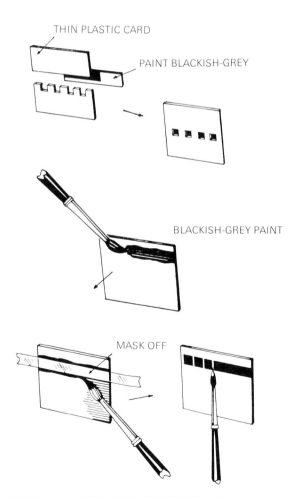

THIN PLASTIC CARD

PAINT BLACKISH-GREY

BLACKISH-GREY PAINT

MASK OFF

DETAILING SUPERSTRUCTURE SCREENS

ively. The smaller scales of most plastic kits of sailing ships often allow the use of stretched sprue instead — this can be produced to any thickness, is quickly and readily secured to other plastic surfaces, is not affected by the vagaries of humidity, and can be painted in the required colours. Reference to Chapter 3 will indicate the scope of this versatile material. Deadeyes, blocks, and so forth can be fashioned from small discs of plastic card. A further advantage of using stretched sprue for rigging is that, since intricate knots are not needed to secure the lengths, there is less risk of damaging the model as the work proceeds, and the absence of any great tension compensates for the fragility of the plastic masts and spars. The lengths required may be accurately gauged by measuring the distances involved with a pair of dividers, and coils and turns may readily be encouraged either by heat treatment before the filaments are fitted or by dampening them with liquid cement as they are positioned. Slackness is rather difficult to imitate with stretched sprue, but with care it can be worked into the material before it is fitted by burnishing it or by forming it over a jig and heat-treating it.

The sails supplied with plastic kits are usually vacuum formed mouldings on a sheet of thin polystyrene which have to be cut out. They are generally too stiff and 'solid' to be realistic, and furled sails produced by this method look quite preposterous of course with their shell-like configuration. 'Dead' and furled sails can be produced from a number of materials depending upon the scale of the model in question. Close- weave linen dyed in a solution of weak tea can look reasonably effective for large scale models, and tissue paper similarly treated can be utilised for those for smaller scales. Joints between individual sail cloths can be shown by pencilling lightly over the material. Billowing sails, necessary of course for scenic settings showing ships under way, and furled sails may be prepared by forming the shapes whilst the linen or tissue is still damp, allowing it to dry over a former or in a jig and then spraying it with matt varnish to stiffen it.

Flags and pennants, where required, may be fabricated by brushing a layer of clear gum over a piece of aluminium foil, slightly crumpled if a fluttering effect is needed, hand painting the designs in matt enamels on one side when set, peeling away the foil and painting the reverse side of the gum film, and trimming to shape with a sharp blade. Paper flags are frequently provided with plastic kits, but like the vacuum formed sails, these are too thick and stiff to give a convincing effect.

The rigging of modern vessels can be tackled in much the same way as sailing ships, taking into

Rigging proper shrouds and ratlines on models of sailing ships is another time consuming task, but the only people who think that such work is difficult are those who haven't tried it!

Top: details from a model of USS *Constitution* (Revell, 1/96 scale), demonstrate how even a little supplementary research and effort can eradicate the toy-like appearance usually associated with sailing ship models built from plastic kits. The plastic sails and 'ratline assemblies' have been replaced with, respectively, lightweight cloth and ordinary household thread. (Model: John Tilley. Photo: Martin R Nale)

Bottom: Heller's *Soleil Royal,* which with 2600 parts must be one of the most sophisticated kits ever produced, unfortunately contains a number of structural absurdities and a very inaccurate set of rigging diagrams. Modellers however are fortunate in that they can draw on a substantial body of research material to help in the rigging of a seventeenth century ship of the line, since the rigging techniques for plastic and wooden models are virtually identical. This model, scaled at 1/100, has been rigged with various sizes of silk thread. The stays and shrouds were spun up cable-laid (left-handed) on a 'rope making machine', the construction of which is described in most serious books on ship modelling. (Model: John Tilley. Photo: Martin R Nale)

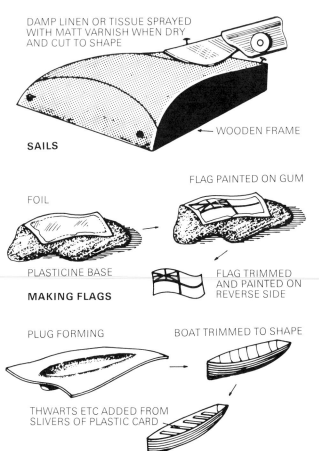

DAMP LINEN OR TISSUE SPRAYED
WITH MATT VARNISH WHEN DRY
AND CUT TO SHAPE

WOODEN FRAME

SAILS

FOIL

FLAG PAINTED ON GUM

PLASTICINE BASE

FLAG TRIMMED
AND PAINTED ON
REVERSE SIDE

MAKING FLAGS

PLUG FORMING

BOAT TRIMMED TO SHAPE

THWARTS ETC ADDED FROM
SLIVERS OF PLASTIC CARD

SHIPS' BOATS

account the requirements of scale and the materials being represented. For very small scales, clear stretched sprue, or clear adhesive such as Uhu drawn out into threads, can look very effective since it has the advantage of appearing thinner than it actually is. Aerials and similar equipment can also be represented using stretched sprue, of course. In all types of small scale model ships, certain liberties will normally have to be taken with rigging. A much simplified system may have to be shown, for example, securing points may have to be compromised by introducing the ends of each length of material into a tiny hole pricked out with a needle or drilled, sails may have to be attached directly to masts instead of lashing them or fixing them by means of stays, and blocks and dead eyes may have to be represented merely by small blobs of glue or paint.

ARMAMENT, SHIPS' BOATS AND MISC-ELLANEOUS FEATURES

With the less obvious features of a ship model, the techniques of refinement, substitution and addition where possible should again be followed. The larger gun mouldings are, as a general rule, quite well produced in plastic kits, and in overall shape are usually fairly accurate. However, barrels can be drilled out, shackles from stretched sprue added to gun carriages, blast covers from filler fitted over turret ports where appropriate and turret front plates, frequently inaccurately represented in order

Right: even where no major structural alterations are undertaken, the addition of extra little details can often improve the overall appearance of a ship model produced from a plastic kit. The decks of this 1/400 scale model of *Prinz Eugen* (Heller kit) look better for some guard rail – made from stretched sprue – whilst the 203mm guns have benefited from the addition of blast covers, made from filling compound, over their ports.
Opposite: leaving the painting of a model ship until its construction is complete is rarely practicable, as the complex camouflage pattern displayed on this 1/700 Tamiya *Prince of Wales* shows. Each sub-assembly is best prepared, mounted on a wedge of modelling clay and painted before it is added to the model. The kit for this model is one of the most accurate and detailed yet produced, but there is still scope for improvement. Note the tiny struts added to the Walrus aircraft amidships and the replacement of some of the mast components with stretched sprue.

to overcome moulding difficulties and to permit the guns to be elevated, modified to the correct shape. Fine detail work with stretched sprue will improve the appearance of all breech loaded guns on open mountings, especially those of small calibre.

Ships' boats are usually supplied as single mouldings in plastic kits and thus whalers, cutters and so on feature thickly formed hulls and solid thwarts, whilst motor boats have a similarly solid appearance and lack cabin glazing and other detail. Careful painting will often go some way towards disguising these shortcomings, but in many instances it is worth making new components by plug forming the hulls and adding fine detail using stretched sprue and slivers of plastic card. Stowage gear usually leaves something to be desired too, with crutches frequently absent or davits consisting merely of plastic hooks which locate into holes in the boats' decking. Again, patient work with the usual materials will considerably enhance the appearance of a model.

Much can be achieved in adding to the realism of a model representing a more modern ship by producing a grid of fine plastic strip or filament or even a closely formed mesh. A tray about 6in by 4in

(15cm by 10cm) may be made up from thick plastic card and suitable graduation marks either pencilled on or etched into the edges. The filaments may then be laid taut across the frame and their ends secured with liquid cement. Once the grid is complete, liquid cement is then lightly but thoroughly brushed across it to secure all the intersections, and when completely set the grid may be sliced away carefully and sections taken from it as required. Depending upon the types of filament used, such items as access ladders, lattice work, guard rail and radar 'bedsteads' may be produced in this way.

PAINTING CONSIDERATIONS

A few general remarks have already been made on the subject of painting model ships, but one or two more specific points which apply particularly to small scale miniatures can be made or re-emphasised.

With diminishing scale, the thinness of the paint

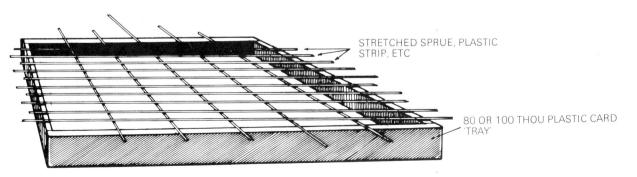

STRETCHED SPRUE, PLASTIC STRIP, ETC

80 OR 100 THOU PLASTIC CARD 'TRAY'

PRODUCTION OF COMPONENTS BY GRID METHOD

coating assumes increasing importance, as do the effects of scale texture and colour. It has been estimated that the average thickness of a coat of ordinary enamel paint approximates to 0.002in (0.005cm), and when one considers that on a model this can represent a thickness ranging from one hundredth to one thousandth of this figure, the size of the problem may be appreciated. In all cases, therefore, particular efforts should be made to ensure that the paint is thinned as much as possible, without detriment to its covering power, of course. The arguments submitted in favour of scale colour and texture is an earlier chapter have even greater validity in respect of ships, especially if they are displayed on a base consisting of a simulated sea, because of the reflective and refractive influence of the water in addition to that of the atmosphere, whilst of course with smaller scales, the effective scale distance is that much greater. Gloss and semi-gloss finishes should generally be avoided, except in special circumstances where it might be desirable to show wetted areas.

The recommendation has already been made that painting a model ship should progress in stages complimentary to its construction. A further suggestion is that larger components be painted before small ones where possible, and horizontal surfaces before vertical ones. Vertical surfaces representing paintwork as opposed to natural materials are moreover better treated by applying the brush strokes vertically. Although this may in some instances be more time consuming than painting with longitudinal strokes, any brush marks or areas of uneven coverage, provided they are not too serious, can be adapted to show the effects of downwash and are far less obtrusive than would otherwise be the case.

Such effects, and others indicating general wear and tear, should always be applied in a very restrained manner. Some modellers, in an attempt to capture realism, brush vast patches of rust coloured or metallic paint over hulls and even superstructures, which in fact more often than not has the opposite effect to that intended. If a specific ship is being considered, every effort should be made to obtain photographic evidence of any erosional features before they are translated on to the model. Otherwise, subtle variations of colour may be introduced using the dry brushing technique — the need to keep paint thicknesses to a minimum do not really permit any other method. As with all types of model and all aspects of modelling, familiarity with the prototype can only be to the advantage of the finished product.

Left: the stern ornamentation of this 1/100 *Soleil Royal* model forms a tribute not only to the artisans of Louis XIV's navy but also to the talented toolmakers of Heller. Very few museum models can boast carved detail superior to this. There is no secret to paintwork of this sort, beyond the use of a fine-grained gold paint (such as Rose Miniatures') and a fine brush. The period ship modeller must develop a good brush technique – an airbrush is worthless for this aspect of the hobby – and for general work water-soluble paints (such as the Polly S range) are a boon.
(Model: John Tilley. Photo: Martin R Nale)

Chapter 9

Special considerations ~vehicles

by DAVE PATRICK

Before any work is started on a plastic model of a road or racing vehicle, a number of basic decisions must be made in order to define just what sort of end result is required. A *concours* model, in all its pristine glory? A model that has a convincingly 'used' air about it? Perhaps the modeller wants to invest the vehicle with an impression of weight and substance, that elusive pimpernel 'atmosphere'. Are doors to be opened, windows wound down, bonnet opened etc? What about the colours to be used? The choice of colours is the most important decision to be taken before construction commences, since the interior colour is related to the body colour, the engine colour to that of the chassis, and so on. This may not apply to racing cars, where a specific vehicle is being modelled, or to custom cars where almost anything goes, but production cars have definite schemes and a little research will pay dividends in selecting an attractive finish which sets off the model's lines. Having made the choices then many and varied techniques will need to be employed to achieve the desired result: different paints for different components to give various textures; subtle colour changes on engine castings; the substitution of proper wire wheels, perhaps, for kit items; toning down or removing the frequently garish 'chrome' plating; the very necessary task of removing all visible mould lines from the components, including those found on the massive rubber 'doughnuts' fitted to current Formula cars. It all comes down to a question of detail, whether of construction, colouring, texture or finish. Many items which the builder might at first consider to have been adequately dealt with by the kit manufacturer may be improved on, and every small improvement is another piece in the mosaic that makes up the model. Very often these detail changes and improvements are not immediately apparent to the observer, but their cumulative effect is of paramount importance in achieving 'atmosphere'.

CHASSIS, SUSPENSIONS AND AXLES

Up until the postwar period almost all road vehicles — cars, lorries, buses, etc — were built round or on a substantial chassis. In many model kits the chassis is combined with the floorpan either to make building easier or, more probably, to cut tooling costs. However, most of the larger scale models (1/25 scale and over), together with the better quality small scale ones, have a separate chassis, and it deserves the attention due to so fundamental a component.

One of the drawbacks of injection moulding is that in order to eject a component from the mould either ejector pins must be used or the side of the cavity must be given a substantial draft angle, or both. These requirements often result in a 'lip' along one side of the component which, when coupled with sinkage marks (inevitable because of the thicknesses involved), produces a rather unsightly effect. As with all modelling problems there are several ways of dealing with it, although many modellers ignore it in the belief that all the moulding faults will be hidden by the body and simply assemble the kit. One technique is to take the modelling knife to the chassis and scrape the sides parallel, at the same time removing the lip formed by the mould split line. This is not so tedious a process as it sounds and it has the advantage of producing a much more elegant component. A second method is to embark on some 'original building' and make the entire chassis from virgin plastic strip, sheet and various gauges of rod and tube, the kit component being used as a guide. Needless to say, this way involves the greatest amount of work — and satisfaction!

The first technique can produce quite adequate results. The knife used needs to have a fairly stiff blade or the vibrations set up when scraping will produce a rippled effect on the component. The plastic-handled Swann Morton knife with a No 1 blade fitted is ideal, but the blade must be free from 'nicks' along its edge. The first step is to hold the chassis so that the light plays along one of the rails. This will show the draft angle on the sides and also the lip or sharp edge where the mould split line runs, which on a normal chassis will be along the top. The knife should next be taken and, with the blade touching the corner of the rail and angled in the direction of travel, gently and smoothly drawn along the chassis rail, producing a very fine curl of plastic. This process will raise a fine lip of its own and this may be removed by scraping in the opposite direction from the other side of the chassis. The whole chassis is treated in this way, including the cross members. Any sinkage marks should be filled and sanded smooth. The result of the exercise will be a more realistic chassis, with none of the lips etc which shrug off paint, and an altogether more accurate appearance. On models where the chassis is moulded integrally with the underbody a similar process may be followed where the rails protrude from the floor pan alongside the engine compartment.

Truck chassis benefit from the 'treatment', too, and are a good deal easier to work on since they are supplied as several parts. The important thing to remember when assembling such a chassis is to use a ruler and make sure that the structure is square and parallel, both horizontally and vertically. Nothing looks worse than a truck with one wheel in the air emulating an errant pup.

The monocoque tubs of the larger F1 kits benefit from having their edges — which are frequently

razor sharp — slightly rounded off, especially round the cockpit area. On custom cars and dragsters with tubular chassis it is very important to remove all the mould lines by scraping or sanding, taking care not to leave a slight flat behind.

As far as painting any type of chassis is concerned, either spray or brush application may be used. It is easier to get into all the nooks and crannies with a brush but the finish produced by an airbrush is generally superior providing a heavy build up of paint can be avoided in all the crevices.

Front axles on older vehicles are usually of the exposed beam type and therefore benefit from having the mould lines removed. Back axles also need to be assembled accurately and have their joint lines disguised.

It is always better on a model to have the front wheels pointing slightly to the left or right (not one each way!) as this helps to 'animate' it. If some form of front wheel steering is supplied all well and good, and the modeller's task is simply to make sure that all the components fit well. If the front hubs are moulded integrally with the axle, as they very often are on smaller scale models, the wheels can still be turned. If they are to be turned to the left a small saw cut is made in the front of the offside hub and the rear of the nearside hub. A drop of liquid cement is placed in each cut and the gap is then closed up. The positions of the cuts may be reversed for a right hand turn.

Road springs on kits representing older vehicles usually leave a great deal to be desired in terms of their authenticity and general appearance, mainly because of cost considerations on the part of the manufacturer. However, a model can be much improved by detailing the kit item or replacing it with a spring made from plastic card and stretched sprue. The kit spring usually suffers from sink marks, poorly defined leaves and inaccurate clamps and 'U' bolts. To improve the kit items, one should be kept aside as a reference and all the moulded detail removed from the other. (Front and rear springs are usually different, both in the number of leaves and in their attachment points, so they should be treated as two pairs.) Sink marks should be filled and the required number of leaves scribed on both sides of the spring. Clamps may be added from pieces of adhesive tape cut to the right width or from stretched sprue, depending on whether they are flat or circular in cross section. The 'U' bolts which hold the spring to the axle are best attached after the spring is cemented to the axle. Making road springs is simply a matter of cutting a number of lengths of 10 or 15 thou plastic card to the correct width and, using the kit component as a guide, laminating the strips together. Particular care

Below: a simple technique can make all the difference to a model car. Posing this Midori 1/16 scale 1904 Wolseley with turned front wheels brings an immediate air of reality to it. Note the effective hood, which is produced from model aircraft fabric, and the 'beading' on the mudguards, from half-round plastic rod.
(Model: Bob Earey)

should be taken to remove the raised lip formed on the strips by the cutting action of the knife, and it is also very important to keep the total depth of the spring identical to the kit item or the model will sit too high or too low when finished. (This facility can in fact be used to alter the sit of the model if required). The clamps and 'U' bolts are made as for the modified kit spring. Plastic card, rod and sprue can easily be shaped by mounting them on a former and holding them in the steam from a kettle. Masking tape is preferable for holding the plastic over the former as ordinary clear tape loses its adhesive qualities in steam. Rear road springs may be dealt with in the same way as the front.

Coil springs on later vehicles are sometimes moulded on to their attendant shock absorbers in kits, but these should be separated by filing and sanding, taking care to leave the upper and lower spring retainers in position. New springs can be made by winding a suitable gauge of soft wire round a former which matches the diameter of the shock absorber. The wire should be wound tightly with each coil close together. When removed from the former the coil can be stretched until the spacings are correct, and each can then be cut to length and slipped over the previously painted shock absorber.

Many kits do not in fact supply shock absorbers but thankfully they are not difficult items to make. There are three main types: friction, lever arm and telescopic. Friction type shock absorbers were fitted to many vehicles until just before World War II, when lever arm and very early telescopic units took over. Today the telescopic shock absorber reigns supreme. To make a friction type damper a number of shaped plates of 15 or 20 thou card are required. These are laminated together alternately to form the damper. One arm is attached to the axle and the other to the chassis. To make sure all the plates are the same shape, the required number of oversize rectangular plates are cut and glued together along one short edge only. The shape required is drawn on the top plate and then filed and sanded down whilst the glued end is held in a vice. The shaped ends are taped together and the glued end cut away and sanded to shape. The plates are then separated and any lips etc left by the shaping process gently scraped away. Some research will be required to ascertain the size and position of these shock absorbers and one tip here is to check whether a larger scale kit of the vehicle exists. If so, a glance at the components and the instruction sheet should yield all the information required.

Lever arm shock absorbers were often fitted to the rear axle when the friction type were still being fitted to the front, so many models will need to have both types fabricated. The lever arm shock absorber

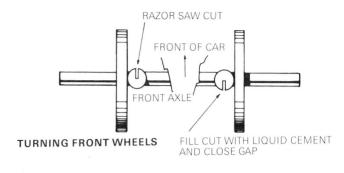

RAZOR SAW CUT

FRONT OF CAR

FRONT AXLE

TURNING FRONT WHEELS

FILL CUT WITH LIQUID CEMENT AND CLOSE GAP

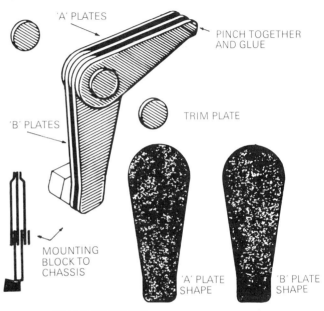

'A' PLATES

PINCH TOGETHER AND GLUE

TRIM PLATE

'B' PLATES

MOUNTING BLOCK TO CHASSIS

'A' PLATE SHAPE

'B' PLATE SHAPE

SIMPLE FRICTION SHOCK ABSORBER

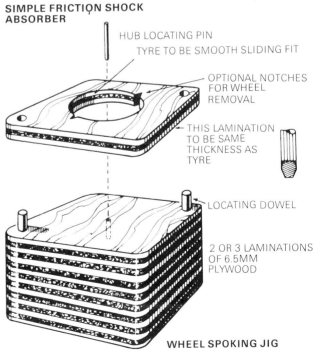

HUB LOCATING PIN

TYRE TO BE SMOOTH SLIDING FIT

OPTIONAL NOTCHES FOR WHEEL REMOVAL

THIS LAMINATION TO BE SAME THICKNESS AS TYRE

LOCATING DOWEL

2 OR 3 LAMINATIONS OF 6.5MM PLYWOOD

WHEEL SPOKING JIG

165

is not at all difficult to make. It requires a backing plate of plastic card, two short lengths of plastic tube, a small block of thick plastic and two lengths of plastic rod. Having worked out the size of the unit, which will of course depend on the scale of the model under construction, the plastic backing plate has its corners rounded off slightly and the two lengths of plastic tube, with their ends blanked off with body putty or Milliput, glued to it. A space is left between them to accept the small block of plastic which should be the same thickness as the diameter of the tubes. To this block, slightly below its top face, one of the lengths of plastic rod is glued. This should be at an angle slightly above the horizontal. When the unit is attached to the chassis the second length of plastic rod connects the axle to the lever.

Telescopic shock absorbers pose no problems and may be produced simply by taking a piece of plastic tube or sprue of the correct size for the smallest diameter and wrapping one or two thicknesses of adhesive tape round it to form the upper cover. Attachment points are made with slices of a smaller diameter tube.

The telescopic damper/spring units fitted to modern racing cars are usually supplied with a separate spring. All that needs to be done to these units is to cement the two lower halves together, having first checked that the upper piece will snap in place easily without splitting the lower components, and then remove the joint line. The damper may be painted the required colour — black, dull gold, metallic blue or dull silver but never 'chrome' plated — straight afterwards. The coil springs themselves

are usually black or dull silver. These can have small colour code bands added to one of the coils on each spring.

Most trucks use massive leaf springs simply because of the heavy loads that they carry. These large mouldings suffer considerably from sinkage and poor delineation of leaves and clamps, and so it is up to the modeller to decide whether they are well enough hidden under the truck to be left alone, or whether they need to be detailed or rebuilt as previously described. If they are to be remade a heavy gauge of plastic card will be needed. On many modern US trucks the problem does not arise for they use pneumatic units in place of leaf springs.

WHEELS
The wheels and tyres supplied with a plastic kit are, apart from the body mouldings, the most important components used in capturing the look and 'sit' of the full size vehicle. Many otherwise beautifully made models have been spoiled by lack of attention and detail applied to the wheels. Models are continually seen with wire wheels carrying spokes like pick handles, or wide racing tyres with prominent mould lines and high gloss sidewalls. Even nicely weathered trucks with bright chrome wheels and tyres which have not had the weathering taken off the tread surface are frequently produced.

Models with wire wheels always seem to hold major terrors for modellers, not because of the complexity of the kit but because of the wheels themselves and the supposed difficulty of replacing them. Even in the larger scale kits with wire wheels, motor cycles included, the representation achieved by the manufacturer is not strictly accurate. Producing a spoke which would seem to be separate at its intersection with the next spoke would be a toolmaker's nightmare. The reasons why kit spokes never look quite right, even after extensive re-working, are that they are usually overscale in cross-sectional diameter and are seen to be joined where they cross each other. This is a small point indeed, but the absence of a shadow at this intersection is a detail that is picked up almost unconciously by the observer's eye and results in a feeling that the wheel is 'not quite right', not really convincing. Some manufacturers overcome the problems of tooling effective wire wheels by adopting a different approach. Instead of trying to force the plastic along tiny spoke forms, they provide jigs and suitable wire or monofilament nylon so that the wheel rim can be 'laced' to its hub. Although this system produces very effective results, it does not help the modeller who has a kit with moulded spoked wheels (usually plated) having the scale effect of being made with scaffolding poles. Spoked wheels are not difficult to make by hand, although this is a time consuming and, at times, infuriating job. There is no doubt, however, that such labours can give the completed model that undeniable 'touch of class'.

In order to make a realistic wire wheel the tyre is set in a jig and either the kit rim and hub are modified or new ones are made from plastic card. It will generally be found best to make new components for there is marginally less work involved with this method. The jig consists of a number of laminations of plywood, with the top lamination the same thickness as the width of the tyre. A centre hole is drilled through all the laminations to take the pin that accepts the new hub. The top lamination is dowelled to the bottom laminations but is left removable. The top lamination is cut to accept the

tyre which must be a smooth sliding fit. The hub pin hole and the tyre hole must be precisely concentric of course or some rather peculiar wheels will result. The hub pin is installed — this must also be a smooth sliding fit — together with any spacers required to ensure that the spokes will not hit the brake drums. Any lips or rims should be removed from the inside face of the tyre, and then the latter is slipped into place. The circumference of the inside of the tyre is calculated or, more simply, a 5 or 6mm wide strip of 15 or 20 thou plastic card is cut and trimmed until a very tight 'snap' fit is achieved in the tyre, the card then being removed from the tyre and measured. The required number of strips on a flat piece of 20 thou card are marked out, remembering that the larger the wheel the thicker the card necessary. The width of each rim is made slightly greater than the width of the tyre where it meets the rim. The lines of the spokes are marked out on either side of a centre line drawn on each rim, and the spoke holes are then pierced along one of these lines. There should be an even number and one will be on the join line between the two ends of the rim. The second line of spokes is marked and pierced, out of sequence with the first row. The marked rims, with the pencilled markings on the outside, are wrapped round a piece of dowel or broom handle of suitable diameter and held with masking tape, and they are then steamed over a kettle for a few minutes and allowed to cool. The tape is removed and, with the plastic still on the former, one rim is cut from the

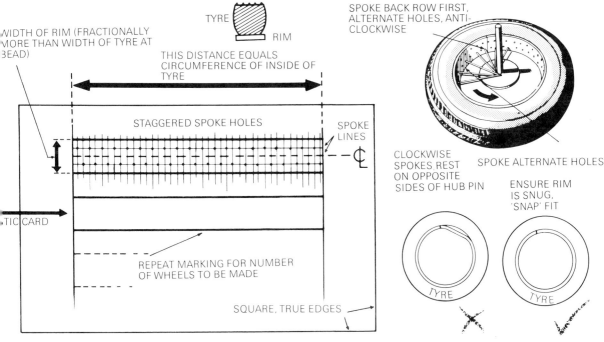

WHEEL SPOKING – MARKING THE CARD

WHEEL SPOKING – FINAL CONSTRUCTION

The problem of scale spokes and some methods of tackling it.
Top left: an Ordinary bicycle, built to 1/12 scale. The front wheel was made by sawing and filing a sliver from a circular plastic drainpipe, the hub is from Plastruct tubing, and the spokes are lengths of wire, heated with a soldering iron and inserted into prepared locations. The figure is adapted from a Tamiya racing car item. (Model: Bob Earey)
Top right: this detail shot of a much-modified Matchbox 1/32 scale Jaguar SS100 illustrates the technique for spoking wheels with plastic rod as described in the text. Note also the hand made cooling fan, fanbelt and timing cover. (Model: Dave Patrick)
Left: a 1948 MG TC, built from the 1/16 scale Gakken kit, with its spokes reduced to something approaching scale thickness through having been slimmed down one by one with a warding file. (Model: Bob Earey)

sheet with a sharp knife. After the edges have been cleaned up, it may be installed in the tyre in the jig. The hub pin and spacers are placed in position and, using a pair of leather punch pliers, a number of plastic discs made by punching through 15 thou card. These discs should be the same diameter as the back of the original hub. A central hole is drilled in each disc to accept the hub pin, and one disc is placed in the jig. Spoking can now begin.

The length of each spoke is calculated and this distance is marked on a cutting surface. Using the required size of plastic rod — G N Slater produce an excellent pack of assorted thicknesses ranging from 5 to 50 thou — the spokes required for one row are cut. Alternate holes, clockwise, are then spoked on the bottom row, using only minute amounts of liquid cement to hold the spokes in position. When these are set, the remaining holes are spoked in an anti-clockwise direction. A disc of card is placed over the spokes where they touch the hub pin and cemented in position. A length of fairly large diameter plastic rod is then filed to a semi-circular section, formed round dowelling as for the rims and trimmed to fit inside the rim on its centre line. The

rod is then cemented into place. The hub proper is made from plastic tube, calculating the distance between the inner and outer row of spokes and trimming it to this length. The hub is fixed into place on the card disc making sure that no cement touches the hub pin. Another card disc is cemented to the hub over the pin and the outer row of spokes is tackled in the same way as the inner. The last plastic disc is cemented over the hub pin on to the spokes. When the assembly is thoroughly set pliers are used to ease out the hub pin. The top lamination is removed from the jig and the completed tyre and wheel assembly eased out. All that now remains is to install a valve and paint the wheel (best done with an airbrush after masking off the tyre), and then repeat the process until the required number of wheels have been produced!

The wheels fitted to modern racing cars carry a variety of finishes: anodised gold or black, as cast, or polished. Polished wheels are usually 'chrome' plated in kits and should really have the harshness of the chrome reduced with a wash of semi-gloss varnish. Where single centre lock nuts are used to hold the wheel to the hub these are often colour coded, metallic red for the offside and metallic blue for the nearside. Since early 1970 most Formula 1 cars have eight bolts, four to each side of the wheel, spaced around the rim to retain the tyre bead in the event of a blowout. These can be represented by tiny pieces of plastic rod glued to the rim at 90° intervals. The latest kits have the cast-in 'lands' moulded into the rims but still require the bolts themselves. The screws used to hold the kit wheels onto the hubs are best discarded and replaced with brass tube. The tube is fixed into the hub with epoxy resin and when the wheel is seated on its drive pegs a nut, which has had its centre filed out to be a smooth fit over the tube, is similarly glued over the tube against the wheel. Retaining clips can be bent up from fuse wire and placed through two holes previously drilled in the tube. 'Chromed' truck wheels need, at the very least, a wash of dark grey paint in thinners to dull them a little and point up the fine detail that the 'chrome' often hides. It is even better to repaint them in a colour that matches either the chassis or the main body, or the most prominent of the secondary colours used in the overall scheme.

Tyres can look unconvincing on a model unless they are toned down, either simply by continuous handling during construction or by deliberately dulling the sidewalls and tread. A pencil-like fibreglass eraser is very useful for this operation. Medium and fine sandpaper may be used on the tread itself to take the 'newness' away. A spare tyre on an older car can have most of its tread removed to portray a well worn item. The pre-slick era Formula 1 tyres often require a great deal of sanding to remove the central mould line; a fairly coarse file will be found best for this task, with the fingers inside the tyre to support the tread. When mounted on its wheel the tyre may have to be filled with sponge rubber offcuts to remove the slight concavity in cross section. Current slick tyres also need to have the mould line removed, this time with medium sandpaper, and really the whole tread face needs to be treated in this way. The shoulders of the tyre can usually benefit from being rounded off a little more. One tip here is to leave the inside edge of the left hand tyres fairly rough and treat the outside edge of the right hand tyre in a similar fashion. This gives the impression of a car that has just come into the pits from a circuit made up of predominantly left hand corners.

Truck tyres are often supplied in two halves, though happily this practice is dying out. Eradicating the mould line from this form of tyre is a little tricky for the tread depth is minimal. Where the tyres are one piece mouldings the process of dulling down is not so difficult, requiring only the use of the fibreglass eraser and fine grade sandpaper.

ENGINES

An engine is, for many people, the focal point of the model they are working on. If the model is being built 'straight from the box' then detailing the engine offers the best method of adding authenticity and atmosphere to the model. Colour is important, especially with the older cars and lorries. Model T Fords did not roll off the production lines with bright yellow blocks and chrome plated cylinder heads. In fact, very few components were chromed; smooth cast aluminium and, on the better cars, polished castings were present but not the lurid 'chrome' plate offered by so many kit manufacturers. Custom cars and dragsters are the exception for on these vehicles anything can be (and probably is) chromed.

There are certain basic constructional steps common to all plastic model engines, whether car, truck or motorcycle. These are the removal of the locating pins on each block half (for they are very often more

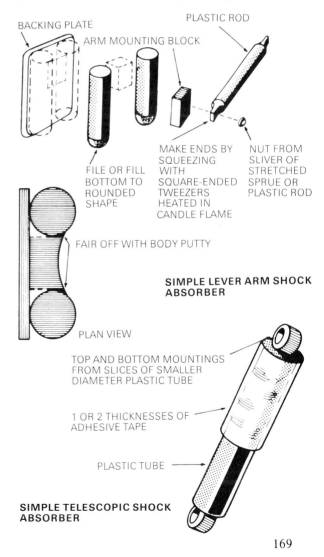

BACKING PLATE

ARM MOUNTING BLOCK

PLASTIC ROD

FILE OR FILL BOTTOM TO ROUNDED SHAPE

MAKE ENDS BY SQUEEZING WITH SQUARE-ENDED TWEEZERS HEATED IN CANDLE FLAME

NUT FROM SLIVER OF STRETCHED SPRUE OR PLASTIC ROD

FAIR OFF WITH BODY PUTTY

SIMPLE LEVER ARM SHOCK ABSORBER

PLAN VIEW

TOP AND BOTTOM MOUNTINGS FROM SLICES OF SMALLER DIAMETER PLASTIC TUBE

1 OR 2 THICKNESSES OF ADHESIVE TAPE

PLASTIC TUBE

SIMPLE TELESCOPIC SHOCK ABSORBER

of a hindrance than a help), the careful truing up of the mating surfaces with fine wet-and-dry paper on a flat surface, the eradication of the joint line when the halves are cemented and the removal of all gate marks from the components. Once the block is assembled and the join disguised the cylinder head, or heads, may be added, having first drilled out the spark plug holes. The rest of the components are cleaned up and test fitted (inlet and exhaust manifolds, timing cover, water pump, sump, etc) making sure that their mating faces do in fact mate. Nothing looks worse than, say, a four branch exhaust manifold which is obviously held on by only two pins, with daylight between the centre pipes and the cylinder head — very noisy!

The fan belt is a component that is dealt with properly by only a few manufacturers, and then only in the larger scales. It is best, even in the small scales, to remove the massive moulded 'belt' and replace it with one made from clear adhesive tape cut to the correct width. This also enables the demon modeller to file a 'V' section in the rim of the pulleys not covered by the belt which can then be painted silver to simulate the highly polished inside faces of the pulleys.

Carburettors are often found covered in 'chrome' in kits whereas it is rare to find them so finished on vehicles outside custom car shows. The careful use of silver paint with a touch of white, grey or light blue adeed can point up the different castings that comprise a complete carburettor. For instance, twin SUs on a vintage car would be a dull aluminium colour, ie silver with a touch of grey. The domed dashpot cover would be a fairly light shade (it is the easiest part to polish on a Sunday afternoon) and the float chamber and base castings a darker shade. The very tip of the dashpot should be painted to represent the brass damper. Post war SUs would have this little cap painted black as brass gave way to plastic. If air cleaners are not fitted, the venturi should be drilled out. Modern carburettor castings tend to have a slightly more yellowish appearance, especially the gargantuan 'four barrel' instruments fitted to many US cars. Modern British carburettors are a dull aluminium colour, sometimes with a very slight bluish tinge. Once again, the float chamber and cover castings may be picked out in two slightly different shades.

Throttle linkages can be tricky, varying, according to the scale, from a little awkward to near impossible. The only way round this one really is research, coupled with a little inspired guesswork. The twin SUs would have a properly engineered positive rod linkage from the accelerator pedal, although current practice is the cheaper and easier cable operation. This cable usually describes an easy curve from the bulkhead to the rear of the carburettor.

If a distributor is supplied (and it is not unknown for manufacturers to omit this component) then its cap can be drilled to accept the fine wire or nylon monofilament used for plug leads. Where the size of the model justifies the inclusion of material for these leads in the kit they are generally much overscale and are best replaced. It is very important, when fitting leads, to make sure that they follow realistic scale curves and take an accurate path. Nothing looks worse on an otherwise nicely detailed engine than plug leads describing vast cathedral-like arches to their respective plugs, or leads with sudden right angled bends in them. The thickness of the leads is of considerable importance for even a small divergence from scale accuracy will be picked up by the well informed observer. Many of the better class vehicles have their plug leads led through a conduit. This can be made from a suitable piece of fine, thin-wall aluminium tube or a length of drilled plastic rod — not drilled right through, just at the ends to accept the leads.

A distributor may be made by first selecting a piece of plastic rod or tube of a suitable diameter. One end is then filed to a dome shape and the other end to a slightly more tapered shape. A piece of thin plastic card or adhesive tape cut to a suitable width is wrapped round the centre section and the cap retaining clips simulated with two small strips of thin card. The cap end (the domed part) is drilled to accept the required number of plug leads with an extra hole for the coil lead. The cap end is painted semi-matt black and the housing end dull aluminium.

As far as fuel injection tubes or pipes are concerned, these are treated in very much the same way as plug leads. On the larger scale racing car models, the black piping supplied for the plug leads can be used from the injection pump to just under the throttle slides. Nylon monofilament is then placed into the tube to connect it to the injector head which has been suitably modified and drilled to accept it. The tubing used on the full size cars is a translucent material and discolours in use to a yellowish straw colour.

Painting model engines requires some thought. In production cars the colours used are uniformly dull — it is only on custom cars that really garish colours occur — so dark reds, blacks, greens and blues are the order of the day. The finish should be neither high gloss nor dead matt: as usual the middle course is best, ie semi-matt. On production engines, most of the steel pressings such as the sump and rocker cover(s) are painted the same colour as the block. Starter motors and dynamos are gener-

Top: large scale, high quality kits, for example the Tamiya 1/6 Yamaha YZ250 from which this model has been built, pose few problems regarding wheel spokes as the latter are close to scale thickness already. Kits for motorcycles like this one are indisputably in the 'de luxe' category – many have parts in simulated chrome and aluminium, red and amber perspex and rubber. On occasions it is not essential to paint *any* part of the model to create a realistic effect, but in these cases flawless assembly work is vital.
(Model: Peter Hancock)

Centre: Tamiya's 1/12 Tyrrell 003, with detachable components removed. This partcular model has been researched in minute detail and certain features of the kit corrected: the 'textured' seat has been replaced by a fibreglass moulding, much of the 'chrome' has been stripped off and repainted more realistically, and additional detailing has been worked into the engine etc.
(Model: Dave Patrick)

Bottom: the 1/12 scale Chevrolet V8 engine from the Tamiya Lola T-70 Mk III kit, with carburettors modified for fuel injection requirements. Note how the materials making up the engine are simulated by using different shades of paint. The rocker covers and bellhousing have been coated with a mixture of enamel paint and talcum powder to give the impression of having been 'cast'.
(Model: Dave Patrick)

ally black and inlet manifolds aluminium or, as with 'V' configuration motors, the same colour as the block. Alternators are invariably natural aluminium.

For most engine blocks and especially those in racing cars, a small amount of fine talcum powder can be mixed with the paint and stippled on over a thin coat of the base colour to give that rough cast look. It should be remembered that on racing engines, though made up of many castings in the same material, colours will vary from component to component. So on an engine with a cast block the dry sump will be a slightly different colour, as will the front and rear covers, cylinder heads, bellhousing, etc. Nuts and bolts can be picked out in suitable colours: very dark grey for bolts, a lighter grey for nuts and flat silver, brass or metallic red and blue for oil pipe unions. This process need not normally be carried out on production engines for these are often painted as a complete unit.

Gearboxes are sometimes the same colour as the engine but can be finished in flat silver, steel or semi-matt black. If the car is fitted with a separate bellhousing or clutch housing, this can be picked out in flat aluminium with talcum powder added. Gearboxes fitted to production cars, whatever their finish (natural cast iron, aluminium or painted), often have pressed steel cover plates etc and these should be of a smooth finish against the cast finish of the gearbox proper.

EXHAUSTS

Exhausts are oft-neglected model components yet their correct treatment is very necessary to overall authenticity. Their painting depends on the type of vehicle and the state or condition in which it is portrayed. Vintage vehicles finished to *concours* standard would either have a polished aluminium manifold or a stove-enamelled, cast iron manifold in black or very dark blue, whilst a car used fairly regularly might show a painted silver or maroon finish; a working vehicle on the other hand would have a somewhat rusty and possibly flaking casting. The first two finishes are easily achieved with semi-gloss paint; a convincingly 'rusty' manifold, however, requires a slightly different approach. First a thin coat of light flat brown is applied and left to dry, and then some small patches of a darker brown are applied to represent the areas where rusty metal has flaked away. Finally a thin coat of matt varnish and, whilst this is still wet, a light dusting of brown or grey powder paint are applied. The downpipe and silencer require painting in the same way but using slightly darker shades throughout.

A little life can be given to chrome tailpipes and manifolds by lightly using various shades of blue and yellow marker pens to give a 'blued' effect — this is especially relevant for motorcycle manifolds. The intricate systems fitted to most racing cars are usually finished in a semi-matt black, except for Ferraris, of course, where matt white is the order of the day.

Trucks are a law unto themselves as far as exhausts are concerned, very many hard-used vehicles retaining polished alloy or chrome covers to their 'stacks'. These large silencers, standing vertically like sentinels on each side of the rear of the cab, are usually chromed in kits, but may be more accurately depicted by being wrapped in gloss or semi-matt Metalskin, or by using a compound such as Rub 'n Buff. A point to remember if using the latter product is to remove *all* the chrome and make sure that the component is free from blemishes, for the gilt will highlight any marks not removed.

INTERIORS

With all but the very largest scales, fitting out a vehicle with fabric carpets, trimming the seats, etc, is really a waste of time. The scale effect of worn leather is difficult enough to duplicate by painting, without adding the complications of finding leather thin enough and with the right grain. It is not possible to trim the seats of, say, a 1/32 scale interior without the seats becoming grotesquely out of scale due to the thickness of the covering material. Painting is definitely the best way to finish interiors so long as proper attention is paid to representing the different textures encountered.

Floor carpeting can be effectively simulated either by using matt paints or by adding talcum powder to semi-matt paints and stippling this on to the floor. Smooth surfaces such as leather, leather-cloth, plastic and fabric may be portrayed by using oil based paints, enamels (semi-matt or semi-gloss) or acrylic colours. Seats can be awkward, especially those in older cars, since they are usually trimmed in leather, and in the case of the driver's seat mightily abused over the years. As most kits are supplied with pristine seats, some alterations are called for. The cushion on the offending seat can either be built up round the edges using body putty, Fine Surface Polyfilla or Brummer Stopping, or carved away in the centre and then lightly scored and sanded. Once a convincing 'sag' is achieved then the seat can be painted with semi-gloss colours and given an overall wash of very much diluted paint, several shades darker than the base colour. Small items such as door pulls and retaining straps can be made from stretched sprue and adhesive tape. When the model is a convertible and is made with the top down, a piece of tissue handkerchief glued to the moulded tonneau will give a convincing fabric effect. Of course if the hood itself is used then it too will benefit from a tissue covering.

Generally speaking, interiors are keyed to the body colours and not vice versa. Therefore choosing the right colour for the model is important, as is the careful preparation and painting of the body mouldings.

BODYWORK AND FINISHING

If the kit being worked on has doors, bonnet and boot supplied separately, all well and good. These can be prepared, checked for fit and painted together. Models with a one piece shell, wing assembly and separate bonnet, however, may require the doors or boot to be opened. Rather than use a hot wire to open the doors, the back of a knife blade can be used to great effect. This method produces a fine curl of plastic and cuts through cleanly, whereas using the cutting edge of the blade or the hot wire raises ugly lips each side of the cut which can be very awkward and time consuming to remove without spoiling the surrounding detail. Needless to say the knife can slip from the moulded groove with equal ease whether one is using the back of the blade or the cutting edge, but gouges fill more easily than cuts!

Particular care should be taken when cutting round door window frames, and it is best to tackle this area first before pressing on to the sides and bottom of the doors. If the model has a 'bathtub' type interior then the moulded door panels on this part must be cut away and cemented to the outer door panel, taking care to see that the panels retain their original alignment when the door is shut. This

Top: the 1/25 AMT Chevy van depicted here incorporates a lot of additional detail and a 'personalised' paint scheme. The doors have been cut from the kit mouldings and hinged; the 'customised' interior features a bench and cabinet built from plastic card, a floor covered with Fablon heat-resistant fabric, and a TV set from plastic card with a 35mm colour transparency mounted inside it; and the 'padding' inside the door is scored plastic card. The outside body panels were first painted by spraying the 'sky' over a paper mask cut to the shape of the 'buildings'. The latter were then sprayed yellow and the black detail was drawn in with a draughting pen.
(Model: Mike Burt)

Centre: the wheels and tyres for this 'customised' 1/16 scale Ford Escort are taken from a commercially-produced kit, but the rest of the model is made up of hand built components. The initial stages involved cutting two side profiles from plastic card, followed by the front and rear panelling, after which the body contours were built up and smoothed out using Milliput epoxy putty. The chassis was next built as a detachable unit, thus allowing the interior fittings to be added. Windows (cellulose-acetate), wheels, engine and exterior fittings were left until last.
(Model: Gary McCrudden)

Lower centre: a flaw-free white finish is a difficult challenge on any model, not least a large vehicle with plenty of body area like this one, and especially when the basic plastic colour, as here, is very dark. It is absolutely essential that all traces of dust and fluff are removed from the model before any painting is attempted; it is just as important that the paint is 'pure', and straining this through a muslin cloth before use is a prudent measure. The model in the photograph is the Tamiya 1/12 scale Lola T-70 Mk III but features a different scheme from that recommended in the kit. Note the carefully masked body trim.
(Model: Dave Patrick)

Bottom: the model in the previous photograph was airbrushed, but with a little care and patience there is no reason why a finish equally as good cannot be achieved with a paintbrush. The 1/12 scale Matra MS11 F1 (Tamiya kit) depicted here has been brush painted with several coats of thinned enamel gloss paint, as described in the text.
(Model: Dave Patrick)

entails filling the gap between the interior and body mouldings round the door aperture and between the inner and outer door panels. Plastic card (5 or 10 thou) and body putty are best for this job. It is a matter of personal preference whether door hinges work or not; however, the model is generally stronger if the doors are firmly fixed in the open position. Opening the boot may possibly be considered unnecessary, for nothing much happens within, and cutting new floors, sides and a bulkhead entails a lot of very painstaking work.

When all the modifications to the bodywork are completed then painting can begin. The parts should be washed in a weak lukewarm, soapy solution and allowed to dry. They can then be either taped to handles made from wire coat hangers or held on a board with double sided adhesive tape or modelling clay. A matt undercoat is normally required, especially if one will be spraying a light top colour over a dark plastic — a neutral mid-grey is ideal. Several light coats are sprayed on until the colour of the plastic is completely masked. The undercoat is allowed to dry for 15 minutes or so and then the top coat spraying commences. It is much better to carry out the complete cycle in one session as this avoids the chance of dust settling between coats.

For gloss paints a 50/50 thinners to colour mix is a good starting point. Matt paints may require less thinners; however, these paints often suffer from very heavy sedimentation and will need to be strained through some fine muslin or old net curtaining after being mixed, in order to remove all the lumps. Most model car kits have enough body parts to enable a 5-minute cycle to be used. This entails spraying a light mist coat on each part in sequence, by the time the last component has received its initial coat the first is just slightly 'tacky' and a second coat may be sprayed. The process continues until a sufficient depth of colour is achieved. It may take 5 or 10 coats but it is better to have many light coats than one or two heavy passes with their tendency to 'run' and 'sag'. Heavy coats of paint also seem to act as a magnet for any stray speck of dust or fluff. Only during the last two passes should the gloss be worked up by spraying slightly closer to the model. Too close a pass, or holding the airbrush in one spot, will result in a run or unsightly blotch, causing torn hair on the modeller's part! When the parts are finished they may be placed in a box which has been lightly dampened to keep any residual dust down and covered with a damp, lint free cloth.

It is not normally necessary to spray a varnish coat over gloss paint, for if the spraying is carried out properly a good medium gloss will result, but should the chosen colour be available in matt only then a coat of gloss varnish will have to be used. Varnish applied over matt colours, it should be remembered, will tend to darken the finish. On models which have been correctly sprayed, sanding down, or flatting down, and finally polishing the surface is rather a nonsense, for not only is it extremely difficult to sand small models evenly and to get into all the nooks and crannies, but the process produces light dust which must be washed off, leaves light score marks and removes paint from raised detail. In general, it trebles the work and effort needed to obtain a good finish. If the model is prepared and sprayed correctly all this unnecessary and frustrating work is avoided.

Brush painting is becoming something of a lost art, it seems — a pity that, for it is certainly a lot cheaper than spraying, and also a lot easier! The preparation for brush painting a model is just as important as for spraying it. New pots of paint should be used, especially when one is painting the top coat, and brushes should be cleaned in new thinners. Once again, wire handles for all the various components should be made so that they can be manoeuvred and set down without tipping over. Because the paint may not be thinned it will not normally be necessary to undercoat the model unless a particularly garish shade of plastic has been used. The paint needs to have a fairly long drying time — say around 30 minutes. For this reason Testors and Pactra paints are not recommended, for although excellent for spraying they dry almost instantly when being brushed, which makes the blending of the brush strokes almost impossible. The parts must be absolutely dust-free of course, and kept that way whilst brushing is in progress. As with spraying, if the painting begins to go wrong for any reason it is best to remove the paint instantly and begin the preparatory process again. The colour should not be left to dry before one attempts to remove it. Soon after painting has started, say on the roof panel, the quality of the brush that is being used will become apparent, for even a medium-priced brush will begin shedding hairs to the detriment of the modeller's temper. Provided that the paint is laid on the model in a smooth operation working from roof to side panels to boot and that putting too much on in one area is avoided, then the cross and fore and aft strokes used to spread it over the body will coalesce and blend into one another as the paint dries, leaving a smooth surface with a good gloss. The application of decals, a time-consuming business in respect of modern racing vehicles, US trucks, dragsters, and so on, may be tackled following the guidelines set out in Chapter 4, particular attention being paid to correct alignment.

One feature of road and racing vehicles that is less applicable to other forms of model is the fact that many if not most of the full size specimens remain in private hands and as such tend to be well cared for. Motorcycles, veteran cars, saloon cars and F1 racing vehicles for example are generally kept in tip-top condition, and flawless finishes are therefore frequently desirable. Moreover, faults on such models cannot normally be 'hidden' beneath a deposit of scale mud or rust. The key to success in this respect is cleanliness — washing the model during its construction cannot be carried out too often, and special precautions need to be taken to ensure that even the smallest flecks of dust are removed before (and during) the painting stage. Dust, paintbrush hairs and so on are never 1/32 scale, 1/24 scale or 1/12 scale — they are always 1/1 scale!

Chapter 10
Presentation

Plastic models tend to be built to a comparatively small scale and completed in a relatively short period of time, and so it is hardly surprising that those involved in the hobby of building these models are usually collectors as well. Sooner or later, therefore, the problem of how best to keep the models in good condition arises. In addition, most modellers will wish to exhibit their handiwork in some way, whether this be to their own personal satisfaction and sense of personal achievement, to interest friends and relatives, or to impress the judges of a competition. The standards of workmanship in the field of plastic modelling have never been higher than they are nowadays, thanks largely to the high popularity of the pastime and the consequent dissemination of information and publicity via its several media, and it is true to say that, for exhibition and competition purposes at least, the method in which one model is presented may very well be the factor which decides its superiority over another. Before these rather complex topics are looked at, however, some more fundamental issues will be considered.

DISPLAY AND STORAGE
The function of a plastic model, as opposed to a plastic kit, will vary according to individual interpretation, but quite obviously, since it will generally be static in character, its prime purpose is to be looked at. If sufficient interest is aroused, it is liable to be studied and discussed critically, in which case its function may also be seen as being educational. Further, a model may stimulate the imagination of the onlooker, allowing him to capture in his mind certain real life events or situations. If two or more models of broadly similar subjects are placed together, they may be compared, especially if they are compatible in terms of scale, thus again serving an educational or stimulative purpose. Quite apart from a desire to continue with his hobby by

constructing more models, the modeller may also wish to extend his collection, the size of which will be determined by the time, money or space at his disposal or by the length of time in which he sustains his interest in it.

Assuming that a model or group of models is to be displayed, the first requirement is one of space, and assuming that the intention is to preserve the work for as long as possible, this will normally be arranged in such a way that the risk of accidental damage is minimised. A shelf or similar piece of furnishing might be allocated exclusively for the purposes of display, where the models might be conveniently viewed but less conveniently touched. If unprotected from the atmosphere, however, the models will very quickly gather dust and other unwanted matter, and so they will need to be cleaned periodically. This can be done by using a soft paintbrush kept especially for the purpose and blowing away the dust as it is agitated. Alternatively, a photographer's puff brush may be used which, by means of squeezing a bladder attached to one end of a hollow tube, will clear away the dust freed by the bristles at the other. More resistant deposits, which will inevitably build up over a longer period, may be removed by carefully washing the model in tepid water which has been reinforced with a few drops of liquid detergent. Direct handling of a model should be avoided as much as possible, although this is less important where glossy finishes are present.

The risk of damaging a model through cleaning it is very great, and many modellers with the necessary wherewithal prefer to take steps to obviate these rather hazardous measures. Some sort of covering, which will both protect the models from dust and allow them to be seen, is therefore desirable. Individual models may be enclosed by commercially-produced clear covers such as those marketed by Titan, which consist of blow-moulded plastic

Two types of display case.

Top: a Titan showcase, consisting of two vacuum formed mouldings, a base and a clear plastic cover. These cases are available in a variety of sizes and are flimsy but functional. The model displayed is the same Matra MS11 as that depicted in the previous photograph.
(Model: Dave Patrick)

Bottom: a home made glass case, displaying a Ferrari 312B F1 which has been produced using the Tamiya 1/12 kit as a basis. The 'floor' consists of a piece of hardboard edged with wood and fitted top and bottom with self-adhesive baize. The glass panels are bonded together with 24-hour Araldite, the corners being trimmed with plastic card fixed with 5-minute epoxy resin.
(Model and case: Dave Patrick)

domes accompanied with a base upon which to stand the model. Individual display cases may be built by the modeller using acetate sheet or, more expensively, glass, with a removable or permanent base. Clear acetate sheeting will provide a light, easily transportable case that is quickly produced and virtually unbreakable, although it will be susceptible to scratching and staining and is liable to lose its clarity with the passage of time. However, such a case is easily produced by cutting the individual panels with a blade and fixing them together with acetone or butyl acetate. Thin beading may be arranged along the edges so as to disguise the joints and then varnished or painted as required. Glass panels will require a stronger and more elaborate framework to enable them to be supported adequately, and though the work needed to produce such a case involves a heavy financial outlay and is both exacting and time consuming, the result will be completely permanent, resistant to the effects of normal handling and immune to atmospheric influences and chemical decomposition. A collection of models may be conveniently housed in a larger display cabinet, which may be purchased, adapted from other types of storage furniture or hand built on the workbench, with shelving arranged to suit the modeller's personal taste.

Where there is an acute shortage of display space, or where the modeller is wont to transport his work from place to place for the purposes of exhibition, competition, and the like, some thought will need to be given to packing the models in order to protect them from physical damage. The containers used for this purpose should be light yet strong, and ideally should be enclosed to prevent dust from reaching the models and perhaps to enable several such containers stacked together, although an open tray may be sufficient if only one or two models require temporary protection for transportation. Certain types of tough cardboard box will normally provide the necessary container, but for complete protection it is generally advisable to introduce some form of internal stiffening, especially if stacking is contemplated. This can be made from additional strips of cardboard or even thin lengths of wood glued at the most vulnerable places, for example within the angles formed by the faces. The model inside the container will need to be packed in such a way that it does not move about. Where it is mounted permanently on a base, double sided adhesive tape may be adequate to hold it in position, but if this is not feasible, strips of ordinary adhesive tape may be laid across suitable parts of the base, prevented from actual contact with it by means of pieces of tissue or other non-abrasive material, with each end pressed on to the floor of the container around it. Free standing models may also be fitted into their containers in this way, with the tape stretched across surfaces of the model that are not liable to be damaged in the process. Where the natural support for the model is delicate, for example in the case of an aircraft's undercarriage system, additional support may be required beneath other areas to help take the weight more evenly. This may be achieved by introducing crumpled tissue paper or shredded paper inside the container, building up cradles from expanded polystyrene blocks or pieces of foam rubber, or cutting jigs from cardboard to fit selected areas of the model. A carefully devised jig, in fact, is often the only form of support that may be required to hold a model firmly in place.

STANDS AND BASES

With one or two notable exceptions, stands and bases are not provided as part of a plastic kit unless the configuration of the model poses problems of stability. Thus kits representing vehicles and water-

line ships are rarely if ever furnished with such items, whilst those for figures and full-hull ships generally are. Aircraft kits may or may not be provided with display stands. Many such kits were years ago moulded in flying attitude only, some gave a sort of grudging option on undercarriage positions, and only a few permitted a full choice between retracted or extended configuration. Display stands, which usually were fitted by means of a slot below the fuselage, were thus very necessary items, since without them poise was, or could have been, absent. Nowadays, in the pursuit of realism and complexity, the policy is completely reversed, and a fully detailed landing gear is the norm. This has resulted in the once necessary stand becoming largely redundant, and many kits omit it altogether.

Models such as figures obviously require a base to enable them to be displayed in a realistic pose, and whilst this may be regarded as primarily functional and as enabling the model to be safely

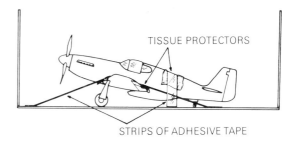

TISSUE PROTECTORS

STRIPS OF ADHESIVE TAPE

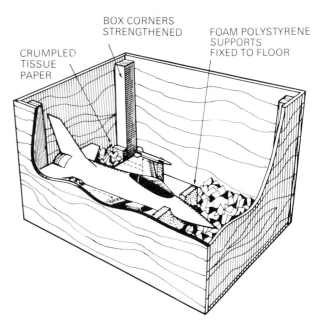

BOX CORNERS STRENGTHENED

FOAM POLYSTYRENE SUPPORTS FIXED TO FLOOR

CRUMPLED TISSUE PAPER

STORAGE CONTAINERS

Top: an uncomplicated but very effective diorama involving simple scenery but indicating much activity: Hasegawa's 1/32 scale Focke-Wulf Fw 190 posed with a pilot and mechanic. The pilot is a reworked 1/32 scale Revell item with parachute harnessing etc added, whilst the mechanic is essentially of 54mm Historex origin with cap and trousers made from soft paper. Note the carefully simulated 'wear' and 'mud' on the aircraft. (Model and photo: Jacques D'Heur)

Bottom: producing a cast base is a straightforward operation, and once the basic shape has been produced all manner of refinements can be worked in by painting and detailing it according to individual model requirements. The 54mm Salm-Kirburg Hussar in this photograph is posed on a resin base cast from a silicon female mould which was in turn made from a Plasticine master pattern — an inexpensive and quick means of producing an effective setting. (Model: Alan Edwards)

Opposite: an attractive polished wooden base has few peers in displaying a model or diorama to its best advantage, as is readily apparent in this photograph of an abandoned 1930 Ford Model 'A' (Monogram, 1/24 scale). The model itself has an atmosphere of utter desolation about it — the carefully administered dents, the crazed windscreen, the 'rusty' finish, plus a dead 'tree' and a couple of birds hopping about, all being contributory factors. (Model: Sheperd Paine. Photo by courtesy of Monogram Models Inc)

handled, the opportunity may at the same time be taken to make it attractive and relevant to its subject. There is no reason why this approach should not be adopted for other types of model either. The provision of a base for a plastic model can be as simple or as complex a task as the modeller wishes. Small bases for figures and so on may be produced from offcuts of wood or pieces of glass or metal, or cast in resin; larger bases for vehicles, ships and aircraft may be fashioned from blockboard, hardboard, chipboard or plywood, suitably prepared and finished. Quite often, an ordinary household item may be considered a suitable base — such things as the plastic tops from aerosol cans, pieces of glass, mirror tiles, ceramic tiles and even teapot stands are regularly used by modellers.

Although it is obviously impracticable to discuss in any depth all the possibilities that exist with regard to the manufacture of a simple model base, the number of such being limited only by the individual modeller's skill or imagination, a general appraisal of one or two of the more straightforward types can be offered. A simple cast base may be made up by first obtaining or constructing a tray from wood and lining it with household aluminium foil. The creases in the foil should be smoothed down as much as possible, in order to save work cleaning up the casting at a later stage. Polyester casting resin is then prepared and poured into the tray to the required depth, thick castings being built up in several separate layers rather than in one. When set, the casting is taken from the tray, smoothed with a file and abrasive paper, and then polished to give a lustred surface. The casting thus produced may either be used directly as a base, in which case care will have to be taken to remove any trapped air bubbles by drawing them out with a needle before the resin has set, or it may be used as a master to produce a number of identical bases. If the latter course is chosen, a silicon rubber mould similar to that referred to in Chapter 3 for casting model components may be prepared, the master sanded and polished to a flawless finish, and the casting proceeding as before. By introducing colouring media, mineral chips, and so forth into the resin, all manner of attractive surfaces may be produced. The undersides of the bases may be lined with felt or baize if desired, in order to protect any surface on which they are placed and to assist grip.

A simple wooden base may be made up by obtaining a piece of ½in or ¾in (1.27cm or 1.9cm) hardwood of the required dimensions, bevelling the edges, sanding it completely smooth on each surface and then varnishing or painting it according to personal fancy. A cheaper method of making a large base is to cut a rectangular piece of plywood or hardboard and edging it with picture beading. An attractive finish will require some very precise measuring to fit the beading and the use of a mitre block to achieve neat corners. The edging may be varnished or painted as before, and the base itself covered with felt, flock paper or painted sandpaper to give it additional appeal. A variation on this approach is to make up a tray similar to a photograph frame, with a wood base and a piece of glass to place over it. A sheet of paper to fit the tray might carry a suitable design, picture, diagram or information area, and be placed beneath the glass.

A base prepared for a particular model might need to bear a title denoting the subject standing on it, and this can very simply be made up using dry print lettering such as Letraset. The lettering can either be burnished directly on to the base, in which case the latter should be completely smooth and preferably gloss finished, or it can be transferred to a nameplate made from a strip of plastic card or other suitable material.

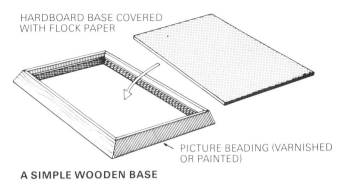

HARDBOARD BASE COVERED WITH FLOCK PAPER

PICTURE BEADING (VARNISHED OR PAINTED)

A SIMPLE WOODEN BASE

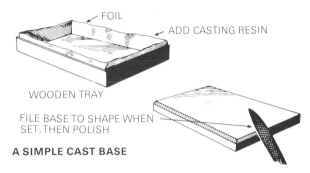

FOIL

ADD CASTING RESIN

WOODEN TRAY

FILE BASE TO SHAPE WHEN SET, THEN POLISH

A SIMPLE CAST BASE

The provision of a base for a model is never necessary, of course, but such an addition does enable it to be displayed in an eye catching and professional manner, and if neatly produced can even give the impression that the model on it is better made than it actually is. However, a base such as those described need only be the starting point for a much more involved way of presenting a model, as will be outlined in the following section.

SCENIC BASES AND DIORAMAS

Displaying a model on a scenic base can be but a very short step from displaying it on a plain base, and it does not require much perception to realise that by developing the scenic base concept it is possible to build up a complex diorama consisting of several models which relates an event or depicts a particular situation. The scope for such methods of model presentation is quite literally infinite, and for the modeller with imagination, an eye for detail, perhaps not too much display space at his disposal, an urge to experiment, a high level of artistic ability possibly, an interest in historical events, or simply a good sense of humour, the creation of a diorama may well be the ultimate pleasure derived from the hobby of plastic modelling.

The setting of a model in a simulation of its natural environment will clearly require a certain amount of planning, and since the work involved may be likened to the production of a three dimensional painting, certain guidelines will usually need to be observed. The first requirement is one of authenticity, and this is not perhaps so straightforward a topic as one might think. A scenic base might be one of three fundamental types. To start with, it might be merely a representation of a piece of groundwork that will immediately convey to the viewer the nature of a model's 'home' environment without elaborating further, and this will normally be a flattish area not much greater than that occupied by the model itself. Examples of this type of setting might be a section of roadway for a vehicle, a piece of runway or grass for an aircraft, a pathway or pavement for a figure, or a sea base for a ship. Secondly, it might strive to represent a typical setting that will give more atmosphere than a simple piece of ground but will not attempt to portray an actual historical event. As such, a good deal of licence is permissible provided the overall realism is not destroyed, since anonymity is preserved. Instances of this kind of presentation might be a figure leading a horse to drink, an aircraft shown as having crash landed, or a vehicle undergoing a wheel or engine change. It should, however, be remembered that only what is possible should be attempted for this type of scenic model — even

improbable situations might best be avoided. The third type of setting is the diorama that relates to a real and usually well-documented event such as the sinking of a famous ship, the portrayal of a famous personality or the representation of a well known place or building. In this case, considerable research may have to be undertaken by the modeller in order to obtain accurate details of the models' surroundings, and care will also have to be taken to ensure that the model or models are as correct in appearance as possible.

Another consideration for the modeller contemplating the construction of a scenic setting for his model is that of balance. The size of the base will obviously be important, not only for the purposes of indicating correct scale distances between the objects upon it but also because the right amount of space will need to be left around the edges of the principal subjects so as to strike the correct proportion between overcrowding and emptiness. Further, the dimensions of the base and the arrangement of the objects upon it may have to be compromised by the height of the objects, what may be considered as the focal point of the diorama, and the direction from which it is to be viewed. If, for example, a diorama features undulating ground or large buildings, it will usually only be possible to show those sections in the immediate vicinity of the focal point, and so where they meet the edges of the base they may have to be finished abruptly as vertical cross-sectional surfaces. In this way, the directions from which the diorama may be viewed will be determined. It is important, therefore, that the modeller has a clear idea of the appearance that the finished diorama will take on before he attempts actually to construct it. The initial inspiration is likely to originate from a photograph or from a recollected experience, and the focal point or points will be decided at an early stage in the planning. A broad appraisal of the diorama's general layout will be made, but it is usually best to construct the principal models involved before any building work on the scenic surroundings is begun. Once the models have been made and the base produced, various arrangements might be tried out before a decision is taken as to the final appearance of the diorama. Some pencilled lines and annotations at appropriate points on the base might then be sketched in before the materials to be used are gathered and prepared and work in earnest is started.

It will already have become apparent that, although reference was made earlier to three main types of scenic presentation, it is, in terms of their construction, rather impracticable to attempt to make distinctions between them. In considering

Above: some diorama subjects give the modeller the opportunity to work on the models themselves rather than on any major scenic features. Being drastically dismembered here is a 1/48 scale Focke-Wulf Fw 190A, built from the Monogram kit but incorporating hand made engine, engine mounting and hoist components, together with a wealth of other 'extras'.
(Model: Y Kosaka. Photo: Susumu Yoshida)

construction materials and methods, it is also impossible to do other than give a general indication of the sort of work that might be undertaken. Modelling is to a large extent a very personal hobby, and although ideas for techniques abound, the modeller will generally adopt his own particular ways of achieving a given objective. Moreover, the huge variety of materials and techniques that are available, and are perhaps yet to be discovered, make a comprehensive guide to diorama building a quite unrealistic aim within the specifications of this book. However, it is appropriate to consider a few of the more orthodox materials and methods that are useful in the creation of model scenery.

A diorama will consist of natural features, man made features, or a combination of the two, in addition to which a number of intrusive objects will be present. Natural features encompass the terrain of the landscape, any areas of water that may be included, plus any living matter such as vegetation and wildlife. Man made features comprise such items as roads, fences, walls, signposts and build-

ings, and may be regarded as permanent parts of the scenery. Intrusive features are those which are temporary in character and would include, for example, human beings and movable objects such as implements and pieces of machinery, together with any general litter and debris. Since the natural evolution of any scenic setting would follow this pattern in real life, it is logical for the modeller to build up his diorama in the same order.

Having sketched out the general distribution of the features that will be presented in the diorama, the edging to the base, if it is fitted, may be masked off to prevent damage whilst scenic work is in progress. The broad contours of the terrain may then be considered. If severe undulations are involved, it may be necessary to erect cut-off points from planed wood or hardboard around the edge of the base, and this should be done before any of the ground proper is tackled. A skeletal framework may then be fashioned from oddments of wood or board and fitted securely to the base by pinning it or gluing it in position, and when completed the shaping of the contoured ground surfaces may be built up with plaster, cellulose filler or plaster-impregnated material such as Mod-roc. If the terrain is fairly flat, the skeleton may be dispensed with and the contours fashioned using plaster alone. Thicknesses of more than about ½in (1cm) should generally be avoided owing to the tendency of the material to shrink, the unnecessary weight that such thicknesses would involve and of course the unnecessary expense entailed, although a product known as Tetrion, being polymer-based, can fairly safely be built up in deep layers.

The surface features of the terrain may next be considered, and these will usually take the form of bare rock, scree, sand or other kinds of loose deposit, mud or soil, or ground vegetation such as grass or low-growing plants. For each, a fairly fluid mixture of plaster may be prepared. Applying a thin coating of this mixture and modelling such features as joints, gullies and crags with a spatula whilst the plaster is still workable will produce a rock-like surface which may be painted when set. A smoother, more level application will be necessary to show soil or mud, and if this is to be bare it may also be left until dry and then painted with appropriate colours. Superficial deposits such as sand, gravel and boulders, together with the representation of low-growing vegetation, are best added before the plaster dries, in which case a medium such as powder paint may advantageously be added to the plaster while it is being prepared to give an effective working ground colour and obviate some tricky painting later on. Mineral matter from the garden, suitably sifted and graded, crushed salt, sand or plastic swarf may be sprinkled over the wet plaster to represent boulders, sand, pebbles, rubble or general debris, and this may be painted with a thinnish wash as it is applied. Cropped grass can be simulated by sprinkling dyed sawdust or flock powder over the wet plaster, and longer tufts can be prepared by dyeing sisal string and pushing short lengths into it. Other features utilising the wetness of the plaster can be incorporated into the diorama, and some of these will be mentioned later.

Modelling water is a task that seems to cause problems for very many diorama builders, but no great skill or inspiration is required to achieve something approaching realism. Muddy ground may be shown by applying varnish over the base colour, thereby darkening it, although high gloss finishes should be avoided. Puddles and shallow muddy pools may be represented by gloss varnish, mixed thoroughly perhaps with a little paint to reduce its clarity. Greater depths of water are best tackled with clear polyester resin similar to that used for casting bases and model components. Care should be taken to get the bed of the stream, pool or sea to look right, and weeds, plants, floating matter, and so on can be introduced into the material after it has been poured and before it has cured. The clarity of the resin can be reduced, and a greater impression of depth conveyed, by building up the resin in several individual layers, tinting each mixture with progressively lighter colours. Ripples on the surface can be produced by lightly crumpling aluminium foil and laying it over the built up layers of resin, and then pouring a thin top layer of resin in such a way that it creeps beneath the foil. Heavily disturbed water may be simulated by building up local areas of resin with a paintbrush or similar implement and applying a wash of thinned matt white enamel paint at appropriate places.

Prominent vegetation such as hedges, bushes and trees is possibly the most difficult aspect of a diorama to reproduce convincingly. Various companies produce accessory packs containing miniature features such as these — materials including foam rubber, sponge, rubberised horse hair and flock and brass-etched particles being used to simulate branches and foliage — but all save the very expensive tend to be unrealistic in appearance to say the least. However, the garden or the local woodland will again yield many suitable items that can be used to great effect on a diorama. Several species of moss and lichen produce long fronds which when placed close together can form very effective bushes; placed in a row, a very realistic hedge can be produced; mounted on short twigs, they can be built up to form realistic shrubs. Selected twigs, roots, and so forth, can be used for sundry vegetational features, and all can be made to stand firm either by mounting them in the wet plaster base or by gluing them in position with epoxy resin. A tree in full leaf is a rather difficult proposition, but modellers with patience have produced realistic effects by using a skeleton of twisted fuse wire, smoothed out if necessary with cellulose filler around the trunk and major branches, and then fitted with patches of rubberised horse hair sprinkled with flock powder. It is also possible to arrange the diorama so that it supports the growth of bonsai trees, although provision for watering, trimming, etc., will of course have to be made.

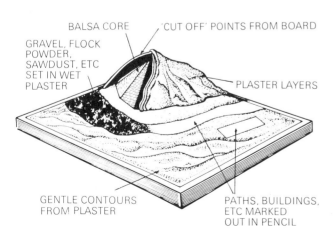

BALSA CORE

'CUT OFF' POINTS FROM BOARD

GRAVEL, FLOCK POWDER, SAWDUST, ETC SET IN WET PLASTER

PLASTER LAYERS

GENTLE CONTOURS FROM PLASTER

PATHS, BUILDINGS, ETC MARKED OUT IN PENCIL

PREPARING THE DIORAMA BASE

Dioramas featuring crashed aircraft always give the modeller scope to use his imagination, but it is the attention to small details that is essential in order to convey a truly convincing picture.

Top: The setting, pose and general appearance of this 1/48 scale Monogram Boeing B-17G are enough in themselves to fulfil the above requirements, but the feathered inboard propellers, the broken off mainwheel, the quizzical postures of the relieved crew figures, and a host of other little touches, all add up to an absorbing and very believable spectacle.
(Model: Sheperd Paine. Photo by courtesy of Monogram Models Inc)

Bottom: the importance of close attention to reference photographs when dioramas are being constructed cannot be overemphasised. The shearing of the fuselage just behind the cockpit was characteristic of crash-landed Messerschmitt Bf 109s, and the effect has been carefully reproduced in this model of a 109E completed as a 9/JG26 machine, together with fractured panelling at other typical points. The groundwork in the diorama was produced from lime, sawdust and chalk, the 'vegetation' being low-growing alpine grasses. Note the size of the base – the model is based on Airfix's 1/24 scale kit – and how the fact that none of the edges is in evidence in this photograph adds to the overall sense of reality.
(Model and photo: Ludwig Thoma)

There are fewer difficulties involved in the portrayal of man made landscape features, thanks largely to the wide variety of quite excellent diorama accessories that are available to the modeller. Pathways and dirt roads may be produced by shaping the plaster base accordingly, applying fine grit or sand if required, and painting in appropriate colours when dry. More regular surfaces such as concrete and tarmacadam may be represented by using card or suitable grades of abrasive paper glued securely in position. A good range of embossed plastic sheeting representing cobbles, flagstones, paving, etc is produced for those modellers requiring special effects, although such surfaces may quite readily be made up by hand using ball bearings, lead shot, suitably shaped pebbles or pieces of card, either embedded in the wet plaster or glued on top of it. Simple wooden structures such as fences and gates are best made from painted strips of balsa, although, again, plastic card with a wood grain effect is available for these purposes. Balsa wood is one of the more time-honoured modelling materials, and it still has considerable value today since it is light, easy to work and relatively cheap. It tends to bruise easily, however, it is fairly coarse grained and thin sections tend to be rather flexible, so that although shapes may easily be prepared with a sharp knife it is not always suitable for exterior surfaces. If so used to represent anything other than wood, its surface needs to be sealed, either by applying a coat of emulsion paint or, for a smooth finish, a light filling compound such as Plastic Padding or Fine Grain Polyfilla or a mixture of clear dope and talcum powder. As a core for a solid structure such as a wall, building or piece of rising ground, balsa wood is an excellent medium and may be used in conjunction with plaster, cellulose filler, paper, papier mache, card or polystyrene sheet. It can be glued with balsa cement or PVA glue, or else pinned provided care is taken not to split it. Expanded polystyrene is a material that may be used in much the same way as balsa wood and shares some common properties. However, it is not generally suitable for exterior surfaces, although it can produce certain effects if used in conjunction with other materials. It may be cut easily enough with a sharp knife or saw, but to avoid the consequences of its electrostatic qualities a hot wire or pyrogravure is often preferable. Polystyrene cement should never be used for fixing expanded polystyrene as the latter will simply dissolve on contact with it, but most universal adhesives can be safely applied. Polystyrene foam such as that used for meat trays can, being much finer in texture, be employed for a number of exterior effects such as rough concrete.

Mention should be made at this point of the very extensive range of model buildings that are available to the diorama enthusiast. Many of these are produced principally for model railway enthusiasts, and items manufactured by companies such as Hornby, Lima, Peco and Airfix may be readily

Top: *Somewhere in Sinai,* a simple diorama centred around the 1/50 scale Fujimi A-4 Skyhawk. The kit has been extensively modified by relocating all the control surfaces, detailing the cockpit and upgrading the configuration from A-4E to A-4H. The ordnance trolleys originate from the old Revell 1/48 Skyhawk kit. The diorama is constructed from a piece of chipboard, with cut-off points from hardboard and 'rock' from plaster over a balsa core. The 'sand' is simply crushed household salt, suitably painted. Note the 'current bedded' rock strata — a common sandstone feature.

Modelling 'water' can involve a number of techniques, but for small scale 'seas' it is not generally necessary to use a material that is transparent. **Centre:** Tamiya's 1/700 scale *Kumano,* prepared for 'listing' by sawing at an angle through the hull moulding, is set in an expanded polystyrene ceiling tile. Tile adhesive has been used to fix the model — polystyrene cement is not suitable for this since, as one might expect, it dissolves the thin 'honeycomb' walls of the material. (Model: Reg Hale)

Bottom: a Polyfilla base has been built up around the capsized hull of Heller's 1/400 *Prinz Eugen* to represent the ship's final moments following the post-war US A-bomb tests in the Pacific. The plaster was spread evenly over an edged chipboard tray, contoured with a putty knife to show the basic wave forms and then 'flecked' with a piece of damp tissue to bring out the wavelets.

Opposite: the effectiveness of selected mosses and lichens is well demonstrated in this small 54mm scale diorama *Evening Picket,* showing 25th Dragoons and French infantry figures. Fronds of moss stay green for a long time — and even when they do eventually die off they convey the impression of dead bracken — although they can of course be painted if required. The fence in the diorama is made from matchsticks and strips of balsa. (Model: Alan Edwards)

Somewhere in Sinai

adapted. Most of these are supplied either as ready-built polystyrene models or as injection moulded polystyrene kits and can therefore be treated in the same way as other plastic kits for the purposes of construction, alteration and painting. Some plastic kits, apart from those representing buildings, notably the 1/76 scale range of AFVs manufactured by Matchbox, contain sections of landscape structures and other dioramic features which may be incorporated into scenic models, whilst firms such as Fujimi, Tamiya, Nitto, Hasegawa and Italaerei market special injection moulded kits for a range of items including brick walls, signposts, street lamps, telegraph poles, and so forth. Vacuum formed features are also produced, the best-known range perhaps being that manufactured by Bellona/Micro Mold, who market formings for battle terrains and a variety of structures and buildings. The fragility of some of these mouldings generally means that reinforcement is desirable, and this can be achieved by inverting them and smearing the interior surfaces with a coating of plaster.

Intrusive features may also be obtained from kits, some of them, such as items of machinery, figures, livestock and tents being kits in their own right of course, and these may be adapted or animated according to the methods outlined in the previous chapters. A number of other items such as barrels, buckets, boxes and similar containers,

tools, implements and weapons, sandbags and lengths of chain are obtainable either from kits of vehicles and figures or as individual accessory packs. Alternatively, they may be built up by the modeller, and, being for the most part small and unobtrusive, will not require a great deal of effort or skill to produce them. Natural debris such as fallen branches or logs may be shown by using twigs from any garden and positioned appropriately; dead leaves may easily be produced from sifted tea leaves suitably stained or painted; rubble, scree and general litter may be shown by using a variety of materials such as grit, gravel, flecks of paper or card, and so forth. The scope of such work, as with all aspects of diorama construction, is limited only by the individual modeller's skill, experience, imagination and ingenuity.

It will have been noticed that several important considerations regarding the building of dioramas have not yet been referred to. One of these involves the question of scale. Although this will be determined by the size of the principal subject or subjects of the whole model, there may be difficulties when the matching of certain other features such as buildings, bridges and signposts is undertaken, and some scales are very deficient in respect of scenic accessories. For example, although a great many buildings are produced to the standard model railway scale — OO or 1/76 — such items in, say,

1/48 or 1/35 scale may be difficult if not impossible to find, and the modeller will have to produce much of his work by hand. Similarly, a large aircraft diorama in 1/24 scale may pose problems if it is the intention to include figures or vehicles. The overall scale of the diorama, and even the subject depicted, may well therefore be determined by whether the

Left: large buildings for dioramas may pose special problems since it is not always practicable to include their total ground area. Ruined buildings are much more popular with modellers and in many ways more suitable since, apart from the fact that their ground area may be very ill-defined, there is less chance of the scenery dominating the model subjects, perhaps to the point of obscuring them. This diorama, featuring the Monogram 1/32 scale Jeep, has building structures made from wood faced with appropriately textured plaster. The 'rubble' is ordinary road gravel.
(Model: Sheperd Paine. Photo by courtesy of Monogram Models Inc)

Weather in miniature. These photographs show two of the effects that can be worked into dioramas to simulate certain weather conditions.

Top right: *Winter Patrol,* comprising two French 5th Line Lancers (Historex, 54mm scale), has 'snow' on base and twigs made from Polyfilla mixed to a normal consistency, with that over the greatcoats from Polyfilla made up to a watery consistency and applied with a paintbrush until a sufficient density of deposit had been produced. Note the 'huddled' appearance of the rider. (Model: Mick Miller)

Centre: Eustace of Boulogne (AD 1066) has his cloak and gonfanon carefully modelled to give a simulation of blustery conditions. A pyrogravure has been used to tease out the horse's mane and tail to complete the effect. The models are from extensively reworked 54mm Historex components.
(Model: Alan Edwards)

Bottom: carefully selected low-growing grasses and fine beach sand was used to form the base for this desert scene centred on a modified Italaerei PzKpfw IV, a Tamiya SdKfz 232 and a Heller donkey (all 1/35 scale). Note the track marks in the foreground, created by pressing lengths of track from kits into the sand — a job best tackled with the sand dampened.
(Model and photo: Ludwig Thoma)

required accessories are available. Natural features such as terrain, areas of water and vegetation are not quite so restricted, since much of the work showing these aspects will probably be completed by hand, and strict scale consistency is not necessary anyway. Grass matting, for instance, though it ostensibly may be produced for 1/76 scale dioramas, will not necessarily look out of place with a 1/32 scale model, and flock used as foliage is quite acceptable for a wide range of scales. However, it is important that the general proportions of these features in a diorama are kept within reasonable scale compatibility, and this is something that the modeller should be aware of at all times.

The overall colour effect of a diorama should also receive some consideration. Scale colour effect has already been discussed at some length in an earlier chapter, and this phenomenon, or apparent phenomenon, is even more important when a diorama is being prepared. Contrasts should be gentle, colour boundaries indeterminate and brilliant hues avoided so far as natural features are concerned. Even man made features will show the effects of atmospheric attack once they have been exposed for a number of years, and weathering will soon take its toll of any bright colours and hard edges. Dirt, downwash, mosses and other forms of staining will all combine to help blend man made structures into the surrounding landscape, and subtle painting will enable this impression to be successfully communicated.

There are also some less obvious aspects of diorama construction for which it is difficult to lay down any specific recommendations but which nevertheless, if properly administered, can impart an enormous sense of realism to a model. One of these concerns the weather, and though it is obviously impossible to represent weather as such in a model, it is quite practicable to depict the sort of weather conditions that are prevailing at the time the event shown by the diorama is taking place. Snow may quite straightforwardly be represented by sifting powdered cellulose filler such as Polyfilla, or even flour, over the appropriate places on the model and then fixing it by applying a very light spray of hair lacquer or gloss varnish over the top. The spray should be very carefully applied so that the air current does not disturb the powder, and it may be necessary to mask off certain regions of the diorama to localise its effects. Drifts may be built up using balsa wood, expanded polystyrene or foam rubber cores and by shaping these with plaster or modelling clay before the coating of powder is applied. Light dustings of snow over the ground may be shown by spraying the model with a very light mist of matt white paint delivered vertically

down on to it, and frost may be depicted by spraying the same material lightly from different directions. Dew may be shown by spraying a mixture of gloss varnish and matt white paint in a similar way. The varnishing techniques already mentioned for showing pools of water may be adapted to give the impression of wet ground, and if the varnish is thinned very liberally and applied with a brush it will tend to run under gravity and collect in depressions to give a most realistic effect. Melting snow can be portrayed by using a combination of the methods outlined above, combined with patches of thinned matt white paint applied directly with a brush. All these techniques require considerable practice, and constant experimentation on prototype materials is strongly recommended before they are committed to a full model.

An impression of the prevailing weather conditions can also be conveyed by more subtle methods, especially by posing and clothing any figures that may be present in a suitable way. Tightly buttoned, thick garments, bare torsos, stretched out limbs on reclining figures, crossed arms that are wrapped around the chest and huddled groups all suggest certain types of weather, and if trees are swept, clothing billowed and hair ruffled, it is possible to convey the impression of wind. Wintry weather is quite easily recognised, but carefully selected colours for foliage, the absence or presence of leaf litter and the appearance of dots of colour to represent different kinds of flowers can all suggest a particular season of the year too. Tinting or shading all the colours used over the model landscape could possibly give a visual impression of the time of year as well, and even one of the time of day — sharper contrasts being used for clear, sunny conditions and less obvious ones for overcast or dark conditions — but this technique is very difficult to apply convincingly and can very easily be spoilt by the natural lighting surrounding the diorama. In an attempt to overcome this difficulty, some modellers provide their work with a suitably painted backdrop, encase it in a two or three sided box arrangement, or even totally enclose it within a glass fronted cabinet. This last method of presentation permits the lighting conditions in the immediate area of the model to be very strictly controlled, and such features as flickering fires, torches, lanterns and even moonlight can, using wire, batteries, bulbs and fibreoptics (not to speak of considerable ingenuity), be incorporated into the display.

Another effect that is difficult to reproduce convincingly is that of movement. Although techniques such as careful figure animation, pressing tyres and tracks into soft plaster, sculpting footprints and creating ripples on the surface of water

are well known and easily appreciated, suspended matter such as smoke and dust particles created by moving vehicles and natural effects such as swirling leaves and falling snow are quite impossible to model realistically unless an enclosed cabinet is used for the diorama and complicated mechanisms for creating air currents are installed. There are certainly modellers around who interest themselves in scientific approaches such as these, and the results of their work are fascinating to say the least. However, very specialised skills and interests are necessary to produce these desirable but rather involved phenomena, and the vast majority of modellers will feel that such work is outside their terms of reference.

In most respects, the building of a diorama follows the same general guidelines as those required for the construction of a single specimen model. An authentic visual impression should be the primary aim, subordinate to meticulous accuracy which, taken to its extreme, is an unlikely proposition anyway. It is as necessary to get a 'feel' for a scene as it is for an individual model, and the importance of the close observation of one's everyday environment as well as a careful study of

relevant photographs cannot be overstated. The elements of originality and surprise, translated by depicting the unusual situation, are regarded by many modellers as being of equal importance as the qualities of neatness and accuracy. The building of a diorama is indeed a task requiring many different propensities.

Above: the position from which a model is viewed is a critical consideration when one is assessing a piece of handiwork – most models tend to be viewed from a vantage point at the top of the scale equivalent of a 100ft tree! – and if 'eye level' is the optimum level then there is a good argument for providing a scenic backdrop to complete the illusion. Here, Revell's 1/32 scale P-47D Thunderbolt is posed effectively in front of a piece of flock paper backed by a hand painted tree, horizon and sky. (Model and photo: Jacques D'Heur)

Overleaf: a little ingenuity can create effects of a quite startling nature. Monogram's 1/48 B–26 Marauder has here been modified to show an aircraft awaiting final assembly; it has then been installed in a 'box' diorama supplied with appropriate fittings, the sides of the box consisting of mirrors. The result speaks for itself.
(Model: Sheperd Paine. Photos by courtesy of Monogram Models Inc)

Index